Nazis' Nightmare

Nazis' Nightmare

CONQUER
How an Arkansas Country Lawyer
helped bring Nazi War Criminals
to Justice

William G. Walker

Deep Water Productions, LLC

Nazis' NIGHTMARE
A Journal from 1942 – 1945
First person by G.D. Walker

Cover Art by Greg Mack
Cover Design by Annie Lorton

Edited by
Michelle Moore, Katelyn Smith and Pam Horowitz

Layout by Annie Lorton

All inquiries should be addressed to
Deep Water Productions, PO Box 662, Rogers, AR 72757
WgWmarketing@gmail.com

1st Edition

ISBN:
978-0-615-52201-2

Printed in the United States by Morris Publishing®
3212 East Highway 30
Kearney, NE 68847
1-800-650-7888

Contents

Acknowledgements - viii

25 Words or Less - x

Foreword - xi

Preface - xiii

Words - xv

Chapter 1 ~ Camp Robinson & Ft. Leonard Wood - 1
Chapter 2 ~ Omaha & Kansas City - 11
Chapter 3 ~ Chicago G-2 Training School - 16
Chapter 4 ~ G-2 Training - "Lessons Learned" - 28
Chapter 5 ~ Omaha, Camp Richie, New York & At Sea - 81
Chapter 6 ~ Great Britain, Rear Eagle - 91
Chapter 7 ~ Great Britain, Glasgow, Scotland - 104
Chapter 8 ~ Great Britain, England & North Wales - 119
Chapter 9 ~ France, Brittany - 132
Chapter 10 ~ France, St. Germain Report & Paris - 149
Chapter 11 ~ France, TUSAG/Verdun - 175
Chapter 12 ~ Germany, France, Belgium, Holland & Germany - 187
Chapter 13 ~ Germany, Aachen & Munchen-Gladbach - 193
Chapter 14 ~ Germany, Ahlen, Braunschweig & More - 235
Chapter 15 ~ Germany, V-E Day - 258
Chapter 16 ~ The Braunschweig Gestapo Report - 268
Chapter 17 ~ Germany, Frankenburg, Marburg & Braunschweig - 304

"He Goes Quietly" - 333

Maps - 334

Glossary - 337

Acknowledgements & Thanks

Thank you, thank you, thank you Dad, for letting me do this. You are such a great man, with such a great mind, and your writing is inspiring. Thank you Mom, Rosemary and David, Alex, Kent, and all the family, far reaching; thank you Jesus, thank you Lord. A special professional thanks goes out to Al White, Tom Dillard, Kris Katrosh, Robert Rhoads, Steve Grilletta, Graham Gordy, Randell Williams, Mara Leveritt, Joshuah Barrett, Katelyn Smith, Michelle Moore, Copy King, TaylorMack and of course "Ye Ole Regulators" (a special group of good, old friends).

There have been so many people throughout the state of Arkansas and way beyond to really list, because I would leave someone out. Each person has encouraged me over the past six years and the thousands of letters, documents, artifacts, etc. I simply can't thank them all. I hope each person knows that I am thinking of them when I simply say <u>thank you</u> for your tired ears and strong support.

Lastly, there are some incredible happenstance meetings with former military men I was able to meet at the U.S.A. BSA Training Camp who served in the post-war occupied Germany: the WWII gentleman that was a war reporter for the U.S. Government and actually had been to Camp Ritchie, Braunschwieg Prison, interviewed Hermann Goering and knew of these CIC men; the Holocaust survivor writer in McMinnville; the retired CIA young gentleman and his beautiful wife at the airport, the sharp and alert young couple on their way to a San Diego for cryptology convention that had a collective 31 years in military cryptography; the US Marshall at King Biscuit Blues Festival that was enthralled (even with "no horse in the race"); thank you all for being so enthusiastic and encouraging.

It goes on and on, but I won't anymore, as the story is in the pages ahead. Without you all, the grace of the wings of angels, Dad's writing and his evidence, there surely would have been no book called <u>Nazis' Nightmare</u>.

A special thanks to the United States Military Academy Department of History, The American Red Cross, USO, The American Field, Look Magazine and Wikipedia.

This book is dedicated in loving memory to G.D. Walker, Alan Latourette, Jim McElduff, Andrew Walker and all those who have, do, and will serve this great country to keep us free and strong.

25 words or less

His stance is justice;

His advice bold.

Romantic literature

Touches his soul.

A living green river,

Fishing his strong hold,

Life, love, freedom

Growing old.

Foreword
by Bill Walker

We all knew G.D. Walker as the lawyer's lawyer; he was a man of respect and authority. Dave Walker was not to be underestimated or overlooked– mostly he took care of business in an unusual manner: simply.

When I was about seven, Kennedy was running against Nixon, and then came along the Cuban Missile Crisis; I had no idea what my grandparents meant, or how far-sighted and brilliant they were about politics and history. I had asked a question about war and if we should worry about our country being bombed. They assured me that I didn't need to worry about a foreign invasion, and went on to say that our great country would some day fail and crumble from within, but not from a foreign invasion.

My grandmother wrote a story about her mother living in the Delta and going to college in 1866. My great-grandmother felt a responsibility to get a college education. After all, how many girls living in Marianna, Arkansas were fortunate enough to go to college during the 1800's?

My grandfather's uncle and father came to Helena in 1866 with a St. Andrews University law and business acumen. They came to take advantage of the richest free expanse of cotton, timber, land, live stock and labor in the world. All were available and opportune. Notably this was a position of envy for any people, century, time or place.

Mother, Dave, Grandfather & Grandmother

George David Walker was born in Helena, Arkansas in 1910. He went by "Dave," but among family, he was called "Bud."

It was no mystery to Dave that he would be a lawyer: he said he knew his calling by age six. Everything he ever did or accomplished was done because it was expected of him.

Dave was an Eagle Scout and graduated at age sixteenfrom Helena High School, where his mother and sister taught Latin and other courses. His hard work paid off as he was the valedictorian and proceeded to the University of the South in Sewanee, Tennessee.

After being a Delta Sigma in high school, Dave pledged Kappa Sigma at Sewanee, where Dave's father and oldest son were also Kappa Sigmas. At Sewanee, George David Walker once again graduated valedictorian, Phi Beta Kappa, Blue Key, Universities Meridiana, lettered in football, four years in track, and then went on to enter law school at the University of Arkansas in Fayetteville.

Dad passed the Arkansas Bar in 1933, graduated in 1934, and taught law at the university until 1936. He then entered the Burke, Moore & Walker Law Firm as a partner and was drafted in February of 1942 as a "buck private."

Preface
by Al White

The CIC is not well documented through existing history sources. It is mentioned, but does not have much detail. The case may be the practice of not talking to family members, or that it was confidential for 55 years, and they just couldn't let it out.

This may not be the most adventurous story of the war, but it is one which has yet to be told. Its importance to the general population in France, and throughout Europe, was to deal with those who created such harm upon them, after the allies liberated the good people and ran the Nazis off- back to Germany. The people of the countryside showed them how to live, however, both Nazis and their sympathizers were arrested and their fates determined.

Language barriers and other factors of chaos were the environment these men had to work in daily.

They helped create order so peace could be a functioning concept while political, social, and economic activities could be restored.

The CIC had its new beginnings within three weeks of Pearl Harbor. CIC was used initially to "collect information." It was said to be inefficient and disdained by the established "regular Army" military. But in endeavors of chaos, it proved effective: especially in combat zones.

As in any chaotic situation, level heads rise like cream, and in this particular slice of historic time, the CIC's ultimate accomplishment was to go into newly-occupied, more specifically German, territory and ferret out:

A) Gestapo

B) All bad guys

C) Put them in jail

D) Be a point of information for "whomever," so a logical and calm format could determine each individual's involvement and future.

This is the story of one individual from Helena, Arkansas

who was among the best and the brightest, whose behavior contributed to giving Germany back to the good Germans, by arresting the bad ones.

It is told by his letters, especially to his wife, and through the CIC TRT 4 Daily Journal. His footprints on the continent can be followed by his prose, and he did it without causing undo worry or alarm for his personal well being.

The CIC earned their right to be proud; they performed their duty. As peace presented, perhaps a better story could be told of the politics which this agency became, when the men who actually made it work went back to their civilian lives, and not into politics, the CID, or the CIA.

This story, the bigger study, is how effective was it in reacting upon reality? The CIC worked in the ETO. Were lessons learned? If so, applied? How can this knowledge be useful today? History repeats itself, but human nature doesn't change, only our options.

"WORDS"

…**Words** on Hitler (GDW - Chicago G-2 Training School notes 1942)

Volk (people) & Geist (spirit) are the key words of German "Mythology of the Blood." Theory that Volk are a superior race, whose qualities are hereditary, and must be kept pure and free from inter marriage. This theory is built into fanatical religion.

Hitler says strength is in disciplined obedience of the people to the leader, whose word must be as God's. Every German everywhere remains German.

…**Words** of Dorothy Thompson - U.S.A. 1939 (from her review of the complete 1933 Edition of Mein Kampf, by Adolf Hitler)

"The State as Movement is something new in the modern world. It is not, however, new in history. The State as Movement was conceived by Mohamet and by Genghis Khan; Hitler is their offspring - not Napoleon's. He is not the bastard child of anything western. Islam would understand him, and the Hunnish riders; and so, no doubt would Trotsky and perhaps Stalin."

The following individuals were committee sponsors for the publication of this annotated and unexpurgated addition. (Hitler removed the complete Mein Kampf from circulation some years prior).

Pearl Buck, Dorothy Canfield, Edna St. Vincent Millay, Ida Tarbell, Cyrus Adler, Charles A. Beard, Nicholas Murray Butler, Theodore Dreiser, Albert Einstein, Morris Ernst, Reverend Harry Emerson Fosclick, Reverend John Haynes Holmes, James M. Landis, Thomas Mann, Bishop William T. Manning, Eugene O'Neill, Theodore Roosevelt, Jr., Monsignor John A. Ryan, Norman Thomas, Walter White, and Rabbi Stephen S. Wise

…**Words** of George D. Walker - Germany, Saturday 20 January 1945

"If anybody knew what the answer was, it would be easier for all concerned, but we are all wondering what comes next. All I know is that it is a tremendous problem, and most of the people who venture to say they know the answer don't even know what the question is. Whatever they decide to do with Germany, I hope they will send somebody with some sense to do it; it isn't a job for broken down politicians, nor the New Deal type of day dreamers."

Chapter 1

Camp Robinson & Ft. Leonard Wood
U.S.A. 1 February – 1 May 1942

Private Geo. D. Walker: Everything is confused here… I will be glad to get assigned to something definite. Today I am assigned to Company A…

I am still fighting fiercely, and, like the British battle reports, the situation is still confused.

Yesterday afternoon we were transferred to Company B, which is the step before getting permanent assignment. This afternoon I was ordered to report to the assignment sergeant at Headquarters, and this may be news. It could mean that I am to get a chance to be on permanent staff here, which would be fine from a personal viewpoint but not so hot as far as getting anywhere in the Army is concerned. However, I don't think there is any future in the Army anyhow.

Today I successfully dodged all the duties and details, and the Army life isn't so bad under those circumstances. I still don't know when I'll get away from here, but I'll be glad to go unless I can get something in the permanent set-up here. This temporary organization is a pain in the neck. A big bunch left today and more tonight, including a lot who came in with me. However, some stay here as much as a couple of weeks. That would be all right if I could get out.

Today I got an office job at the Reception Center. They told me over there I would be here two or three days more, which may mean a week. I met a boy from West Helena who has been transferred to the Headquarters Company at the Center and has been there a month. That isn't bad at all, as he can get out whenever he wants to. However, he says he won't be there much longer, as they have to get eight weeks of basic training sooner or later. I wouldn't mind staying over there for a while like he is, but you can't do any good toward getting a promotion until that basic training is taken.

I have been doing very little work at the Reception Center, as the flow of draftees seems to have slowed down this week. It's hardly enough work to keep from being bored, but it certainly beats K.P. and cleaning up the whole camp.

The things I miss the most are tables and chairs and places to put things. It's a nuisance to have no place to sit except a bed, which likewise must serve as a table if you want to put anything down. Also, living out of these glorified laundry bags isn't so good, as everything you want is invariably at the bottom.

However, I'm getting a little used to it, and life isn't so bad, as long as I can cuss.

Last night I walked up to see Jackie Cooper and Phyllis Brooks in a USO show. They didn't overwork themselves, but Phyllis is certainly a cute number. The main feature of the show, or rather the main entertainment was Ada Leonard and her all-girl band. They put on some good numbers, especially comic tumbling and acrobatics. All in all, it was a pretty good show, but can you imagine me walking fifteen long blocks and back just to see a show? Truly, circumstances alter cases.

There's no news and nothing of any consequence going on. It seems that men may come and men may go, but I stay on forever. I am getting so I sort of like this place, and wouldn't mind getting transferred to the Headquarters Company, especially since they can get out whenever they want to, without getting gray hairs over it.

I have a notion that this is contrary to all rules and regulations, and I will probably be court-martialed if they find me using Uncle's time, stationary and typewriters this way. However, they won't give me any selectees to select, so I might as well spend my time in a good and pleasant way.

I have been over here three days now and have done about fifteen minutes work. For some reason there are not nearly as many coming through as there were last week. I don't mind not working hard, but I would just as soon have enough to keep me more or less occupied.

My good job just played out, on account of they put every-body at Headquarters to taking training. We were just temporary workers but they sent us along with the rest. So all afternoon I have been busy drilling. However, that is still better than K.P. and cleaning up, and I am learning things that will make it easier for me when I am permanently stationed.

Practically everyone has been shipped out of camp except me, and I still have no news.

Ft. Leonard Wood

I got in here about 10:30 this morning. Left Camp Robin-son at 7:00 a.m. yesterday, and the Mo. Pac. train was an hour late, with the result that it failed to connect with the Frisco at Hoxie, and I was stranded in that lovely metropolis from noon until 9:30. I went over to Walnut Ridge, a mile away, and saw a movie and visited with a law school classmate, so it wasn't too bad. The night train reached Springfield at 3:00 a.m., where I had to change again and wait until 5:45 and ride again to Newburg. There we were met by a six-wheel Army truck.

Here I am just thirty miles past the end of the world. It will always be a mystery to me how the man that found this location for a camp ever got back to civilization to tell about it. If I did not know they were long since dead, I would think this place was located by the bishops who discovered Sewanee. This is undoubt-edly the most desolate, God-forsaken spot I have ever laid eyes on. There are no signs of civilization for miles around, except good roads, and the place has that bare newness and sameness of all Army posts. To add to the general cheer, it seems to have rained last night, and the place is muddy and the skies are overcast and gloomy.

I suppose I should be flattered at being assigned to this outfit, as I understand that they take the highest I.Q. ratings and assign them to the Engineers. It is a fact that these boys seem a little above the general run. However, I would just as soon be a

3

little dumber and get a little less of this hard work, such as bridge building, pick-and-shovel work and hard running under a full pack. I don't know whether I ever will learn all this stuff, but I guess if these other lugs can do it, I can too.

This outfit seems to be composed of boys from Chicago, Ohio, Texas, and seven boys from California that came in with me. So far as I have observed, I am the only one from Arkansas.

We are in barracks, which seem to be very comfortable. There are about thirty in this room, which is upstairs, and room for an equal number downstairs, but it is still empty.

We are in quarantine and confined to our company area for two weeks. Can't even go over to the Post Exchange across the street. Maybe things will be relaxed a little when we get settled, but that is what we have been told.

Things will be better here, as we will be issued foot lockers (small trunks) and will have a place where we can put things and keep them in order. Also, we will be able to send out laundry, which is approaching the point of necessity with me. Furthermore, we are getting started on our real training, and it's more like an Army and less like a mob.

This morning I was ordered up to see the Post Intelligence officer and got a nice, cool walk of a mile or so up to Headquarters. He interviewed me regarding the Army Intelligence, and I believe I will get in. That means that at the end of my eight weeks here, I will be sent to school, probably at Chicago, with a sergeants' rating, and if I complete the school course successfully I will be a 1st sergeant or technical sergeant with a good chance of becoming an officer. Naturally, I am a good deal pepped up about it, and the prospect makes this training a good deal easier to take.

By the way, if you haven't already said anything about what I wrote about the military Intelligence, it might be wise not to mention it. They didn't tell me so, but I think it is more or less confidential.

We are really getting lots of new things. Today we started learning the manual of arms with the rifle, and we find a thousand different things to keep clean. How I'm going to find time to clean and polish everything that has to be shiny for inspection is more than I can figure. I'm becoming an expert with the scrub brush and polishing rag.

Tonight our outfit has guard duty. I am on the fire guard and don't have to walk post, which is decidedly a break. All we do is sit around in a building for 24 hours and wait for a fire. If there is one, we are supposed to assist the firemen in some way they haven't explained to us, so I guess we will just blow the fire out. Anyhow, there isn't supposed to be any fire, so we are settling down to catch up on our sleep, reading, and correspondence.

The rest of the company, or most of it, will have to walk post or guard prisoners at work, two hours on duty and four hours off, for 24 hours. Some of them have never fired a gun, and hardly any have ever fired one of these rifles, so they should be a big help in the event of invasion.

I don't know whether I will ever get to be a soldier. Just when I begin to catch on to what I've been shown, they give us a thousand and one new things to learn. There are all kinds of equipment to be taken care of and no time to do it, and I don't think I'll ever learn how to use all the tools and gadgets we are supposed to understand. Every day I appreciate more how well off I was before.

There is an old saying that if our foresight were as good as our hindsight we would be better off by a damn sight, and I am appreciating how true it is.

Today we went out and learned some combat tactics - how to cover and advance while keeping protected. The idea is to run a little way and dive behind the nearest tree, stump, etc. That's all very well, but the catch is that the woods are full of sticks and stones and very rough indeed. I haven't felt this way since I quit playing football. However, I am getting in better shape, losing a little weight and a little waistline, and even though somewhat stiff, battered and tired, I feel pretty good.

We had another tough day today, although not as rough as the two preceding. This morning we had lots of drill, both close order (parade formations) and extended order (combat formations). We also had some of the famous pick and shovel work, although not enough to hurt, and did I look dignified wielding them! This afternoon it was a long hike, partly cross-country and down a mountainside. I was already sore as a boil from all the bouncing around, running and diving on rocks of the past two days, and tonight I will need rocking to sleep. However, I'm getting in better shape daily, and this soreness ought to begin to work out tomorrow.

You asked about the food. I guess the less said about it the better.

Through Friday this was about as hard a week of work as ever I went through, and after hours about all I could do was drag through the cleaning up that had to be done and get to bed.

During the first part of the week I was so stiff and sore that it seemed sometimes I wouldn't be able to get going next time. Friday morning was worst of all, and that was our toughest day - drill all morning and then about two miles with eight packs out to where we practiced combat work in the woods. More drill after lunch, and then a six mile hike with full field packs (about fifty or sixty pounds), and after getting in we had to scrub the barracks and clean all our equipment for Saturday inspection.

I went to church this morning and feel very virtuous. It does make you feel better to go, particularly for someone who needs it as much as I do after the things I say and think during the week about this life.

Our quarantine ended this weekend, and about half the boys immediately applied for passes and went charging off in all directions. No doubt they will all come staggering in tonight blind running drunks and feel like hell tomorrow. And will my halo shine?

Some of the boys were pretty fairly charged and rather amusing when they got in, so there wasn't much sleeping early. I nearly choked laughing at two of them. There were also a few A-grade hangovers.

Well, I am now one-fourth through this damned course, and I've made it this far. It reminds me of the first quarter of a mile race, when I used to start thinking, "By golly, they're running this too fast." But I always finished my mile, and I'll finish this too, and maybe be a soldier when I'm through.

We have been learning how to shoot rifles, and tomorrow we have our first day on the range. It has to be done the Army way, and I have a notion I won't be too good at it. My method of shooting a gun is to take aim and shoot it, but in the Army you have to harness yourself up with the rifle sling and get in the most uncomfortable position you can find first. When I get through aiming it and getting all fixed up, I am so cramped that the sight is waving like a nightshirt on a clothesline.

I hear the Intelligence Service has been investigating me in Helena, and it is very encouraging.

For the last few days we have been working on the rifle range and will continue to do so until we shoot for record about the middle of this week. Of course, I like to shoot and have been doing fairly well at it so far. With a little improvement I should qualify for a sharpshooter. The only drawback to shooting is that we leave the barracks early in the morning and stay away all day, eating in the field. Then when we get in there are lots of things to be done, particularly cleaning rifles and mess kits. The ammunition has some sort of powder in it which fouls the rifles worse than any I ever saw, and after they have been cleaned once they have to be attended to over and over again every few hours, as there are some salts that sweat and corrode the barrel.

Today we had another full day in the field, leaving the barracks at seven-thirty. We were working on combat principles and running around the woods pretending we were attacking somebody. The day wound up with a big attack by the whole company. We had live ammunition and tricky little moving targets, and made an attack with real shooting. After shooting I came home and wrapped up in my pup tent like an Indian chief. I looked almost as military as General MacArthur.

Today I became a machine gunner, and now I will turn to other military pursuits, maybe the bayonet. While we were on the range, a terrible wind came up, and some way a fire got started in the woods so the Army had to quit fighting the targets and go fight the fire. It was a most unpleasant mess, but such is life. You have no idea how pleasant a meal can be with the wind blowing smoke into your eyes and grit and soot in every bite and swallow.

While we were fighting the fire, a rain blew up and put it out. Of course, I had to go off without my raincoat, and with all the enemies we had to make an attack and bayonet charge down one mountain and up the one opposite. It's a wonder I didn't fall down and cut my throat.

Today we worked on road obstacles and tank traps. That sounded very interesting and important, but really it consists of digging deep holes and setting up small saw logs in and about them. All this is done by hand, and I do not love either pick and shovels or toting trees around.

Tomorrow we go to pontoon school, which is a separate school down on the river about five miles from here. We have to pack our barracks bags and then march down there with full field packs and equipment. We will be there until Thursday and then get a nice hike back – uphill. It's rather primitive there - no lights or other conveniences and eating out of full mess kits.

I was out on the river Friday when we were digging fox-holes and trenches, and it is a pretty, clear, little mountain stream. However, I have a notion it is plenty cold, and I have a picture of the whole thing running in my boots.

Last week got pretty tough towards the end, when we were working on field fortifications, tank traps, road blocks and trench-es. Digging foxholes is particularly fun - you lie flat on the ground and dig a hole big enough to lie in it full length.

We marched down here this morning, about five miles, with everything but the kitchen stove hung on us. The hiking wasn't bad, but, as usual, the weather turned off bitterly cold, and we have been having snow flurries all day. It was certainly an un-pleasant day to be messing around a river, and of course one poor devil had to fall in.

We have been working plenty hard, but we have a good crew and have been getting through early. This pontoon work is interesting, although the timbers really get heavy. The only disadvantage is that we stay dirty all the time.

Today we went through the gas chamber. First we wore gas masks, then went back in with masks on, took them off, and walked out. That was to show how good the masks are, and they are good. I couldn't have cried much more if you quit loving me.

I got a lucky break today when I missed out on guard duty. About half the platoon caught it, and they will have a day of nice long walks with very little sleep between.

Today is a beautiful Easter morning, and I just got back from the big outdoor Easter service. There was a choir of about 125 voices, a big band, organ and piano, and the music was fine. I guess there were over a thousand men there, and the service was really inspiring.

Our training is nearing an end here, and after next week some will start leaving, and the whole outfit should be gone about the 18th. I probably won't go with the rest of the company. I probably can't get out until my orders arrive. What I'll do then depends on whether I go to the officers school or to the Intelligence Service.

Yesterday was one of those days that made me wonder why I ever was a soldier. I was just congratulating myself on getting out of both guard duty and inspection, when they came along and picked me up on a labor detail. I spent the whole day unloading coal out of trucks.

If I get any tougher, I'll just nail my clothes on instead of buttoning them.

I am on guard at the demolition area, about four miles from camp, and have just finished my third two-hour shift, guarding the dynamite magazine; one more and I'll be through.

It is a beautiful day, and this is a pretty place. I am stretched out on a blanket between two big trees in a little grassy valley. There is a noisy little brook about fifty feet away, and the trees are beginning to bud. Redbud and wild plums are blooming on the hillsides, and dogwoods are just beginning to open. Across on the ridge a quail is whistling, and doves are cooing and birds singing everywhere. It's a good day to be alive, even in the Army.

I hear, unofficially, that I have been accepted for the Intelligence Service and am supposed to leave within a couple of days.

Yesterday I got another piece of good news. I have applied for and been approved for the Finance Service Officers Training School and passed the physical, but now the captain tells me that this camp has no quota for that service, so I am stuck here until they get one. He says I may be here for as much as four months, and if something does not turn up in that time I will be shipped out to an Engineer outfit, which is about the same as a chain gang. While here I won't be so bad off - my status will be that of acting cadre (the permanent training personnel). As such I will have no K.P. or work details and will have a class A pass, which allows me to leave the post whenever I am not on duty. However, I didn't come here to be stuck as a private or maybe a corporal in this God-forsaken hole.

If I didn't have a sense of humor, I believe this business would run me crazy, but there's always something funny about my troubles.

I am going to Omaha. This Intelligence work should be a good thing. I don't know exactly what my address will be except Ft. Omaha.

Chapter 2

Omaha & Kansas City
U.S.A., 3 May - 30 July 1942

We reached Omaha late last night after a tough trip. Our train to Kansas City was late and missed the morning connection, so we stayed over and caught the afternoon train, which was a streamliner just like the Delta Eagle.

This business we are getting into is kept so much on the q.t. that nobody seems to know anything about it, and those who do just smile wisely and say nothing when asked. All I can find out is that we will be moved out of the post and sent to school.

I am continuing my important work for national defense. Since I got back I have been working on the moving van, moving the household goods of all the officers and non-coms who move on and off the post. It could be a lot worse, and anyhow there isn't much I can do about it. There are some signs of activity in the office downtown, and I have hopes of knowing something soon. As well as I can observe, everything the Army does is a masterpiece of inefficiency.

Yesterday I arranged an interview with the major who runs the Omaha Intelligence office, and he informed me that he had just received word that I was definitely accepted. He says my transfer papers will come through in the next ten days. One of my best friends was accepted today.

The long-anticipated day has finally arrived, and I am sitting here waiting for my orders proclaiming me a sergeant and transferring me to military Intelligence. Thereupon I will report downtown, purchase $140 worth of civilian clothes, and take up residence in a hotel. The new pay is going to look almost respectable, too. Under the present schedule it is, with food and lodging allowances, about $130 per month, and under the new bill it will be around $150. I will check in all my uniforms and equipment for storage. I am a bit proud of the uniform and hate to give it up, but that will be compensated by turning in the fatigue clothes.

It looks like we will have plenty to do here. We have to work seven days a week, and as I understand, frequently at night.

Another thing - from now on my doings are supposed to be more or less confidential, so forgive me if I don't write too much about them, and if anybody is around, you don't know what my service is or what I'm doing. Forget all about my Army. This Army that I now belong to is a very heathen one and thinks that people should work on Sunday - and all the rest of the time, for that matter. They want us to work all day and then come back at night to finish up. That might not be too bad if the night work was like you see in the movies, but so far I haven't heard anything about drinking champagne with beautiful babes and tricking them into giving themselves away, or something. It seems that we are more concerned with checking up on a bunch of bums who have no social value whatever. It looks as if I will do a lot of traveling, sometimes for a week at a time. I have gone right to work and am now on my first case. There's one thing about this work - it is really thorough, and anyone who is investigated by this outfit is really checked on, whether they are trying to get him a job or get him shot. Maybe some day, when all the fifth columnist are in hell, and all the ambitious young men in the Army have been proven to be model citizens...

Left K.C. this morning about 9:45 and I have had a pretty good trip, in that I had no trouble and found it pretty interesting. I covered more than eleven hundred miles in seven days, in addition to making the Lord knows how many interviews. For the next couple of days I will be busy writing up final reports on my cases, and then I will be ready to go again.

After a good day's work I had to take off tonight and spend a couple hours down town on some interviews that couldn't be done by day, so I've had a pretty good session.

Everyday they are crowding more cases on us.

Unless the school is discontinued, I should certainly go to the next one, which will be about August 1st.

As for foreign services, there is no telling, but definitely a large number will go. If I have to go, I am not afraid of it, but I certainly don't want it.

These aren't reasonable times, anyhow, are they? Today I was on duty all day. I intended to take off and go swimming this afternoon but just as I was getting ready to pick up and leave the major decided to have a conference. So for two hours we sat and listened to him and two looeys shoot off their mouths about some utterly immaterial matters.

Chatham Hotel

BROADWAY AT THIRTY-SEVENTH

KANSAS CITY, MO.

Then we came back to the hotel and moved to the address on the letterhead. The major is having a grand time playing detective, so we are not to reveal our identity under any circumstances, which is very mysterious, and our mail is to come to the office, 319 Porter Bldg., 34th and Broadway. If you should want to call me, you can reach me at Logan 28149, the office, or here under the name of Apex Novelty Co.

I had expected to leave today on a pretty long trip which would take the rest of the week and maybe longer, going nearly out to Colorado. However, we are snowed under with office work, and the whole outfit has been in typing, which is most dull, hot, and tiresome.

Our major is the most unreasonable man I ever met in the matter of taking off, as well as some others. Furthermore, he is now in a vile humor, suffering severely from big-shotitis since getting his promotion, and complicated at present by the fact that we are way behind in office work.

It is hotter than hell here, and I am not at all happy. We have started getting up every morning at 6:00 for exercise, and have to dash across town to a gym and then back to dress and have breakfast. I enjoy the exercise, but losing the sleep is a pain, and all the rushing around is a nuisance. That is just one of the fool ideas our C.O. has come up with. These road trips are unpleasant, but it would be a blessing to get away from him.

Tonight Seminara and I went to see "Eagle Squadron," and had lots of fun watching the gadgets zoom and shoot each other up. It's a pretty good show.

Ryan has grabbed his little gun and black jack and gone charging off to catch a spy or something - real glamorous. I am still super-sleuthing with a typewriter, but may take off shortly for the Kansas wilderness.

There's still no news about going to school. The major says we will go, but that is just his guess and probably wrong if he thinks it.

Last night we all decided to go out to Swope Park and go boat riding in that lagoon. We got one of the motor boats, four of us, and sailed merrily away. However, we came to grief, on account of we got too close to the bank and cut off a citizen's fishing line, and was he unhappy! He came around to the dock and was going to have us all arrested or maybe throw us in the lake until he saw that we were fairly well matured and not averse to a little throwing. Finally we told him we would buy him another line, but then it developed that it was a very fine line and cost $1.59. The war almost started sure enough then, as any fool could see that it was rotten and never cost that much anyhow. The upshot was that we finally went off and bought him what we considered a suitable line, and when we got back he was gone, so now I am practically ready to go fishing.

It's a lovely moonlit night that I ought to be spending with you, but instead I've got to go charging out and mess around with a bunch of bomber plant employees to see if they talk too much when they're full of beer.

It looks as if the school will definitely go on. The boys from the last one got in last weekend, and they say the next one will start Monday. I am the first on the list in this corps, so I guess I'll be there. It lasts four weeks. However, I still have no orders, and they'll probably wait until an hour before train time.

Yesterday afternoon all of us took off and drove out to Excelsior Springs, about 25 miles, where there is a salt spring, and a salt water swimming pool. We had a swell swim, and then came back to the apartment to have a supper of Italian salami and cheese which Seminara's folks sent him, with beer to make it good.

We had pistol practice tonight, the first time I had ever shot one except to plug away a few times at a tin can. I had the best score in the crowd, although it was not too impressive.

I rather doubt that I'll get back to Kansas City, as two new men have come in to replace us. The other possible assignments are Omaha, St. Paul, St. Louis, and Denver.

I'll be at school until about the 29th of August.

Chapter 3

Chicago G-2 Training School
U.S.A., August 1942 and February 1943

Headquarters Seventh Service Command
Service of Supply
Office of the Commanding General

Letter No. 6-1970   *Omaha, Nebraska,*
AG 220.48-(Conf)   *30 July 1942*
xAG ea 201 (7)-(Conf)
Subject: *Detached Service.*
To: *Assistant Chief of Staff, G-2, Hq Seventh SC, Omaha, Nebraska.*

       Each of the following named sergeants, DEML (CIC), Hq Seventh SC, Omaha, Nebr, is placed on detached service with the Investigators' Training School, Chicago, Ill, and will proceed thereto on or about 1 August 1942, reporting upon arrival to the commandant, that school, for duty.

SCHWEERS
WILCOX
ST VRAIN
HARDEN
DALY
WALKER
SEMINARA

       Travel will be performed by rail and the Finance Dept will pay each enlisted man, in advance, the monetary travel allowance prescribed in table II, AR 35-4520, at a rate of $3.00 per day for rations for one (1) day, it being impracticable for the government *to furnish cooking facilities for rations for the round trip.*

It being impractical for the government to furnish cooking facilities for rations in kind, while on detached service at Chicago, Ill, the Finance Dept will pay each enlisted man, in advance, the monetary allowance prescribed in Table II.

AR 35-4520, for a period of thirty-one (31) days, at a rate of $2.25 per day for rations   for the first three (3) days, $1.65 per day the next three (3) days, and $1.40 per day for the remaining twenty-five (25) days.

The travel directed is necessary in the military service. FD 34 P 434-02 **A 0425-23.**

By command of Major General UHL: **DF Fesler,**
Captain, AGD,
Asst Adjutant General.

G-2 Courses of Training & Advanced Training of CIC agent & special agents in 1942 & 1943

Aerial Photograph Reading	*Aims & Methods of Japanism*
Alien Registration Law & Investigation	*Anti-American Ideologies*
Applicant Investigation	*Bombs & Explosives*
Bombs & Infernal Machines	*CIC Detachment in Theatre of Ops*
CIC Rules & Regulations	*Civil Service Act & Regulations*
Codes & Ciphers	*Conspiracy*
Contacts & Sources of Information	*Counter Subversive System*
Crime Laboratory Equipment	*Disloyalty Investigation*
Espionage & Counter Espionage	*Examination of Evidence*
Examination of Hand Writing	*Explosives Laws*
Field Stations of Immigration, Naturalization	
& Border Control	*Fingerprints*
Fingerprinting	*Firearms Laws*
General Principal of Investigative Procedures	*Handwriting*
Impersonation	*Informers*
Inspection of Quarters	*Interrogation of Witness & Prisoners*
Investigative Table of Violations	*Investigative Photography*
Jiu Jitsu	*Latent Fingerprinting*
Law of Arrest	*Law of Evidence*

Law of Search & Seizure	Methods of Communist Infiltration
Methods of Searching	Methods of Surveillance
Microphone Installation	
Military "Assignment to Temporary Duty"	
Modus Operandi – Arsonists	Moot Court
Mulage	Observation & Description
Organization of the Army	
Organizations & Functions of the Military Police	
Organizations having Communist, Nazi, and Fascists Leanings	
Organizations of the German Army	
Personal Description	Photography
Plaster Casts	Plaster of Paris
Police Lab Work	Post Office Inspectors
Practical Work	Preservation of Evidence
Report Writing Practical Problem	Report Writing Summary Report
Russian Section of the 5th Column	Sabotage & Saboteurs
Safeguarding Military Information	Search & Seizures
Signal Communications	Surveillance
Systems of Identification	Telephone Installation
Telephone Supervision	Total Espionage
Treason	Treasury Department Agencies
Undercover Investigation	Undercover Work
Uniforms & Insignias	U.S. Courts Federal Procedures
Warrant	1, 2, 3, March...

G-2 Training School August 1942

The Tower Town Club used to be some sort of women's club and hotel, but has been taken over by the Army and Navy. We are on the 11th floor, and our room looks out over Lake Michigan, which is only a couple of blocks away. The first ten floors are taken over by some sort of naval officers' business, about 1200 of them. We have our meals and our classes here.

Classes start tomorrow, and will last about 7 or 8 hours a day, including two hours of exercise and jiu-jitsu. We will be able to get up at a reasonable hour and will have Sundays off.

Chicago is overrun with soldiers and sailors. The Air Corps has taken over the Congress and Stevens hotels. Also, the

18

Great Lakes Naval Station is here.

We decided to see something of the town and went down to the College Inn. The idea was that we could stand at the bar and wouldn't have to pay a cover charge, but it wasn't such a hot one, as the bar was so far away you needed a radio to hear. Drinks are fifty cents a throw, and there was a mob there, besides which the music was nothing to write home about, so I considered the evening rather a wash-out.

I saw Paul Whitman's band on the stage at Omaha Friday, heard Duke Ellington for a few minutes Saturday, and Ozzie Nelson last night, so I'm pretty well up on my name bands.

There are too many people in Chicago, and I don't care too much for it. I guess I am truly a country boy. If you were a millionaire, you might be able to have a good time here one or two nights a month, but I'd rather spend the night at Bear Creek than a month here.

We have been having eight hours of lecture a day, which is a lot to try to absorb, and I don't know whether I'm learning anything or not. Yesterday afternoon I had my first class in jiu-jitsu, and no doubt I'll soon know how to twist off somebody's arm and club him to death with it, all in one simple twist of the wrist.

I'm just in from exercise, which consisted of a good swim this afternoon. It felt good, too, as seven hours of listening to bull and taking notes thereon is truly tiresome. This school is not too hard, but there is certainly a lot of it. There are bales of material to be read and studied, and so far all I've done is take it down. I'll have to take off over the weekend and read it all over, as our first exam is Monday.

I used to be able to absorb and retain things without too much study, and I hope the gift has not deserted me.

They are certainly giving us plenty to do. I don't even have time to put things off, and you know how I hate that.

The exam yesterday wasn't too hard, and I think I did fairly well at it, although I doubt I'll duplicate my collegiate grades. Somehow I can't get very enthusiastic about studying too hard on this stuff. There is too much of it, and a large part is the purest bull.   From now on our work will consist of more practice of things we are supposed to have learned and less class work, and I think it will be more interesting. I am getting so much like a cop that I even have flat feet.

Last night I was out galloping around the city playing cops and robbers. I was the "hare" and two other guys were the "hounds" and supposed to follow me all around to see what I was doing, just like I didn't know they were there.

Tonight we had a test blackout (the whole city) from 10 to 10:30. Of course, it would come when we were all busy as the devil writing up a long-winded report that is due first thing in the morning, so half an hour was wasted. It certainly was black with all the lights everywhere turned off.

This afternoon we had to practice undercover work - snooping around a restaurant supposed to be suspicious. We had all afternoon to do it, and I couldn't possibly think of a way to kill more than an hour in the damned joint, which didn't even sell beer.

We have been getting lots of work, and I have been plenty busy. We haven't received many grades so far, but the ones I have got have been very satisfactory. None of this is hard, but there is so much of it that at times I get tired and feel like saying to hell with it.

All day today I was downtown riding around with a couple of A.T.U. guys learning all about practical copping. However, the bootlegger they were supposed to catch failed to appear, so we just sat and waited most of the time, and I didn't learn how to be a super-sleuth.

Grades are beginning to come in, and I have done pretty well so far. We have another exam Monday, for which I have a world of reading to do, so it looks like another peaceful week-end.

Counter Intelligence Corps

This is to Certify, That

SERGEANT GEORGE D. WALKER

has successfully completed the course of instruction in the

INVESTIGATORS TRAINING SCHOOL

For the Assistant Chief of Staff, G-2:

Commandant
THEODORE J. WALKER,
Major, M. I.

HUGH D. WISE,
Major, F. A.,
Chief, Counter Intelligence Corps.

Date 8-29-42

Copies to

Original to Studen...
The Adjutant General.
A. C. of S G-2, ____th____ Corps Area.

SUPREME COURT
STATE OF ARKANSAS
LITTLE ROCK

October 15, 1942.

TO WHOM IT MAY CONCERN:

      I have been requested to make a statement regarding Sgt. G. D. Walker, D. E. M. L., Denver, Colorado.

      I have no hesitancy in emphasizing the fact that Mr. Walker is one of the best young lawyers in Arkansas, he having been admitted to the bar in 1934. Not only does he handle his cases well, both as a trial lawyer and in appellate work, but he is a young man of exemplary habits, fine personality, initiative, courage, and adaptability.

      He will do well any task assigned. His legal training has been with one of the state's outstanding firms, the members of which think very highly of him.

      This letter is written in all sincerity and not as a mere formality, or for the purpose of accommodating interested parties.

Yours very truly,

GRIFFIN SMITH

(Chief Justice Supreme Court
of Arkansas.)

Advanced G-2 Training School February 1943

The school is located just off Michigan Ave., but down south in a run-down part of town, about a block from the Stevens Hotel and just across from the Illinois Central station. We are in what used to be a women's club, but it is older and not as well fitted up as the one we were in before.

Lt. Mohr was officer of the day when we got in and seemed delighted to see us. The officers live here too, and he had Tom and me come up to his room when he got off at midnight. We received all the gossip, and he has apparently been having a large time for himself. He says the school is as silly and boring as ever, and since he didn't want to come anyhow he is not enthusiastic about this higher education.

Apparently there is no particular reason to anticipate foreign service as a result of this school. At least, that is the general opinion, and the best information I can get.

When I got on the train, I was much surprised to see Seminara there, visiting with the boys and waiting to see me. He was supposed to have gone across but was turned down on account of a bad appendix. He was quite enthusiastic about the foreign service set-up and said it looked like a good deal, but he is welcome to it.

Again I have fallen in foul company, on account of I have been out with Lt. Mohr. That is funny, because I was out with him last night and the night before, and always the same. In a minute I have got to go back upstairs and help put his best buddy to bed. He was too drunk a while ago and wouldn't go.

Two days of my higher education have now passed, and, aside from the fact that the remaining number has been reduced to twenty-five, I can't say that anything has been accomplished. So far there hasn't been a single new idea, and I don't think there's going to be. The officers in charge don't know what to do with us, as they say nobody told them that this was to be a refresher course for old men.

I went up to the Lt.'s room tonight and typed a report for him. If he passes this school, it will be a wonder. Hopper came in, and we chewed the rag over a couple of drinks a while. Then the Lt. was invited out with the officers to visit Vargas, the artist who draws the beautiful babes in Esquire, etc. I don't know whether the babes were to be there in the flesh or just the pictures, but anyhow they were told that they could look but mustn't touch. Hopper and I went out for a light beer and then hurried home for bed check.

While I was doing the Lt.'s work for him, I neglected my own, so I guess I'll sit up a while. Of course, I could have passed up that beer and done mine, but one can't give up everything for duty.

All these boys with me are corporals or newly made sergeants, and they are fighting fiercely to get the work done. I think they consider me a subversive element on account of I don't give a damn.

There are no other old men in this school besides those from our Command, except four - two master sergeants and two techs - who came from Hawaii. They had been there ever since Pearl Harbor without going to school, and they could teach the faculty.

The Lt. is very unhappy. It looks as if he is going to pass the course in spite of his worst efforts. He made 91 on his second exam and he's passed everything so far in spite of never studying a minute. Will he be surprised when he gets back to Omaha and finds himself sober for the first time in a month!

This afternoon we had a practice surveillance and got hold of a no-good bum who wouldn't cooperate. He walked us all over Chicago, and he could really walk fast. I am a tired citizen.

The days all ride past on caterpillars, and another week has finally dragged by today. I just asked my roommates if this was Wednesday but no such luck. The past ten days seem ten times longer than the whole fall, and I could swear that I have been here forever.

The Lt. got his final grade this afternoon - 94.5! He is passing with flying colors, and still without one minute's study. Everyone wonders how he did it. He was about half tight all after-noon in class, and they have gone out tonight to make a thorough job of it. I just don't know why I bother to study. This school isn't hard, but it certainly is boring.

This afternoon I again spent with the Lt., having a few be-fore pouring him on the city of Denver. It looks like that's getting to be a habit with me. He is to be in Omaha before he takes off for Bismark. He says he is going to try to promote it for us to get up there. Maybe he'll drop me a line to let me know the deal, but he's not much of a line-dropper. He graduated with flying colors - 13th in the 13th class at the school on Feb. 13th, if that means anything. I sure hated to see him go, but I wouldn't wish it on anyone to stay here, although I did offer to go out and open up the office for him if he would stay here and complete the course for me. Strangely enough, he wasn't interested.

On the way back from the station, I stopped with another Lt. who was a friend of Lt. Mohr and had supper at a Chinese restaurant down in the Loop. They have excellent Chinese food. He is here in the room now, sleeping loudly while waiting for his train to leave at 9:00. I will pour him on, and that ought to be about my duty by the country for this weekend.

The Lt. called me from Omaha about noon today. He had forgotten to check out of the school, and I had to go down and sign him out.

I had another nice letter from Mo. He said that they have in six new men, making eight altogether since we left. I guess I take some replacing!

I had a note from the Lt., returning his room key for me to turn in. He said he had not had a chance to get any dope at Headquarters.

School has been a little better this week. We've been doing practical stuff like installing microphones and tapping telephones, which is more or less interesting. Being a veteran, I am supposed to know how to do it, so the rest of my group stands around while I pitch in just like I had seen the damned things before. The result is that I have learned a few things that I ought to have known already, and that is the first thing I have learned.

Tonight I indulged one of your favorite desires and went to a burlesque show with two of my roommates. Both of them are married, so we made good chaperones for each other. This end of town is full of them, but we had to walk way up to the Loop to see the one that is supposed to be the best. I must say that I was never so gypped. You can walk down the street on a windy spring day and see more and better scenery, and the dancing was ordinary, the singing lousy, and the jokes unbelievably corny. I am a sad citizen.

After the show (we went early) we went up to a restaurant which is supposed to have fine steaks, where I paid $1.40 for a smack club steak, which was not too tender and altogether about a 40¢ steak. That made me a sadder citizen. Food prices here are absolutely outrageous, and the quality in the best places is nothing to brag about. The only exciting thing is that another week is nearly by - only eight more days here!

Your Wednesday letter came this morning and found me in the middle of directing my squad in a giant man-hunt which would have kept J. Edgar Hoover in the headlines for weeks. We had an all-day problem, in which we installed a microphone in a citizen's room, listened to his conversation, trailed him around town, and finally trapped him and his accomplice with the stolen plans - the rats! You should have seen your dashing husband pinch off a 1st lieutenant, who was the spy, and brutally twist his arm behind his back in the very best jiu-jitsu arrest. Great stuff - and it will help me to no end in finding out if Johnny is a good boy and whether his grandmother smokes. It really was interesting, though, and may someday be helpful.

Having been the squad leader and directed this monster spy hunt, I was greatly exhausted by my efforts, so I commanded one of my trusty sides to accompany me as a bodyguard and went to the Chicago Theatre, where we saw Claudette Colbert in "Palm Beach Story" and Beatrice Kaye on the stage.

This morning Bridewell called me and invited me up to the Chicago University Club after I got off. I went up about four and got a good workout in the gym and a good swim. It is quite a swanky establishment - eleven stories, with libraries, dining rooms, gym, squash and handball courts, and numerous other such. Bridewell says that the Navy has advised him that they are full up with admirals and can't use him, so he is a sad citizen. He will probably be drafted right into the fighting Army. I am supposed to call him and have lunch one day next week if I can get off.

This afternoon we got our first exam papers back, and the old gentleman made 94. There were three or four higher, the highest being 96.5, but I was very well pleased, considering the time and effort I had put forth. Your friend Hopper made 78 - 80 being passing. We have a three-hour exam Thursday afternoon to finish up. That is too long, but I am not going to worry my pretty head too much about it.

Tonight I did an awful thing. Having re-read the two letters I got from you, and read the paper and the American Field from cover to cover, there was nothing left for me to do but study. After doing that for a couple of hours I was so ashamed and in such a desperate nervous condition that I had to go down to Danny's Saloon on the corner and have a couple of beers to drown my sorrow.

I haven't heard any more from the Lt., which does not greatly surprise me. I guess I'll have to wait until I get to Omaha to find out what the deal is. I'm not sure whether any other boys will be sent back here. They are somewhat confused about that.

I found out about my train today. It leaves here at 12:45 and is supposed to reach Omaha about nine.

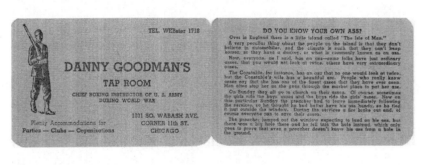

Chapter 4

Lessons Learned

G-2 Training School – GDW Notes
August 1942 & February 1943

Immigration & Naturalization
Sedition
Disaffection Investigation
Disloyalty Investigation
Conspiracy
Treason
Treason: Impersonation
Communism
Fascism
National Socialists (Nazi) Party
Organization of German Army
Uniforms & Insignias

CIC Policies & Regulations
CIC to PIO
Codes & Ciphers
Espionage & Counter Espionage
Evidence
Personal Description
Observation & Description
Method of Searching
Interrogation
Undercover Investigation
Undercover
Sabotage & Saboteurs

Not True to U.S.A.
Synonyms ~
Unfaithful, inconstant, treacherous, deceitful, false

Immigration & Naturalization

Established 1891 in Treasury Dept. to enforce Chinese Exclusion Act 1906 to Dept of Comm and Labor 1913 – Dept of Labor 1933 combined with Naturalization 1941 – Dept of Justice administers all provisions of laws relating to immunization, naturalization alien registration.

Immigration Section - admission – deportation.

Naturalization Section – testing and certifying to courts of persons entitled to citizenship.

Border Patrol – to prevent illegal entry between ports of entry manned by immigration inspectors.

Alien Registration Section – enforcement of Alien Registration Act.

First alien act was Chinese Exclusion Act covering Asiatic races, except as students, professional men, and visitors.

Basic act was that of 2/5/17 – deportation of undesirable aliens and those who entered illegally.

1921 Selective Immigration Act – set up selection. 1924 National Origins Act – quotas based on number according to national origins. 1890-1910 .

Law now provides not more than 153,000 per year can enter for permanent residences. Provides for deportation of aliens involved in moral turpitude, convicted of 2 felonies, and public charges.

Public 670 - 76th congress Omnibus Sedition Act. Provides for deportation of alien violating Alien Registration Act or convicted of carrying automatic weapon or riot gun. Alien Act provides for registration and fingerprinting of aliens entering country and all of those in U.S. over 14 years of age; parent or guardian required to apply for younger. Files are confidential but available to CIC upon proper application.

Alien residents are required to notify comm. of immigration for each change of address within 5 days; others every three months. Alien questionnaires sent to Washington and filed in comm. of Immigration - fingerprints to FBI.

El Paso border control office has 100,000 fingerprints of aliens returned through that office for illegal entry.

Sedition

First sedition law under John Adams prohibited any criticism of conduct of government which interfered with orderly administration.

First amendment prohibits passage of any law abridging freedom of speech or press.

Constitution cannot be construed to uphold attacks on existence of government.

Sedition is the stirring up of disorder in state, tending toward treason, but lacking the overt act. Advocacy of force or violence in overturning the government is sedition. A revolt against legitimate authority, a factious commotion within a state, the stirring up of such a commotion, the incitement of discontent against government, and the disturbance of public tranquility, as by inflammatory speeches and writing, or acts or language tending to breach the public order.

In this country the words must directly tend to foment riot or rebellion or other breach of peace. Must obviously create a clear and present danger among the people. Schenk Case by Holmes recognized that war could make words seditious which might not be in peace.

50 U.S.C. ~33: Whoever, when U.S. is at war, shall willfully make or convey false reports or false statements with intent to interfere with the operation for success of military or naval forces of the U.S. or to promote success of enemies, and whoever in war shall, willfully cause or attempt to cause insubordination, disloyalty, muting, or refusal of duty in military or naval forces, or shall willfully obstruct recruiting or enlistment, shall be punished by fine of not more than $10,000 or 20 years, or both.

8 U.S.C.~ 137- Unlawful: To knowingly advocate, abet, advise, or teach the duty, necessity, or desirability or propriety to overthrowing or destroying any government of U.S. by force or violence or by assassination of any officer; (2) with intent to cause overthrow or destruction of any government in U.S. to print, publish, edit, issue, circulate, sell, distribute or publicly display any written or printed matter advocating, advising or teaching duty, etc., of overthrowing or destroying any government in U.S. by force; (3) to organize or help to organize any society, group, or assembly of persons to teach, advocate, or encourage the overthrow of any government in U.S. by force or violence, or to affiliate with or be

a member of any such group, knowing purposes thereof; $10,000, or 10 years, or both.

Disaffection Investigation

Disaffection - may be violation, 96th Article of War. State of alienation of affections from U.S. government, a disgust, ill-will, or hostility toward it.

Disloyalty is a pure lack of allegiance. Unfaithfulness, inconstancy, perfidious, deceitful, faithless, untrustworthy.

Necessary to prove (1) act, and (2) intent.

"I cannot see how the government can compel troops to go to France. If it was up to me I would tell them to go to hell. It is a damned shame. Why have not the socialists of America the same privileges as they have in Germany?" Held guilty of inciting insubordination.

Directive on "Basis for Transfer of Personnel to Specific Organizations." (1) If S is in subversive activity. (2) When S has strong sympathy for enemy. (3) When party has parents or close relatives in enemy country and refuses or objects to fighting a particular enemy. (4) Those who have been members German-American Bund, employees in German foreign office, or employees of enemy government or enemy quasi-governmental agency. (5) S served in enemy armed forces in recent years. (6) S's activities in our own Army demonstrates that he is pro-Army. (7) S is fearful of reprisals on family in enemy country. (8) S entered U.S. from enemy country subsequent to January 1, 1939 and have shown no positive evidence of loyalty.

In all cases where transfer is made, it is based on Safety.

Disloyalty Investigation

Loyalty investigation is made where nothing derogatory is known. Disloyalty is where adverse information to loyalty is known and the basis for investigation.

Characteristic of disaffection in the element of affection for another country.

Disloyalty may (1) endanger the safety of the nation; or

(2) cause damage to the nation; (3) or injure the prestige of the military service among (a) military or (b) civilians.

Affidavit form: (name), serial no., being duly sworn under oath, deposes & says: That he is a member of the armed forces of U.S. & is now attached to _____.

Affidavit further states _____ (details of birth & residence).

Affidavit further states that he has read the above affidavit, & that same is true, that he understands it fully, & that he makes it voluntarily without any duress, coercion, or promise of any kind and that he has been warned of his constitutional rights & that this affidavit may be used against him. Subscribed & sworn.

Conspiracy

One of the oldest known crimes ~ Conspiracy: an agreement between 2 or more persons to do an unlawful act or to do a lawful act in an unlawful manner. There may be a conspiracy even if person charged made no physical attempt and if actual undertaking failed. The charge will reach those in the background with no physical connection or participation. Conspiracy charge may reach small fry in the plot and coerce informers. In ~37, U.S.C A - Criminal Code

(1) Must have unity of design or purpose; essence of crime is confederating together for common purpose.

(2) Must have intentional participation, Mere intention to form conspiracy, solicitation, acquisition or approval is not sufficient.

~ 37 Crime Code, if 2 or more persons conspire to commit offense in U.S. or to defraud U.S., and one or more does any act to effect the purpose of conspiracy, each shall be guilty - $10,000 or 2 years, or both.

Four Elements:

(1) An object to be accomplished: either commission of offense v. U.S. or fraud on U.S.

(2) Must have a plan or scheme.

(3) There must be an agreement between parties to commit the crime.

(4) There must be an <u>overt act</u> by one of the parties in further-ance of the scheme.

Great latitude is allowed in proof of conspiracy. <u>Any per-son encouraging, advising, or assisting in prosecution of scheme, with understanding of illegal purpose, is guilty of conspiracy.</u>

If only two persons are charged both must be convicted, or neither can be. Husband and wife cannot conspire together, but may with a 3rd person.

<u>Agreement</u> in conspiracy need not be formal - merely nec-essary to have acted together for common purpose with common intent, with any mutual understanding, expressed or implied.

<u>Parties</u> - All persons working together in furtherance of conspiracy are conspirators, and liable for acts of any member committed in course and furtherance of conspiracy. The guilty knowledge is the test.

<u>Intent</u> will be inferred from the unlawful acts.

<u>Overt Act</u> must be a separate, subsequent, independent act in furtherance following the agreement. The overt act of one is the act of all.

<u>Jurisdiction & Venue</u> - Conspiracy may be prosecuted in any district where agreement was formed or any overt act oc-curred.

<u>Statute of Limitations</u> - 3 Years except capital offenses. In conspiracy the 3 years begins to run from the last overt act.

Three Questions in Conspiracy:

(1) Does conspiracy exist?

(2) Can proposed defendant's connection within 3 years be shown?

(3) Can an overt act be shown?

Wide latitude in introduction of circumstantial evidence is allowed in conspiracy. Because of secrecy of the crime, direct tes-timony is rare. Disconnected overt acts by persons shown to have associated are sufficient. Exact place & time of agreement are not essential.

Co-conspirator is a competent witness. "As a man thinketh in his heart, so is he." Conspiracy is a crime of wrong thinking,

33

even though no crime results. It is planning, not the act.

Treason

Treason is aimed at existence & continuance of government itself.

Constitutional Act III, Section 3 (only crime defined in Constitution): "Treason against the U.S. shall consist only of levying war against them, or in adhering to their enemies and giving them aid & comfort."

Treason is a breach of allegiance to a government, committed by a person who owes allegiance to it.

Allegiance - the tie or duty of obedience of a subject to a sovereign under whose protection he is.

Insurrection is the open & active opposition of a number of persons to the execution of federal, state, or city laws, and constitutes a defiance of government of lesser magnitude than that of treason.

Sedition is the incitement of discontent against government by means of factious commotions produced by inflammatory writings or speeches designed to breach the public order.

Overt act is one which manifests a criminal intention & tends toward the accomplishment of the criminal object.

Levying war is the actual assemblage of men for the purpose of executing a treasonable design by force.

Misprision of Treason is the concealment of treason with knowledge thereof and a failure to make it known to the proper officers.

1909 - Title 18 U.S.C.~ 1 - "Whoever, owing allegiance to U.S. levies war against them or addresses to their enemies, giving them aid and comfort, within the U.S. or elsewhere, is guilty of treason.

Alien in U.S. owes allegiance and may commit treason. Overt act in levying war is the assembly of men with necessary force.

"Adhering to enemy & giving aid & comfort" - must take place in time of war, adherence alone is insufficient - aid & comfort must be given. Success is immaterial if aid attempted would have helped. Must be some overt act.

No accessories to treason: everyone taking part is a principal.

Any act clearly indicating want of sympathy with government & sympathy with enemy and which advances cause of enemy is treason.

Mere expression of opinion indicative of sympathy with enemy, although sufficient to justify public indignation and suspicion that he is a traitor, are not sufficient to convict for treason. Disaffection alone is not a crime.

Evidence to convict: No other evidence is admissible until overt act is proven by two witnesses to the same overt act, or by confession in open court.

Misprision of treason - concealment of known treason & failure to make it known to proper authorities: (1) President of the U.S.; (2) governor of state; (3) state or federal judge. Reporting to any constituted officer would probably be sufficient.

Penalties: Congress has power to declare punishment of treason, but no attainder shall work corruption of blood & forfeiture beyond life of person attained. Prohibited even to hold public office.

Treason; Impersonation

At present, MI has no jurisdiction over impersonation of officers by civilian; this is FBI matter. However, in many cases by close collaboration, MI handles cases until completion & turns over to FBI. Usually there is another crime involved besides mere impersonation. Air Corps uniform is favorite.

Treason: Conviction automatically carries both fine & imprisonment (5 yrs & $10,000 to death). Proof requires overt act by testimony of two witnesses or confession in open court.

Statutes: 18 U.S.C.A. 76a - badge statute - misdemeanor - $250 or 6 months - use of badges or credentials of known agency; it must be an existing agency, not a fabrication.

18 U.S.C.A. 76 - impersonation with intent to defraud a federal

officer - felony - $1000 or 3 years or both - Essentials: (1) intent to defraud - mere effort to obtain prestige is insufficient for conviction, but may be ground for arrest - not necessary to attempt to obtain money, but anything of value; (2) there must be false impersonation of an agent, employee, or officer of U.S. Govt - does not apply to member of Armed Forces covered by Articles of War - it is not necessary to have an existing agency; (3) the mere acting as officer or demanding or obtaining something of value.

People v. Hamilton, 170 N.Y.S. 705, held that impersonation of naval officer existed where private detective wore blue uniform without insignia & used name "Capt" in arresting naval deserters; also held, that Army or naval officer has power to arrest deserter without warrant but civilian does not.

18 U.S.C.A. 77a - arrest of person or entry of building while impersonating officer or agent of U.S. - misdemeanor - 1 yr. or $1000 - fraudulent intent need not be shown, mere arrest or entry under pretended authority.

F.B.I. has fraudulent check file & fraudulent signature & handwriting file useful in impersonation.

10 U.S.C.A. 1316 - govt. uniform, insignia & equipment not to be worn without authority. Authority given to cadets, R.O.T.C., not guard, men given honorable discharge, (for 3 months).

Communism

N.B. Two Russian: "Who do you have a date with?" "Maria"

"She is too young for you - she has no hair on her." "She will tonight."

It is necessary to keep an eye on Russia & Communists. They change sides as suits their needs. Note change in names of organization: League Against Fascism & Communism; League for Peace Mobilization; League of Peoples Mobilization.

There is a school in Chicago, another in New York: Advanced course in communist and labor theories.

To understand communism it is necessary to understand differences between various schools of thought. Their common purpose is overthrow of capitalistic system. Their differences have prevented effectiveness.

Communism dates back to Plato's Republic, 400 B.C. - theory of goods distributed in proportion to work. Spartacus, Roman gladiator, 71 B.C., started peasant revolt. Walt Tyler, 1381, England tried peasant revolt. Numerous other peasant revolts, all arising out of desire of poor people for social equality & overthrow of economic system. These rose out of spontaneous movements of people.

Procedure today is the opposite. Leaders come from top, who recruit masses and stir up trouble.

American Revolution grew to some extent out of Industrial Revolution. It produced a great change in living conditions, and the first radical movement began. Adam Weishaupt arose out of the industrial uprising - former Jesuit, Prof. of Law in Bavaria - founded Order of Illuminate; favored:

(1) Abolition of family & religion
(2) Abolition of nationalism & patriotism
(3) Abolition of capitalism
(4) Abolition of property rights
(5) Abolition of inheritance rights

Weishaupt has been considered grandfather of communism. Order of Illuminate was divided into Adepts, who were Leaders, and Dupes, the body of members flourished from 1776 - 1785, when secret existence was discovered, and it was disbanded. Leaders continue to operate underground in Germany, France. Jacobin Club of French Rev., 1789, had some of same members.

Labor organizations grew up after Industrial Revolution, but were never able to organize internationally.

1848 - Karl Marx, "Communist Manifesto" - 1st international workers movement. Marx was father of communism. Highly educated, and in course of studies came across Weishaupt. Frederich Engels collaborated in Communist Manifesto and financed it. Rallying cry of workers from Manifesto: "Workers of the world unite! You have nothing to lose but your chains & all the world to gain."

Marx divided people into bourgeoisie & proletariat - the haves & have-nots. Consider that they had nothing in common, and that they should fight. Advocated workers' revolution. Founded 1st Internationale.

3rd Internationale - began 1915. 1st meeting in Switzerland 1916, not attended by U.S. socialists, or German, French or English parties. Manifesto issued is policy of party today, calling for arousing the spirit of protest & resistance to grow into the overthrow of capitalism.

Russian Revolution of November, 1917, was backed by Germans, who sent Lenin & staff in sealed train into Russia. The Bolshevik Party & Mensheviks grew up in Russia. Bolsheviks were the party of violence and direct action - party survived in Trotskyites, the pure revolutionists & bloody Reds. Mensheviks were the party of moderation, believing in education and taking over country by ballot.

3 Aims of party in Russia:

(1) Inclusion of farmers in proletariat

(2) Immediate expropriation of capital & socialist administration

(3) Arming the proletariat & disarming the bourgeoisie.

At convention in Moscow, 1919, 4 American parties were represented.
I.W.W., Workers International Industrial Union, Socialist Labor Party of America, and Left Wing only of Socialist Party of America.

Trade Union Unity League conducted an industrial propaganda campaign among poorer workers.

Neither Socialist Party of America nor I.W.W. is now a member of the 3rd Internationale. Refused to subscribe to 21 steps of platform.

In Russia there is a Union of 21 Republics - Communist Party is divided into 3 branches. All Communist Parties are set up on some plan - from Moscow. 1st - Political Bureau (which runs party); 2nd - Soviet Government; 3rd - Comintern (the propaganda brand set up to communize the world).

<u>Communism</u> - an organized movement which works by force or violence for overthrow of governments not under control of communist and establishment proletarian dictatorship & economic system based on communal ownership of property instead of private ownership. Advocates (1) abolition of religion; (2) private property; (3) abolition of inheritance; (4) social, racial & economic equality; (5) world wide revolution to establish proletarian dictatorship & world-wide union of soviet socialist republics with capital in Moscow.

Under force of expediency; Russia has abandoned international features for the time being.

Communism is similar to socialism in dissemination of unequal distribution of wealth in democratic state and advocates equality. It is like syndicalism in advocating violent uprising of masses.

Socialism differs from communism in advocating gradual change through education of majority and peaceful methods. Communism takes view that only through violence can rule of workers be set up. It opposes middle classes as well as upper.

Modern - 1848- "Communist Manifesto" by Karl Marx & Frederich Ingals. Theory that workers had always been exploited by ruling classes and could be liberated only by revolution.

1st Internationale - 1864 - anarchists got in and broke it up by argument over aims.

2nd Internationale - 1889 - Paris. Controlled by Marxists views. Radical communists considered it too conservative. Failed in WWI.

3rd Internationale - 1919 - Led by Lenin - Moscow still in effect.

4th Internationale - 1938 - Switzerland. Opposed to present regime in Russia.

Stalin, Chairman of Communist Party, got control of government at death of Lenin and exiled Trotsky.

Program: (1) organize workers in industry; (2) confiscate all private property; (3) cancel all debts; (4) take over all agriculture; (5) state to take over all wholesale & retail business and banks, develop consumer co-ops, control all foreign trade; (6) complete equality between men & women; (7) all publications, radio, theaters under control of state.

Russian Government - Union of Socialist Republics, theoretically run by workers, but actually by self-perpetuating groups of revolutionaries headed by Stalin. Only 2 1/2 million party members in Russia. Head of party is Political Bureau of 10 members, controlling (1) Soviet Government; (2) 3rd Internationale. Legislative power in congress of Soviets, meeting every 2 years. Between meetings an Executive Committee of 400 or 500, from which is chosen Prosidium, which is real legislative power, appointing commissars.

Comintern - or Communist Internationale, with 5 bureaus.

NKBD - traced back to 1881 with organization of Dept of Safety to Combat Internal Revolution, replaced by Chika, which was replaced by **Ogpu**. Purpose of Ogpu was to combat economic & political counter-revolutionary movements & espionage. Became most feared agency of government, and in 1934 was curtailed & returned to part of NKBD, which had continued in various individual republics. NKBD - means Peoples Commissariat of Internal Affairs. Divided into political affairs, maintenance of highways & prison camps, militia, and Internal Security under letter of counter-espionage, etc. NKBD supervises individual Russian from registration of birth until death.

Russian informer usually starts off with tale of mistreatment by NKBD.

Professional spies under direction of NKBD. Also, keeps Russians in line by "liquidation" if necessary. Lesser offenders are read out of party and attacked by press if big enough.

Communist in U.S. - originated in 2 left-wing groups after split in Socialist Party. Met in Chicago - 1919- disseminated propaganda for 3rd Internationale. Underground until 1923. Workers Party of America formed in 1921, underground until 1928, when it came out as member of 3rd Internationale, 1939 it renounced membership in 3rd Internationale to circumvent Voorkees Act.

Constitution of Communist Party states that purpose is to educate, direct & lead worker of America to conquest of political power destruction of bourgeoisie machinery, to establish dictatorship of proletariat, to abolish capitalist system and introduce communist society.

One aim which has been partially lost is establishment of Farmer Labor Party controlled by communist minority.

Basic unit of party is branch, based upon precinct, township, or industry. The next higher organization is section, covering area similar to congressional district. Then county organizations, and districts made up county organizations - 35 districts in U.S.

National Headquarters in New York - National Chairman, W. Z. Foster - Sec'y Carl Browder. Secretariat composed of leaders. Political Committee or Politbureau, and National Committee. Also, have a Secret Central Committee, not now operating.

<u>Communist Party Line</u> - Key is to be found during period of Russian-German collaboration. 1919-29. Party line based on outright revolution & opposed to all existing forms of government. With depression in 1929, party turned away from outright revolution and sought to identify itself with unemployed and promised improvement. After 1935, party changed to liberal reform group, posing as red-blooded Americans and began to advocate cooperation with democracies against Hitler & fascists.

1939 - Russo-German Pact - party policy did about face. 1040 American Party dissolved relations with 3rd Internationale because of Voorkees Act. Formed Industrial Emergency Control Committee of North America to direct if party driven underground. CT strategy (complete tie-up) for maritime communications. Policy was to infiltrate quietly into unions; to accept draft but set up cells in Army. Inspired Allis-Chalmers, International Harvester, and Ford strikes. American Peace Mobilization picketed White House for 24 hours a day. "The Yanks are not Coming." Strikes called to demonstrate community power.

1941 - invasion of Russia by Germany. "Dirty Capitalistic War" became "people's war cry." Picketing & strikes ceased. American Peace Mobilization became American People's Mobilization.

Present aims: (1) Party to act as real, open political arm of working classes. (2) Get as many members & friends as possible. (3) Endorsement of joint labor & capital committees. (4) Favor government control of industry & then take over government. (5) Get complete information service in plants. (6) Cooperation with British Communist Party. (7) Concentrate upon Army & defense plants. (8) Get into civilian defense. (9) Repeal Firearms Control Acts. (10) Nationwide drive for military training of workers.

Propaganda activities: (1) Disseminate idea of communism as solution of all troubles. (2) Defend Russia from all capitalistic & rightest attacks. Communist press is organized into national & foreign language sections. Daily Worker & on west coast, The People's World are voices. Have Croat, Serbian, Greek, Italian, Finnish, Polish, Bulgarian language papers. These are "people's" papers, not openly affiliated with communism. Also, have pamphlets, pictures, sound tracks, speakers. Concentrating now on western front, all-out aid to Russia.

United Front technique - arrangement for common action by people with opposing views who are willing to unite for one common purpose. Aim is to extend influence of Communist Party beyond it's own members and fellow travelers by supporting some laudable enterprise. United Front is composed of (1) Communist Party members who control; (2) fellow travelers, the middle class intellectuals & parlor pinks who follow communism; (3) the stooges - men in public life sucked in for personal prominence to allow use of names for publicity; (4) the innocents - those who joined organization without realizing purposes because of attraction of prominent names & outward purposes.

Sam Pevzner, John Gates, and Timothy Holmes were committee on Army organization. Purpose to get in Army: build up good reputation, then begin work. Attempt to undermine discipline by advocating equality between officers & men: soldiers representation on courts, equal rights of leave, no saluting. Idea to create class consciousness in Army. Milorg was one organization and International Workers Order the other used for infiltration in Army. International Workers Order is most active - organized 1930 for fraternal benefit of society for left wing. Has financial reserve of over 1 1/4 million dollars and has founded over 100 schools for teaching loyalty & devotion to workers; also social works; language leaders in each foreign tongue; have publication "Fraternal Outlook." 3 sub-groups to work in Ay: (1) Front Line Fighters Fund, donated cigarette, collected large fund for gifts to soldiers; (2) National Service Men's Welfare Committee, handling forwarding of books & propaganda; (3) Young Fraternalists handling dances, entertainment, and correspondence clubs.

Fascism

Commenced March 1919 - Fascis di Combaltimento. Founded by Mussolini, ex- socialist editor of Milan Populo di Italia. October, 1922 march on Rome & control of government. Founded to combat communism. Developed into National Imperialist Militaristic party. Only party in Italy supported by militia. 1928 fully in power and party membership closed, except for youth. National guild economic structure. Except for Army, Navy & Air Corps, all government officials must belong to party.

Youth education begins at 7. Upon completion of military service, youth is eligible for party membership.

Black Shirt Militia maintains order and supports party; all sovereign power in hands of Mussolini.

Theory of fascism emblem signifies close union and obedience to law, as in Rome. Society does not exist for individual, but individual for state. State is all supreme - a fanatic nationalism.

Differs from communism in its nationalism. Communism is international, aimed at world worker's supremacy.

Fascism aims to hold foreign Italians in allegiance to fatherland and prevent assimilation. Two theories of nationality: One, ix soli (from the land) that birth in a country confers citizenship. Other, ex sangreinis (from the blood) that person of one national descent retains citizenship wherever born.

Special Tribunal for Defense of State is special court for

state and political offenses.

National militia is to maintain internal security and to prepare for national defense and offense. To guard against counter-revolution.

Intelligence - 3 branches of service have their own services reporting to C of S, who is responsible to Mussolini. Each had attaches in embassies. Had OVRA, equivalent to Gestapo. Had CAO, the American Center of Operations, Headquarters in Rome. Members of OVRA receive no pay except favors and immunities. CAO organized December, 1940, Robert Suster of Stephani Agency at head. 1941 reorganized to work under supervision of CAO in Berlin, controlling both North America and South America. There are numerous other propaganda and espionage agencies under supervision of Propaganda Ministry, called Ministry of Popular Culture.

Population Culture Ministry has subsidiary agencies for each group: Fascist Party, University, Youth Group, Advanced Guard for young boys, children, girls, women, officers on leave, sports, after work & after school clubs, Naval League, Institute of Fascist Culture to rewrite history. These groups are closely connected with espionage, teaching individuals to be informers.

Also foreign affiliated groups: Italian Youths Abroad, Italian War Veterans, which has dangerous U.S. branch, Association of Italians Abroad, with American branch in Rockefeller Center, Fascio Abroad.

Foreign Service has espionage agency, attaches and Bureau "V," Bureau "V" had charge of consulates in U.S. and put in OVRA man.

Fascism in U.S. : Purpose (1) to obtain details of vulnerable points in maritime zones, oil fields, war industries and mines and place fascists in key places; (2) to arouse sympathy in press and politics; (3) in elections try to defeat those upholding discord; (4) create discord among racial elements (French-Canadian in Canada); (5) press to conduct Italian campaign and remain neutral in local questions, arouse Italian feeling and listen to Italian radio; (6) instruct agents to stay out of party meetings, away from consulates, justify selves by patriotic demonstrations toward U.S., buying bonds; (7) workers to be organized to hinder production and provoke strikes.

Agents were official groups, diplomats & consular, and unofficial organizations. Many individuals employed by consulates were American citizens and probably organized to carry on.

Unofficial - began 1928 - General Secretary for Fascism Abroad. Diplomatic did part of work and individuals had charge of zones. 1928-29 began to appear as Black Shirts, drilled, pledged to prevent assimilation of immigrants. Schools for education of Italian children established, teachers sent from Italy. Fascist League of North America incorporated in New York, official appointed in Rome and responsible to Rome. Dissolved in 1929. Then established Lictoral for Education of Italians Abroad. New agents sent over - clubs bearing names of Fascist heroes arose. Italian consuls had control and furnished teachers. Tourist bureaus and Italian press organized. Tried to reach all age groups. Order of Sons of Italy tried to reach groups 20 to middle age. National United Italian Associations reached children under pretext of teaching Italian language. Federation of Italian War Veterans Association, Committee Pro-Italian Language, Dopo Scoula (after-school clubs), School Youth Training, Italian-American Youth Group - young people. Lectoral violent and cooperating with Bund. Order of Crown in Italy - five groups - made awards & most decorations after 1922 were for fascist services. Order of Sons of Italy in America was formed independently and then infiltrated by Fascists

American Center of Operations (CAO) in Rome purposes: (1) to act as liaison to organize labor trouble; (2) to organize special sabotage outrages; (3) to organize sabotage aboard ships; (4) to organize propaganda publication and distribution, particularly in armed forces.

Note Italian clannishness and jealousy. Racial and providential differences account for varying appearances and customs.

Nazism

National Socialist (Nazi) Party rose out of economic and political confusion of post-war period. Exploited economic crisis, political confusion, and oppression of Versailles Treaty. Through this and strong-arm methods it came to control of government in 1933.

3/24/33 Hitler became chancellor. At death of Hindenburg he became both president & chancellor and Reichstag became rubber stamp.

Maintains power through semi-military organization and winning over Army by successful campaigns and promotions.

War over labor movement: (1) by destroying unions and substituting idea of leader state; (2) by bringing labor into totalitarian state in idea of classless society; (3) by production efficiency.

Took over government officials by demanding personal oath of loyalty to Hitler.

Organization: local cell, district and region. Control is from top down, each leader appointed by one immediately above him.

4 Types in Party

(1) Leaders

(2) Praetorian guards, elite group of administrators who do not make decisions.

(3) People

(4) Slave classes of conquered.

Aims of program:

World domination on theory that one system of laws is necessary throughout world before peace can be had. Co-existence of national socialism and democracy is denied. Idea is to organize Europe under German domination and the world as colonies.

German intelligence was reorganized after 1918 and sent agents abroad as commercial travelers, bankers, business men, manufacturers, etc. Organizations were set up in Germany and abroad for propaganda and discipline.

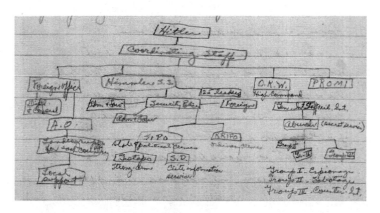

Group I (1) Military Espionage, (2) Naval Espionage (3) Air Espionage, (4) Economic Espionage, (5) Air Industry, (6) Communications, (7) Secret Inks

Group II: sabotage, terrorism, kidnapping key persons, spreading of confusion, etc. - the 5th Column.

II

Liaison   with   Liaison

O.A.W.   Foreign Office

O   A   W

Group A: has change of special assignments & trouble shooting sabotage in connection with Army attack. Planned work in Poland and England.

Group O: divided into 5 sections, covering activities in

East; North Africa, Asia Minor, India, Balkans.

Group W: has activities in West-Overseas Section; Spain, Portugal, Morocco; Ireland and South Africa; France, Belgium and Holland.

Group III: Counter intelligence is broken into 11 main sections: (1) organization and conduct of counter intelligence (espionage, treason, sedition, etc.) in armed forces; (2) security of military intelligence organization within Reich itself; (3) combating economic intelligence; (4) investigation of espionage in conjunction with Gestapo; (5)personal examination and examination of visitors to high command; (6) security of espionage abroad and in occupied territory - protection of espionage agents; (7) deception - planting of agents in foreign intelligence service & originating misleading information; 8) tracing & controlling sabotage in Reich & occupied territory; (9), (10), & (11) drafting legal cases;

Foreign Office (Ribbentrop) is divided into 2 branches: (1) Diplomatic and Consular Services, of which Germany had 4 or 5 times as many as other countries; kept membership of Bund; paymastics; smuggled in Germans; engaged in propaganda, (2) A.O. or Auslanders Organization, originally the foreign intelligence of Nazi Party. Later became controlling agency of foreign nations. Carried on "permanent war" theory. Idea is that defense would eventually undermine power of blitzkrieg unless foreign intelligence obtained information to offset by sabotage of foreign effort. Object of A.O. was to weld together all German in country where working; then to obtain all forms of information; then to organize a 5th Column and subversive propaganda groups.

PROMI is propaganda ministry under Goebbels. Function is not intelligence, but propaganda: cultural & economic; antisemitic; control of press; Fichte-Bund, foreign service training, professional literature; personal letter writing.
Note: All intelligence & counter-intelligence in Germany is a service group for all three (3) branches: Army, Navy, and Air.

5th Column in Poland: Poland allowed German minorities to organize into German associations, teachers clubs, scientific societies, German language schools, sports & touring clubs, children sent to Germany for study. All engaged in propaganda & espionage. Organizations were tied into A.O. and furnished information for intelligence of Army. After outbreak of hostilities saboteurs were sent in to join in direct work of these groups; (1) Collaborated with air corps by directing to objectives; (2) Also tapped or destroyed communications; (3) Destroyed transportation; (4) Hindered Polish military operations; attacked units and signaled location to Germans; (5) Issued false instructions, changed road signs. Seized public utilities; (6) Spread panic among refugees; (7) Directed Germans to objectives and pointed out troops.

Cause of trouble was (1) failure to realize nature of German propaganda; (2) failure to control German organizations; (3) lack of broad counter-intelligence; (4) failure to recognize travelers as spies or to convince government of danger; (5) Polish intelligence too small to cover all agents; (6) Polish Army not organized for military police.

After invasion 5th Column aided Gestapo.

Organization same in Holland & Norway.

We have counter 5th Column plan. In 6th S.C. there are 3 areas, divided from geographical, population, and economic considerations. This is problem of Provost Marshall General. 16 subdivisions set up in 6th S.C. Liaison through Commanding General with other S.C. Plan will be put into operation by Commanding General on receipt of advice from G-2. Forces to be used: (1) M.P branch; (2) non-military forces: state guards; (3) civilian forces & veterans organizations.

Nazism in U.S.: Hitler: "National Socialism alone is destined to free U.S. from its ruling clique." Theory that wherever Germans have fought for land and settled, it is German.

Aims:

(1) To obtain peaceful cooperation from U.S., or at least have U.S. strictly neutral. This would have put him in position to dictate after war.

(2) In event of failure; to plant a well organized 5th Column for aid in invasion.

Had 3 types of agents:

(1) Strictly official - embassy, consuls and their aids &   a t -
taches.

(2) Semi-official - Fortura, Inc., a war aid society to collect and
transmit funds for friends and relatives in Germany; German Service Library of Information-Propaganda; Trans-Ocean News Service; etc.

German R.R. Office, supposedly a travel bureau, but really are
propaganda and espionage. Same for Trans-Ocean News Service,
formally a legitimate news service.

(3) Unofficial - German-American Bund, German-American
Business League, and similar societies and associations. Bund is
typical of Ausland's organizations originated in 1923 as Teutonia,
reorganized by Hitler, 1933, as Friends of New Germany, along
militaristic lines, with camps in N.J. and youth movement. Public
protests led to organization being split to include only American
citizens. German agents remained in control. In 1934 another
apparent split and reorganization. Investigation by Congress in
1935 and reorganization under name of German-American Bund
in 1936. Under Fritz Kuhn there was an enormous growth, leading to investigation (1939), court proceedings and trial of Kuhn
and other leaders for fraud and perjury. Wilhelm Kunz succeeded
Kuhn. Each Bund had a fuehrer, who appointed chief of strong-
arm squad, who wore uniforms, drilled, and were to be nucleus
of storm troopers. Finally driven underground. Some effort was
made to reorganize as sports clubs, etc., but seems to have petered
out.

Recent case of espionage - unnamed subject arrested in Canada,
November, 1942. Landed from submarine November 8, 1942.

Organization of German Army

Organization of German Infantry Division -
Estimated strength - 15,000 men, 3800 horses, 1050 motor vehicles.

(1) Division Headquarters Staff, specialists, clerical help, Division Headquarters machine gun platoon (3 heavy machine guns);
motorcycle platoon; map reproduction section.

(2) Signal Branch, consisting of signal branch Headquarters, mobilized wire company (telephone), and motorized radio company, signal train of 10, 1 1/2 ton trucks.

(3) Reconnaissance Branch: Reconnaissance Branch Headquarters; horse troop (9 light machine guns, 2 heavy; bicycle troop 9 light, 2 heavy machine guns, 3.50 mm mortars, heavy weapons troop, consisting of troop Headquarters, heavy machine gun platoon (4 heavy), 1 gun platoon (2 - 75 mm howitzers), anti-tank platoon (3 - 37mm guns), scout con platoon & motor platoon.

(4) Anti-Tank Branch - Anti Tank Branch Headquarters; 3 anti-tank companies (each 12 - 37 mm guns); 1 anti-aircraft company; anti-tank branch train.

(5) Combat Engineers Branch
    a) Engineers branch Headquarters
    b) 2 combat engineers companies
    c) Bridging train (pontoons & boats)
    d) Engineers tool company
    e) Engineers train (10-1 1/2 ton trucks)

(6) Observation Branch
    a) Headquarters
    b) Sound ranging battery
    c) Flash ranging battery
    d) Balloon battery

(7) 1 regiment light field artillery regiment
    a) Regiment Headquarters
    b) 3 battalion light field artillery (3 batteries) (12 -105mm howitzers)

(8) 1 battalion medium field artillery battalion - medium field artillery
    a) 3 batteries (3 - 105 mm guns)

(9) 3 Infantry Regiments
    a) Regiment Headquarters:
        1. Signal platoon
        2. Mounted infantry platoon
        3. Pioneer platoon
    b) 3 rifles Battalions

1. Each - Headquarters, 3 rifle companies, 1 machine gun company, battalion train
2. Rifle Company: Headquarters, 1 - anti-tank section (3 anti-tank rifles), 3 rifle platoons (4 machine guns, 50 mm mortar), company train of 4 wagons, 1 kitchen.
3. Each rifle platoon - headquarter, 1 light mortar squad (1 - 50 mm mortar), 4 rifle squads (1 light machine gun, 6 rifles)
4. Machine gun company: Headquarters, 3 machine gun platoons (4 heavy machine guns); 1 heavy mortar platoon (6-80 mm mortars); machine company train (19 vehicles).
   (a) Machine gun platoon: Headquarters, 2 sections with 2 guns each.
   (b) Heavy mortar platoon: Headquarters, 3 sections with 2- 80 mm mortars each.

Uniforms & Insignia

Identification of German troops - full info in Uniforms of World by Blakeslee. Training Film 11-225. Japanese Ground & Air Forces, MI - Summary Information Bulletins No. 14. Tr. Manual 30-480, Handbook on Jap Military Forces.

Field uniforms - blouse forest green or slate green - 5 buttons - no shirt worn under - 4 patch pockets. Pants slate gray, tucked into black putters.

Tank troops - black, loose-fitting uniform resembling fatigues, black beret, & half-knee length boots.

Mountain troops - white coveralls in winter.

Paratroopers - loose-fitting coverall & field uniform underneath. Coveralls zip off.

Identification tags similar to ours but perforated in middle to divide if killed. Usually carry "sold buck," pay record & service record, showing full info as to unit & service.

<u>3 reasons to know insignia:</u> (1) In field armies keep history or enemy units opposing; (2) knowledge of unit makes specific questions possible & save time; (3) makes possible identification of officers, non-coms & enlisted.

<u>3 things fundamental to identify prisoner:</u> (1) branch or arms of service; (2) unit to which attached; (3) rank.

Can be made from collar pad & shoulder strap. <u>Branch</u> is shown by color of piping on shoulder strap. White - infantry. Rifle troops - light green. Cavalry & bicycle units by gold yellow. Reconnaissance units by gold brown. Engineers - black. Artillery - bright red. Signal Corps - lemon yellow. Transportation - bright blue. Medical units - dark blue. Chemical warfare - dark red. Armored - pink.

<u>Unit</u> designated by large numeral inside shoulder strap. Enlisted men have embroidered cloth numeral. Company grade officers have gold metal no., as do field grade.

<u>Rank</u> insignia falls into five groups: (1) enlisted men; (2) non-coms; (3) co-officers; (4) field officers; (5) general officer. Pvt. has numeral in same color as piping, & piping does not extend across bottom of shoulder strap. PFC has silver star on right shoulder. Corporal with less than 6 yrs has two chevrons. Corporal with more than 6 yrs has 1 chevron & 1 star. Career corporal has 2 chevrons & star.

1st non-commissioned rank is sergeant. Has silver border inside single strand of piping. Not piping across bottom. Roman numerals designate corps. S/Sgt. differs from buck in that inner silver border continues all around strap. 1st Sgt. has one silver star on strap. M/Sgt. has 2 stars on strap.

Commissioned officers: 4 parallel strands of silver braid inside shoulder straps - gold numerals. 2nd Lt. has no star. 1st Lt. has gold star on strap below numeral. Capt. has 2 gold stars above & below numeral. Maj. Lt. Col. have instead of 4 bands of silver braid 2 strands woven together. Maj. has no star, Lt. Col. 1 star (gold), Col. has 2 gold stars. Gen. has red background on strap, 2 strands of woven silver braid, one of gold. No star Maj.-Gen., 2 stars Lt. Gen., 3 General.

Large letter A - reconnaissance; S - rifle; P - anti-tank; E - engineers; K - motorcycle; B - observation battalion; D - Division; R - bicycle troop; small R - smoke battalion.

Lower non-com often attached to special unit, designated by round disc. on rt. forearm.

CIC Regulations & Policies

CIC organized late in last war, known as CIP. Agents largely picked for speaking French. Need for service recognized earlier in this emergency, & central record system set up. Work began early in 1941 with 250 agts., now 543; 1528 sp. agts., 2500 agents, also clerks. Now shortage in officers, expected to be filled from agts. in officers schools. Definite number is to be assigned to each tactical unit.

Special agents are sergeants of 4 grades - trained in CIC schools. Agents are to be corporals & sergeants of 4th grade, trained in service commands, supposed to do foot work & to be promoted later. School in Chicago to be made advanced course.

Service is rapidly expanding & increasing in importance. Qualifications: age 24-34 with exceptions; at least high school education with college & law preferred; 8 weeks basic training.

Jurisdiction: Delimitation Conference late in 1940 between FBI, ONI, CIC. CIC has jdn (jurisdiction) over military, & civilians employed & paid out of War Dept funds, all personnel in Panama, ports of Alaska, & other territories; also "all other duties required by proper authority." Personnel cases were supposed to be transferred to P.M. but has not been done. There are many cases of borderline jdn, should be worked out by common sense & cooperation.

Assignments to expeditionary forces - powers are broader. Where there is joint jdn of Army & Navy, there should be conferences & cooperation.

Field officers or district officers are set up in each S.C. They were undercover at first, but this has been changed in most places. Undercover & surveillance agts. should be kept elsewhere.

Every agent should be careful of personal appearance. Organization is judged by appearance as well as conduct. Avoid conspicuous clothes but wear good clothes in good shape.

Because of temptations, CIC are picked to avoid misconduct, particularly as to money, women & liquor. Agt. is judged 24 hrs. a day. Also, one slip of tongue or one mistake may be fatal.

Expenses - necessary expenses paid from confidential funds. Travel on orders 3 cents - other travel 5 cents.

Equipment - cameras, movie cameras, & fingerprint cameras, fingerprint kits, amplifiers, moulage, revolvers. Should not be stored in safe or vault but made available for training & use.

Credentials & badges - should be carefully kept, clean & polished. Loss should be reported at once by affidavit for your own protection. There should be periodic inspections.

Don't allow yourself to be placed under obligations to anyone. Don't accept gifts.

Power of arrest - no need for any except those of a citizen.
Gun is issued for self-protection & for defense of fellow agents. It reveals identity of officer & may be cumbersome. Don't wear them when not needed, & don't display it. If used, it should be shot to kill.

Relationship of CIC to PIO

Four parts of lecture.
1) Function of CIC
3) PIO Office

2) Relationship of PIO
4) Miscellaneous cases

1)Trained investigators

2) Go first to PIO & get harmony with him.

If two agents are present, one should do the talking. Agt. may be assigned to PIO

3) PIO divided into inner and outer office. Outer usually handles passes, identification, fingerprinting. Always be courteous. Inner office carries on confidential work. C.S. work usually there. In addition to 7 general classes of cases PIO may handle cases of protection & security, investigation of funds, identification of persons coming on post, theft. Don't get sucked in on these. PIO usually has confidential secretary handling correspondence and files, who may have assistant. Also has chief investigator and assistant chief investigator. Correspond through channels.

Japanese: Hawaiian born & Alaskans mostly OK. Test: Have Japanese parents returned to Japan within last 5 years.

4) PIO usually has officer's personal biography, also all WAC officers and nurses. PIO usually interpreters available.

Codes and Ciphers

Codes & ciphers used since early times. Secret writing may be developed, but code should be sent to trained breakers. It may be invisible - written in secret ink; some inks become invisible after writing. Writing so small as to require glass is considered invisible.

1st classification of codes is <u>visible</u> & <u>invisible</u>. There are also microscopic messages.

Cryptogram - to convert plain to secret language - Dearyptograph to reverse process -

"Cipher" deals with individual letters. "Code" with whole words, phrases, or sentences. Telegraph & cable companies have code libraries - used commercially for brevity & secrecy. Army interested only in secrecy.

Cipher may be worked by transposing or by substitution. Ciphers always transmitted in groups of 5 for simplicity in transmission & to eliminate errors. Key consists of series of numbers indicating order for re-transcribing. Keys are literal & numerical.

Numerical is series of numbers - literal is a word indicating the same numbers by numbering letters in alphabetical order.

Never use common word as a key.

Don't tamper with code message or fool with it.

Cryptogram is a message in visible secret writing. Cryptography is the science of secret messages.

Cryptograph - to put into secret writing.

Cryptographer - one skilled in secret languages.

Two reasons to use are secrecy & economy.

In military use consideration is for secrecy.

Code system deals with a word, phrase or sentence.

Cipher system deals with individual letters.

Code system requires books. Both sender and receiver must have a book. Each book is indexed to show clear text words or phrases in alphabetical order with code equivalent, and vice versa. These are called encoding & decoding books.

Cipher system may be set up by (1) transposition or (2) substitution.

12-13	Trick - Task
13-14	Heggle - Higgle
14-15	Tottle - Taunt
15-16	Tile - Green
16-17	Halve - Hole
17-18	Hand - Handle
	Alt Hail - Freeze
27-28	Rib - Cozy
28-29	Wire - Ring
29-30	Rough - Bell
30-1	Forty - Nine
1-2	Wait - Hurry
2-3	Walk - Along
3-4	Read - Range
4-5	Nimble - Quint
5-6	White - Fish

In <u>transposition</u>, letters retain their original identity, but shifted so that clear text meaning is lost.

In <u>substitution</u>, a different letter, number, or symbol is substituted for the original.

Usually 5 letters in a word group.

<u>Essential that both sender and receiver know what system is to be used.</u>

<u>Cipher system must have key</u> : Key may be <u>numerical</u> or <u>literal</u>. Numerical key is derived from the literal key by numbering letters according to agreed rules.

C A R B U N C L E - literal key

3 1 8 2 9 7 4 6 5 - numerical key

Don't use easily misspelled words which are easily misspelled for keys, or words with repeated letters, or with common geographical meaning.

Espionage & Counter-Espionage

NB Russian agents, brother & sister, came to U.S... Return to Russia, "Everything free. Free dinner, dancing, drinks, breakfast in bed." "Did this happen to you?" "No, to my sister."

Intelligence - (1) positive, (2) negative. Positive intelligence is actual spying; negative is watching spies, or counter-intelligence.

Hannibal one of early spies. Lived in Italy for number of years before campaigns.

Spy is eyes & ears of enemy.

Hague Convention, Article 29 defines spy: <u>"One who, acting clandestinely or on false pretenses, obtains or seeks to obtain information in the zone of operations of a belligerent with the intention of communicating it to the hostile party."</u>

Soldiers in uniform not spies.

Genesis 42:9; Numbers 21:22 refer to Biblical <u>spies</u>.

<u>Emissary</u>: Agent sent out by government openly who may be a spy.

<u>Scout</u>: One sent out without disguise on dangerous mis-

sion.

Simulate: To assume or to have mere appearance or form, without reality.

Quondam: Having been formerly.

Clandestine: concealed, surreptitious.

Dissemble: To conceal.

Feign: To make false show of.

Espionage: The secret watching or observing of the acts or words of another.

Delilah: spy. Achieved complete espionage triumph as Philistine secret agent.

Marshall Nay - spy for Napoleon. Marshall Catonet entered Arras as charcoal burner. Alfred Great entered Danish camp as bard.

Germany under Hess and Japanese use mass espionage; England & U.S specialists.

Frederick the Great - father of organized espionage. Classified spies, patriotic spies : (1) Common spies, recruited from poor; (2) Double spies, the unreliable renegades & paid informers; (3) Spies of consequence, the noblemen & staff officers; (4) Persons forced to turn spy against their will.

Karl Schulmeister - Napoleon's "spy giant." Resourceful, able, daring.

Wilhelm Stieber - "spy master" for Bismark. 36,000 German spy in France under him. Expert on underground and wholesale betrayal. (1) Father of counter espionage. (2) Also instituted military censorship. (3) Instituted military propaganda to spread terror. (4) Organized first central information bureau in Germany to obtain & compile information about other countries. (5) Subsidized banks to obtain commercial information. (6) Put 1000 spies in Alsace-Lorraine (7) Organized bureau to check foreign publications. (8) "Green House" in Berlin, resort for diplomats, etc.

Espionage schools grew up after 1890. Germany now has about a dozen, Fraulien Doktor established famous one in Antwerp in last war after invasion. Schraugmuller was given name. (1) Everyone sent to school known only by letter. (2) Faculty of 7 experts. (3) I.Q. exam on entry. (4) Studied enemy uniforms, ranks & grades of officers, artillery, report writing, disposition of troops & wounded. (5) Mediocrity no bar to getting in school. (6) Studied communications. (7) Factories studied - locations, number of employees. (8) Taught to recognize factories from top as well as sides. (9) Studied labor organizations. (10) Surveillance problems. (11) Rules of spying.

Taking statement from espionage agent: (1) Prove publication of dissaffectionate statement to others. (2) Prove utterance to agent. (3) Get it in writing.

Hess: (1) Everyone can spy. (2) Everyone must spy. (3) Everything can be found out.

Gestapo is large force of secret police. Not a spy ring. Heinrich Himmler head of Gestapo - tried to build it as counter espionage. Himmler always photographed in cap.

Espionage system is separate. Founded on principals of sabotage. Admiral Caraties (former Greek - no pictures) built German system. Worked in Spain and with Mata Hari in WWI. Financed German Free Corps after war. Friend of Heinrich Heydrick - hated by Hemmler, forced by High Command. Carnaris organized Personnel Dept B, list of friends of Germany. Watch for attys for consulates as members.

General Franz Von Epp - former honorary governor of Bavaria and chief of German colonial office - organized African spy ring. Originated cry of "Give us back our colonies!"

Ernest Wilhelm Bohle - born England and naturalized Germany. Organized Germans abroad, especially in U.S. Father of German-American Bund. Fanatical Nazi, crazy to organize America. Joined Hess in mass espionage theory.

Eugene Ott - German ambassador in Tokyo - plenty anti-American & anti-British.

Alfred Rosnberg - Chief of Foreign Political office in Berlin. Specialist in Russian espionage. Born in Rival, Russia.

Hans Oberlindeober - Chief of German World War Society, sponsors of World War II. Chairman of Kyhoffis Bund. Traveling spy over Belgium, France, and Norway.

Dr. Conrad Ferdinand Fritz Grobba (name Arthur Borg) agent in Middle East, organized Iraq revolt, former German ambassador to Baghdad.

Col. Walter Nicolai - Espionage expert, chief of all military intelligence from WWI to 1937. Graduate of famous Kaiser school. Established scientific sabotage in schools, 1924.

Marie Jenks - sister of Ribbentrop, married to apparently obscure commercial attache in Ankara Turkey. Most valuable woman spy today. Assigned by Himmler to watch Von Papen in Turkey.

Capt. Fritz Weidemann - former consul in San Fransico. Contact with Japanese. Tried to crash society. Believed to have had hand in Pearl Harbor.

Eberhart Von Stohrer - ambassador in Spain. Associated with Canaris and active in organizing espionage in Spanish Civil War. Agents in Lisbon & watching Gibraltar.

Joseph Goebbels - Greatest propaganda campaigner in the world. One of leaders in 1943 German espionage.

Rules in connection with spy investigation: (1) Exhibit no curiosity. (2) Keep passive face. (3) Invent information & expound on it. (4) Do not discuss confidential information in public or with suspect. (5) Avoid leaving letters, notes, scraps of paper. (6) Acquire habits of recording notes in commonplace manner. (7) Conceal knowledge of language or ability to overhear conversation. (8) Make appointment with informer away from residence & place of operations. (9) Have informant travel to interview if possible. (10) Get one fact rather than a dozen opinions.

Romantic & adventurous spy is disappearing. Types: (1) Resident spy; (2) Mobile spy; (3) Soldiers; (4) Salesmen; (5) Journalist; (6) Letter box. Commercial spy is usually cheap & unreliable. May be found around beer parlor, stations, lower-paid city employees.

Espionage is the acquiring of intelligence & vital information within the confines of a nation & transmitting the same to an unfriendly or enemy nation, to the detriment of the nation from which it is acquired and to the benefit of the enemy nation.

Counter Intelligence - 1st organized in France under Napoleon, Stieber in Germany organized schools.

3 types of organizations in U.S.: (1) Official, (2) semi-official, and (3) unofficial. Official: German agencies, consuls and diplomats; Semi-official: Trans-Ocean News Service & American Bund & travelers.

Germany supposed to have 45,000 foreign agents in last war. Believed to have 15,000 in U.S. now.

Authority to try spies by military commission - 68 U.S. 243, Walliskan case.

Aerial photographer not in Army is spy. Spy who escapes and is later captured in uniform as a prisoner of war cannot be tried as a spy. (article 31 - Hague Convention - quondam spy.) Spy must be caught in act.

Note necessity of proving intent. Definition of dissimulate. Swearing in not necessary in case of selectee; Notice to report begin military service. Otherwise in case of volunteer.

Intent may be presumed from wearing deceptive uniform. Offense is complete with intent - not necessary actually to obtain information. There must be an attempt to communicate.

Hague Tribunal recognizes as lawful the right to employ spies. They are punished not as violators of international law, but in order to discourage practice.

Obtaining information openly without false pretenses is not espionage.

Spy must collect information:

(1) By actual ground reconnaissance: sportsmen, travelers, etc.

(2) By searching personal effects of individuals and listening to conversations.

(3) By talking to or getting into argument with persons having information.

(4) Burglary, bribery, assault, and other underhand methods.

2 Factors of espionage: (1) obtaining, & (2) transmitting it. Transmission is danger.

6 Classifications of espionage: (1) Commercial, (2) Political (3) Financial, (4) Military, (5) Naval, & (6) Espionage per si.

<u>Lessons Drawn from 5th Column Activity in Europe</u>. Phrase coined by General Mola in Spanish campaign. He did not invent the idea.

In Poland there were several minorities. All were loyal except Germans. Germans had freedom of activity but used it to plot & organize: (1) German citizens, (2) German teachers association, (3) children who were to go to school in Germany, (4) those who claimed Russia was enemy, (5) book dealers for propaganda, (6) sport travel clubs to observe country - All these were taken into German espionage - system and put to work gathering information.

Formed German Patriotic Leagues Volk Bund, German-Polish political organization, Young Peoples League, & Traveling Teachers. Concentrated on working with young people in free Polish schools, and then they were sent to Germany for final training in sabotage & espionage.

Polish Counter-Intelligence was aware of these, but could not get action from political officials. Probably not very efficient.

Many of the agents had government jobs, ranging from parliament to postman & police. Just before attached 5th Columnists were smuggled into the country. Their main achievements were: (1) to collaborate accurately with air force by indicating objective, wind direction, and parachute activities; this was accomplished by markings on roofs, lights in wells & chimneys, marks in fields & crops, secret radios. (2) To destroy or tap communications. (3) To destroy transportation facilities or preventing destruction of those considered necessary for German invasion. (4) To hinder operations of Polish Army through immediate contact by firing from concealed vital places & destroying transport, giving incorrect information, changing road signs, barricading roads, posing as officers & giving false orders & spreading rumors. (5) To destroy public utilities. Other groups created panic among refugees to block Army movements other groups supported German ground troops by acting as guides, pointing out enemy groups, providing hidden fuel & other supplies.

In occupied Poland, German troops had been propagandized to such extent that they showed no mercy. Gestapo moved in, already equipped with list of undesirable citizens in each district to be liquidated.

Success of Polish campaign was due: (1) Poland failed to realize power of German propaganda. (2) Poland failed to realize size & nature of German minority. (3) Insufficient counter-espionage measures. (4) Failure to recognize that students & travelers to & from Germany were spies. (5) Failure to identify spy leaders & halt storage & smuggling of arms. (6) Failure to provide for police expansion to guard transportation & communication facilities - resulting in incomplete mobilization. (7) Success & power of German attack disrupted plans of Poles.

Denmark - Geo-Political Institute obtained complete & accurate information as to resources & economics of Denmark. Invasion was merely an occupation, entirely unexpected by Danes. Few precautions had been taken by Danes. Land along border had been bought by Germans living in Denmark. Communication system was seized to prevent spread of news.

Norway remained neutral in World War I and intended to do so again, although at certain cost. Norway did not realize that it had anything anyone wanted, failed to realize value of fisheries & foodstuffs & strategic value of harbors. Same system was used in Norway as Poland, except there was no minority to exploit. Germans again used total espionage methods. They worked on traitorous discontented Norwegians. Quisling was selected as a leader, but he was unable to organize a party except among youths & discontents. Treason was a minor factor. Norwegian Army was small & ill-equipped. Vanguard of forces was the children adopted during & after World War, also tourists. Consular & embassy staffs were greatly enlarged & used to gain information. Germans explored coasts - went ashore for sight-seeing hikes. German business representatives toured country. Merchant ships loaded with troops were anchored in harbors.

Prime cause of fall of Norway was overwhelming power aided by detailed information obtained. Second, failure of Norway to appreciate danger. 3rd, failure to obtain advance warning by military intelligence. 4th, no precautions were taken against Quisling & other elements.

In Holland, bridges were vital to defense. Two 5th Columnists took over one important bridge, disconnected mines, & held it for parachutists through a trick on sentry.

Evidence

Only those things which tend to prove the ultimate facts at issue should be admitted into evidence.

If this type of evidence is to be transported for examination by an expert, each bullet or cartridge case should be separately wrapped in a wad of clean soft absorbent cotton, then placed in a separate cardboard box with sufficient additional cotton added to prevent the evidence from shaking around in the box. The box itself should then be properly labeled with a description of the evidence contained therein and with the name or initials of the individual who packed the box. Where possible to do so, it is desirable to seal the package or box with a gummed label bearing the signed name or initials of the officer packing and sealing the box.

Course: Evidence as applied to <u>criminal</u> investigation, in <u>federal</u> <u>court</u> procedure. Course does not apply to courts martial, & only federal court.

Pleadings: Allegations by prosecution, & allegations in defense by defendant.

Evidence: Matter brought up at trial to prove or disprove allegations of pleadings.

Practice: Incidental acts & steps in course of bringing matters pleaded to trial & procuring & enforcing judgment.

CIC is confined to investigation & prevention, & trial work is turned over to F.B.I. Handled by U.S. Dist. Atty.

Law is a rule of human conduct, & the law is a system of such rules built up through the ages, by legislative enactment, universal acknowledgment, & state decisions.

Law is <u>adjective</u> & <u>substantive</u>. Substantive: The rules & obligations laid down for conduct of men. Adjective: The rules governing enforcement of substantive law.

Evidence: Any matter of fact from which an inference may be drawn as to another matter of fact. Facts on which inferences are based are called <u>evidentiary</u> facts. Law of evidence is largely made up of negative rules as to what cannot be admitted.

Evidence must be relevant, competent, material. Relevancy & materiality relate to value of evidence itself, competency to the method of introduction.

Competency is presumed. Common law disabilities have been limited by statute to insanity (?). These are not to be confused with privileged communications. At present, in federal court, husband & wife are incompetent - new rule probably pending.

Judicial notice - No greater degree of proof is necessary with circumstantial than with direct evidence.

Presumptions of <u>law</u> and of <u>fact</u>. Presumption of law is binding on court & jury; presumption of fact is a mere inference which may be rebutted by evidence.

Character is what a man actually is. Reputation is what he is thought to be.

Previous conviction of witness affects his credibility only.

Personal Description

N.B. Western American boy delivers telegram to beautiful woman in hotel, robe open, "Come in, someone is coming." "You must have wonderful ears." "Why?" "Party you heard coming was me."

1st system of description ~ expert memory. (2) Photographs. (3) Bertillon system - photographs & bodily measurements. (4) Fingerprint-system, including photographs & personal description.

Name - serial number if military - color - sex - citizenship - age - date - place of birth - height - weight - hair - eyes - peculiarities. To locate by description add description of face & head & hands & feet. Emphasize unusual.

Family, associates, and places frequented are important.

Obtain photograph or note where one can be obtained. Add details of previous record.

Description should be useful (1) to locate in files; (2) to identify on street; (3) to aid in localizing search.

Description may contain personal history; addresses, employment, education, relatives, associates.

Note if photos & fingerprints in file. Criminal record may be noted.

Observation & Description

Two parts of observation: (1) the act of taking note or perceiving, or the acquisition of knowledge through the 5 senses, and (2) the importing of the information gained to another.

Witness is likely to confuse what he actually saw with what he deduced from his observation. Everyone's ability to observe is limited, & this must be born in mind in investigation. Reports are colored by beliefs & prejudices.

<u>Purpose</u> of <u>observation</u> is to obtain information and <u>to be able to describe</u> or relate it later. The real object is to be able to describe.

Observation must be <u>systematic</u>. It is necessary to develop a method suited to the individual.

Photographs, maps, & diagrams are useful in description of places.

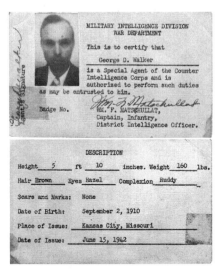

Best way to describe an article is to obtain a duplicate.

Criminal identification has existed since days of branding, followed by days of visual recollection by experts. Photography brought rogues' gallery, & Bertillon added system of body measurements. Then about 1903 came fingerprints.

Modern method is to use fingerprints, photograph, and physical description.

Full & correct name is important, together with aliases & how used. Next, age, date & place of birth, & note difference in apparent age. Height - Weight - color & peculiarities of hair. Eyes - color & glasses & peculiarities. Forehead may be described if unusual enough to identify & same may be said of other features, nose, mouth, lips, etc. Ears won't work unless unusual. Complexion is of little benefit unless extreme - use of medium or ruddy is a waste of time. Neck must be extreme to identify, likewise shoulders. Figure may vary. Hands, arms, feet & legs are not usually described unless deformed or tattooed.

Describe scars according to kind & location; specific location, size, shape, & color are valuable. Applies to marks, moles, tattoos, etc.

Description of clothes is important if to be used immediately. Not reliable. If making a description, describe clothes; if using one, don't rely on it.

Methods of Searching

Rules will not fit all cases. Two axioms: (1) <u>Never underestimate intelligence of subject; and never take anything for granted.</u> (2) <u>The more valuable a piece of evidence is to you, the more valuable it is to the subject.</u>

Searches are of <u>two major types</u>: (1) <u>for specific items</u>, and (2) <u>for unknown items</u>. In looking for specific items, one should not forget importance of other unexpected information which may be found.

Subdivisions: (1) <u>persons</u>, (2) <u>premises</u>, (3) <u>open areas</u>, (4) <u>wooded areas</u>, (5) <u>vehicles</u>.

Normal search of persons covers both types. It should be made immediately upon detaining subject. Know as much about subject as possible beforehand. Should be as thorough as possible at time & should always be followed by complete search. Make sure he is not armed & does not dispose of anything. Make certain that he is continually under observation. Take advantage of surprise, & never be forced on defensive. Deny all requests. Fraction of a second may give opportunity to dispose. Make preliminary search & then transport to place of security & privacy. Handcuffs should be used if possible. Then have him remove clothing in presence of witnesses. Hair, armpits, crotch, between toes, even rectum. Inspect clothing carefully, watching labels, laundry marks, stains. Always have subject watch search.

Anything found should be laid aside & examined later. If there is any possibility, garments should be processed for hidden writing. Papers should also be processed if doubtful. Fountain pens, pencils, etc., may be weapons. Money should be inventoried as to denomination & place carried. Consider each article suspicious until it is definitely shown not to be.

All these principles apply to search of women, but must be by matron, police woman, or reliable woman. In the preliminary search it is necessary to have a witness to avoid accusations.

Search of property should be planned in advance. Permission will be necessary, & if area is large there should be more than one agt. There should be organization, & one should be in charge & obeyed. Either party may act as unit, or part may be assigned to each individual. Chart of area should be prepared. If any article is found, it is desirable to have photograph, & in any event a witness should be called in addition to the agent. If photograph is used, something to identify scene & shows perspective should be included.

To search living quarters without knowledge of suspect, be sure to restore all articles to place. Try to get a key before using force or picking lock. It is essential to make arrangements so that there will be no interference. Lookout should be posted, & it is a good idea to keep suspect under surveillance as well. Restore each article as moved so that you can leave quickly. If microphone is to be installed, do that first.

Quarters may be searched incident to an arrest if within reasonable distance.

Interrogation

N.B. Absent minded professor who kept notebook of dates. Irate husband, "I don't like it." Prof, "Neither did I."

Interrogation is putting questions to one. It is most common method of investigation. It does not employ force - the idea of interviewing is better.

Purpose is to obtain facts from person interviewed about things seen, felt, heard, observed, or known.

Every case involves interviews at some stage. Force does not get results. Use only force which is necessary in making arrest. Then treat suspect well, see that he has cigarettes, a good meal. Get him in a good humor to talk. Investigator should think of himself as a salesman to sell himself & the idea of giving information to him.

Methods of approach in interview: There is no fixed rule to determine beforehand; it depends on the individual, and the first thing is to size him up. Test of the approach is whether it works.

Give the individual the idea that he is helping.

Approaches:

(1) Open & straightforward method - type used with reliable persons. Make full disclosure.

(2) Emotional appeal method - the idea of sparing a relative embarrassment; patriotism, etc. Don't try this on tough boys.

(3) Flattery

(4) Trickery - by getting two suspects to believe that each is betraying other, by fabricating information, etc., pertaining to friendship.

(5) Pretext - posing as someone else. This is dangerous and may lead to embarrassment & refusal to give information. If used, be sure to know enough about subject to carry pretext through.

Types of interviews

(1) With complainants - persons who, on their own initiation, furnish information concerning offenses; may or may not be a witness. May or may not have an interest. To make an interview with complainant, agent must know his jurisdiction & elements of offense under each. Be sure to get full name, address, phone number. Reduce information to writing, even if unfounded. If interview is at your office, there should be a private room for that purpose, be courteous; let them talk & get all the facts; don't call back. Don't refer to another agency if you have no jurisdiction.

(2) During investigation - with person sought up by agent after complaint received & investigation begun. Advance appointments with busy persons are desirable. In a big business go to the top for cooperation. If file is kept, try to see file itself.

(3) Under Pretext - interview to obtain information under guise of being someone else. This is dangerous. Know something about business which you pretend to represent.

(4) With informers - paid or seeking other personal advantage. Do not interview in your own office, nor in his office or home. Try to do so in out-of-the-way place. Fix your own time & place. Officer in charge should know informer's identity, & one agent only. Keep it out of report.

(5) <u>With witnesses</u> - always get full name & address of any. 3 types: (1) Willing & reliable - may be interviewed anywhere if private; let him tell his own story & fill in later with questions; not usually necessary to have statement signed but desirable; anyway take notes. (2) Willing but fearful witness - assure him of protection by keeping information confidential and by use of subpoena; obtain a signed statement from him. (3) Unwilling witnesses: Try persuasion & salesmanship; then try to turn witness against subject; then question as if a subject, may be jailed as material witness. If statement is obtained, by all means have it written, and signed if possible. If witness is a victim, he may fall into any of 3 classes.

(6) <u>Suspects</u> - before interview, obtain as much information about his background as possible. Have interview in your office if possible. Interview in his home or office is unfavorable. Be as friendly as possible. May start by asking if he knows why he is being interviewed. Get complete statement of his activities before, during, and after offense. Ace in the hole is threat of complete investigation to obtain information, with resultant embarrassment, if he doesn't talk freely. Don't lose temper; keep control of situation. Always get a statement.

(7) <u>Subjects</u> - individuals who committed the offense. Interview as soon as possible after crime. If 2 or more are arrested, immediately separate, and interview separately; have interview in private room. Have your back to light. Place him to side where you can observe his entire body. Be sure to advise him your official capacity & advise him of his rights. Talk to him about background & interests before you reach point; get him talking. Don't argue with him or threaten. Never promise anything you can't back up. Get a written statement if possible. Don't write anything until you have complete story. Read complete statement back to him. Do not erase changes. Cross out and initial. Avoid putting admissions of unrelated crimes in same statement.

<u>Types of subjects</u>: (1) 1st offender; you may reveal some of the evidence to him; don't take nervousness as proof of guilt; sympathy with motives & misfortunes may be good approach.

Shifting blame may help. Two offenders may be played against each other. Confession obtained by trickery is good.

(2) Confirmed criminal - the professional. Familiarity will not work. But methods to point out that you will get information anyhow. Expense is no object. Flattery or toughness may help. Ace in the hole is difference between maximum and minimum sentence.

Taking notes during interview - be sure to have date right. Take only pertinent facts. Get correct spelling of names, correct address & dates.

If using a mike, make a notation occasionally so as not to reveal use.

Four classifications of persons interviewed:

(1) Complainants or informers - May be (1) a conscientious citizen; (2) person prejudiced against subject; (3) local law enforcement officers; (4) paid informants - stool pigeons - not too trustworthy, particularly if they have past records. Be sure to fix time and place of meeting to avoid trap, or being used as alibi.

(2) Witness - persons who have first hand knowledge & are competent to testify. 1st type is willing witness, of which best is the original complainant. 2nd type is unwilling witness.

(3) Suspects - (1) in custody, and (2) not in custody, latter are difficult, must be interviewed at home or at their own offices, and are able to control interview or refuse it. This is where salesmanship comes in.

(4) Prisoners - already convicted or arrested with sufficient to hold. 1st class is the prisoner being interviewed regarding another crime.

In interviewing a big concern, go to the top; don't be shoved off to small fry. Get full name & title from secretary if he has one.

Interview a subject as soon as possible after crime. Get any unwilling witness to your office if possible.

Listen to witness' story even if it is not important. If it bears on another matter, report it to proper authority.

Don't be prejudiced at start of interview.

Never promise anything you can't deliver. Never bluff. Never lose temper.

Informers

Underworld contacts are informers. They are very important. Without tips it is difficult to arrive at suspects. In order to obtain information someone must have confidence of suspects & persons who know suspects.

Types of informers:

(1) Patriotic citizen.

(2) Anonymous - be sure to get all information at once, because he cannot be contacted again.

(3) Professional reformer, busy body, crank.

(4) Nuts, mildly insane.

(5) Persons who acquire information in their work - hotel employees, etc., bellboys, house detectives, waiters. In dealing with these types, always be liberal with tips. Taxi drivers usually have information.

(6) Neighbors & children - children usually have information and will talk.

(7) Criminal or criminal associate - most of them like to brag & gossip. May come through fear, but usually will not voluntarily contact officers. Best approach is fear of another charge. Another way is to arouse jealousy or fear of big shot, or suspicion that he is going to hold the bag. Do not make promises other than that you will call matter to attention of court or District Atty.

Petty criminal may act as informer for officers for his own protection. He will hand out information on major crimes in the hope his own minor acts will be overlooked.

There is also the professional informer who wants money. Usually are old criminals. Care must be used not to pay for false information - reward or per diem basis is best. War Department has confidential funds to pay for information.

Many informers act for revenge for a double cross or some wrong.

In dealing with informers, be sure not to let him know what you know. He may be pumping you. It may be well to drop a false hint to one of them and see if it gets back.

In dealing with informers do not show contempt or indicate that you consider him a stool-pigeon. Refer to him as an "informant" or "confidential source" if he is likely to overhear. Always protect his identity. Do not meet him at office or his or your home, or places where he is well known. Avoid using him as a witness. If he gets in trouble, try to help him. Keep your word to him; good treatment usually pays. Discourage their fears as to consequences of informing.

Always run the show; get information & not advice as to how to work case. Don't let him take advantage of his position.

Don't adopt informers moral habits if you have to associate with them, particularly with women.

Undercover Investigation

Undercover is one of the oldest types of investigation. It produces quick results if properly handled. Agents must be well trained & adept. He drops his true identity, mingles with and gains information from suspects. It is necessary to avoid entrapment by showing that criminal intent by subject existed & was not induced by agent.

Undercover requires (1) natural or acquired aptitude for work, ability to drop identity & assume another, and some histrionic ability; (2) must have complete confidence in ability as undercover; (3) must establish an unbreakable background for assignment & under no circumstances permit anyone to frighten or bluff him; (4) must be versatile enough to assume any guise or identity required; (5) Must have strong moral fiber to resist temptation; (6) Must have infallible memory because he does not have opportunity to write notes; (7) Must rigidly suppress all normal habits of speech and action as officer.

Most important is self-confidence. To do this he must have good background. He must have a preliminary check of his suspects to know who they are, where they come from, what they have done, and what they are supposed to be doing. Background should be placed in other city than site of operations, and one unfamiliar to suspects, and familiar to agent as that he can answer questions. Never claim to be a big shot; it may be embarrassing not to have connections. Underworld uses long distance calls and may check on background; have a check arranged.

Suspects occasionally pretend to know more than they do and may try to bluff or test agent.

Care must be given to dress & appearance. All identification should be removed, and it is not a good idea to carry a gun. May be well to remove clothing labels & hat bands. Business or calling cards are useful. Draft cards should be obtained, showing deferment. Deafness or blindness may be simulated, or other infirmity, but it must be practical & carried through.

Street photographer, push cart peddler, or WPA or municipal employee may be useful guise.

Drinking while working undercover is a problem. It should be avoided if possible. Good alibi for not drinking with suspect is ulcers of stomach. Agent must remain sober enough to keep identity & retain observations.

Women are to be avoided if possible. May get suspect's girl & cause trouble. May be unable to get out of involvement. Also not a good idea to take a girl on an assignment. She may get too deeply involved, so that it becomes necessary to reveal identity.

Question of expenses must be watched while undercover. Agent should not live above the means of the person whom he impersonates. Should wear clothes suitable to role.

The expenses incurred should be recorded in a manner meaningless to anyone except self.

Discretion in writing reports is vital. Agent should not be seen writing or mailing. Stay away from neighborhood of office. Report may be made in writing, telephone, or telegraph. Do not duck in a booth at every opportunity. Good reason for disappearance to write report or make a call must be given, and care must be taken to make sure that one is not tailed. If shadowed, one must decide whether to shake him or go through with reason for absence.

Theatre is useful to drop shadow. Turning the corner & entering building may work. Getting on bus & off just as it starts leaves tail aboard.

If used as a witness, do not give interviews.

If assigned to undercover, insist on having all data & facts available as to suspect. Generally no time limit is placed on undercover work, unless there is some necessity for it. Background is absolutely necessary. May be questioned as to neighborhood and geography of the town where he claims to have lived, people known & incidents which have happened there.

How to get entree - best way is to be introduced & vouched for by a contact. Each case must be figured separately.

Question whether to commit a crime in course of conspiracy must be governed by judgment and instructions.

Not advisable to be armed. $2 package of nickels is handy weapon.

Undercover investigation:

2 types: (1) where some other identity than own is used for simple inquiry - the guise; (2) the completely undercover assignment. Preparation requires more time than job. There are few laws in undercover; one is: in every case there must be preliminary investigation.

ONIT-8-10 is excellent investigators' manual.

Suggestions:

(1) Do not confuse regular investigation, no matter how confidential, or how many ruses or pretexts are used, with completely undercover work.

(2) No credentials on any completely undercover

(3) Never begin an undercover assignment without making a complete and exhaustive study of case.

(4) Make your "introduction" to group logical & convincing.

(5) Remember you may be constantly under observation.

(6) Immediately destroy all communications received.

(7) NEVER CONFIDE IN ANYONE.

(8) Have no more money in your possession than you can logically explain.

(9) Never be seen in company of officer. Make contacts carefully & by pre-arranged plan.

(10) Write & mail from post office only.

(11) Never use same telephone twice in calling office. Always try to use dial phone.

(12) Never publicly recognize another agent as either may be on an assignment.

(13) Check up with all operatives on undercover work at regular, per-determined intervals.

(14) Try to avoid making notes. When necessary use apparently innocent figures. Memorize.

(15) Never act mysteriously, never brag, never show off.

(16) Do not admit knowledge of foreign languages except in role; same of military affairs.

(17) "Sacrifice Play."

(18) Be suave & considerate in dealings with women; even if not strictly in character, it will pay dividends.

Sabotage & Saboteurs

The willful damage - or destruction of property or the slowing down of production by attacking of property, material, or personnel is sabotage.

3 kinds of sabotage organizations: (1) radical international organizations; (2) foreign nationalists groups usually Americans under foreign influence; (3) secret sabotage agencies or organizations organized directly by foreign governments. There are also individuals acting independently.

2 types of sabotage: (1) labor and, (2) physical, which is divided into sabotage by (1) mechanical means, (2) explosives, (3) arson.

Labor sabotage includes foreign-inspired strikes, slow-downs, or any other method to hinder production under guise of a labor dispute.

In investigating labor dispute do not take sides but try to get all facts. Get full information from original informant: the company involved, contacts, name of union, name of leader, cause of dispute, violence. <u>Take no steps not authorized by higher authority</u>.

Totalitarians consider war to have begun when secret units move into a nation to prepare it for defeat. They do not follow rules of fair play, and should not have benefit of them. They have well-developed methods of underground activity in 3 groups: (1) propaganda, (2) espionage, (3) sabotage.

Russian machine was model for Germans. Both aim at world domination. German theory is that they are superior race, and will establish domination by force. Russian theory is to establish a world-wide Soviet Union. Ultimate aim of each is world domination, and only means differ.

Sabotage & underground activity is studied in Russia as a science, and is taught in several universities in courses of one to six years. German machine uses only its own nationals; Russian uses others. <u>Propaganda</u> is used and taught as <u>morale sabotage</u>. Morale exists (1) where there is a dynamic central cause or idea around which people may rally. (2) where there is confidence in leaders, and (3) where there is confidence in success. These three may be attacked by propaganda. <u>First attack</u> is to disunite people & break down belief in the central ideal - to cause strife between races, religions, labor & capital, soldiers & civilian, etc.; object is to make a group put its own interests above those of the action & act accordingly. <u>Second attack</u> is to establish suspicion of aims & honesty of leaders, and to bring about demoralization. <u>This attack</u> is to break down people's belief in their own ability to succeed; rumors are spread that officers are corrupt, forces ill-equipped. At same time potential allies are led to believe that the nation is doing well and needs no help.

Bolshevists in this country have quit talking about revolution. Now they talk about socialism instead of communism, and promise that Shangri-La can be found by following Russia. They emphasize civil liberties for protection of their own crimes. They use language & slang of those among whom they work, i.e., "America First."

<u>Sabotage</u> is directed at breaking down economic life of a

nation. It is broader than technical sabotage, i.e., it is not mere destruction of machinery but aims at tying up production through strikes, etc. The strike is the most effective form of sabotage. It is organized, not by urging revolution, but by inventing and urging grievances and stirring up those who are not members of party. The object is to get an unreasonable set of demands which will be refused, not granted for the good of the worker. Next comes the strike, and the demand for the sympathetic spread. The hope is to arrive at the general strike, which becomes political - a revolution. Effort is to stir up violence, to force police or soldier to shoot. Then comes armed resistance, and the possible revolution. Each strike which does not reach these proportions weakens the nation & prepares for the big strike which is aimed for.

If strikes cannot be fomented, next come technical sabotage. The object is to find a key piece of machinery & destroy or to tie up production. The aim of Soviet is to get mass sabotage, not the work of trained specialists. In planes, particularly, it is the desire to get delayed action, so that they will pass inspection and then crash.

Mass saboteur is strike organizer, and technical saboteur is destroyer of machinery. Propagandists is morale saboteur.

Russia is just as dangerous as Germany.

Chapter 5

Omaha, Camp Richie, New York & At Sea
U.S.A., October 1943 - December 1943

(Note: CIC is reduced from over 5000 to around 500 in the late summer, early fall of 1943. Most returning to regular service, and some to OCS, while the cream of the crop went to Camp Richie).

Nothing is happening, and apparently nothing will, but we want to be sure. If everything continues quiet tomorrow when the mines open, the other boys, or most of them, will probably go home, but I think I will stay here until it is clear that nothing will happen.

Elliot went through today on his way to drive his car home. He seemed in good spirits, and we gave him a couple of drinks and sent him on his way rejoicing. He is supposed to leave Saturday night.

I haven't been doing much except lying around a hotel room waiting for the telephone to ring, and it is certainly monotonous. I direct the others to do what little there is to do, which isn't much.

HOTEL KEEN

VIRGIL A. ROBERTS, Prop.

HARNEY STREET AT 18TH
OMAHA - NEBR.

Friday Night

I arrived OK about twenty minutes late tonight. Had a very good trip to St. Louis, arriving on time. I couldn't get a seat on the Eagle, but by swapping off with some soldiers and killing time in the diner I did fairly well until I got a seat at Kansas City.

I didn't have a single beer, either!

Harden was in the lobby when I came in. He says Heard has been called and has gone home. I hope he left my stuff with Jim or somewhere. Six boys from the office are going to Chicago school this week, and Harden says that leaves only three to work besides the resident agents. He says the captain is running in circles. Harden hasn't been called yet, but not many are left.

The best G.I. rumors I can get are that we are all going to Ritchie for an indeterminate period.

Most of the boys are out helling around, but I gave it up after a while. Had a few drinks with Zinsmaster before and after supper, but he went off with a fluff and I came home. I have read over the paper and the American Field and am about ready for bed.

We spent all afternoon out at Fort Crook drawing equipment. I bought an extra barracks bag - which I probably can't keep - and still don't know where I'll put it all. Being a soldier certainly is strenuous, but anyhow I have some shiny new stuff.

Everybody has a different rumor about what we will do, but I don't think anybody really knows. They vary all the way from serving in the cadre at the staging area to going across immediately.

New orders are still coming in, and it looks as if hardly anyone will be left. We are lucky in getting such a good bunch to go with - none of the heels and pains in the neck that I could name.

We haven't done much today except check in our ammunition and arm bands.

I might get some more information today, but all I can get is rumors that confuse things worse. We will leave Tuesday night about 8:30. We will be in Baltimore two, three, or four weeks, according to what rumor you want to believe, and then at Ritchie two or three weeks, or maybe at Ritchie first.

Sutton has gotten his orders - Baltimore on the 1st.

We reach Baltimore about eight in the morning and report about noon. After that, maybe some of the mystery will clear up.

We have just had breakfast and are getting ready to report.

There isn't much I can tell you about what's going on. This deal is just like basic training over again - all hard work and confusion. All of us have forgotten all we knew about soldiering, and it's hard to pick up. I have been trying to act as platoon sergeant, and it will be a wonder if I don't march them into the ocean.

I have seen several of the boys but not Elliot so far. He is supposed to be back Sunday, and I know he'll be happy to see Hopper, Stobbart, and me. I hope so, because there isn't too much here to cheer anyone. However, it isn't too bad, and it will do all of us good.

It's hard to write without talking about what we are doing, but even if we could it wouldn't be very interesting anyhow. This isn't bad, not nearly as tough as the engineers, and I think I'll get along all right. As a matter of fact, it is quite a lot of fun listening to all the G.I. griping. When you consider how well this bunch could do when complaining about the perfectly good life they had, you can imagine how Black Jack, Tom, and some of the others get going now. Mo is always funny, and he keeps everybody laughing at his remarks.

It is now eight o'clock, and M/Sgt. Hopper is in bed - can you imagine that? It's about the only place there is to go at that.

I'm inclined to doubt that our mail is censored, incoming

anyhow, although it is possible. Anyhow, they won't get much consolation out of mine.

Yesterday was rather a full session. Today we have a few minutes to ourselves with only a couple of thousand things to do.

You may observe from the postmark that we have moved, but keep on addressing mail to the old address.

This is a beautiful camp, and the mountains are very pretty at this time of year. However, they look pretty high, too, and the fall air is rather brisk early and late. I'm glad we didn't wait any later to come here.

Of course I can't tell you anything about what we'll do here, but I suppose it's no secret that we'll be plenty busy. It looks as if sleep is about the only thing omitted from the course. They go in for the military manner in a large way, and I love it just like I always did.

Another day's work is behind me, and I still haven't seen anything as rough as the engineers. Aside from pretty long hours, this hasn't been too rough so far.

As a prerogative of great rank I get to live in a squad room with only one roommate, instead of out in the barracks with the common herd. It is a good deal, being more private and easier to keep in order, besides having more room than a bunk in the big room.

I heard today that Harden has got his orders and is coming here shortly. I'll bet the poor captain has blown his top now for sure.

Zinsmaster is in writing letters to make all the girls happy.

We still aren't overworked, but will be out until midnight the next four nights, so don't look for too many letters.

By some mischance we got through a few minutes before supper tonight. We take off on a night problem after supper.

We have been awfully busy. The work is not awfully hard, but the hours are long. This is the third successive night we've been out, and 5:30 comes just as early.

All this stuff comes back pretty quickly, but there is an awful lot about it that we never did know, and I certainly have no desire to use it. This is a good course here, but awfully concentrated. It should have been at least three times as much time as we have for it.

Sunday is just another day in the Army here, and leisure is unknown. Last night we were out from seven to midnight on a compass problem, a nice rainy evening and the third one in succession. I have about forgotten what a night's sleep is like.

Tonight was our night off. Tomorrow is supposed to be a holiday - they have every eighth day in here instead of Sunday - so all we have to do is a 14 mile hike.

We are having quite a rough go, but it is mostly the hours rather than the work. They just don't believe in sleep.

Ft. Meade (Camp Ritchie)

We had one of the roughest days I have hit yet anywhere - a twelve mile hike in a driving rain that was almost sleet. It was really rough going - over a mountain.

After drying out and changing clothes, I intended to spend the evening cleaning my equipment, write you, and go to bed early. However, Mo, Zinsmaster, Hopper, Stobbart, and my roommate wanted to go over to Hagerstown to get a couple of drinks and a decent meal, and talked me into going along. The result was a good seafood dinner and a few drinks, and none of the things done that I should have.

I am all right and doing as well as can be expected, but I don't like this old line soldier stuff.

We are getting in sight of the end of our stay at this miserable hole now, and everybody is looking up. Last night we had our last night problem, and tonight we will actually get a short nap. I have had about as much sleep as a débutante, and everybody has circles under his eyes like an old hell-raiser after a week's bender.

When or where we are going is a deep, dark secret, but it is generally conceded that we are going somewhere.

I don't believe we are going across at once, although there seems to be little doubt that it won't be long.

What is so secret about it is more than I can figure out, as we don't do or learn anything that isn't common routine to any infantry private, and not much of that. I guess the whole idea is to get us in a frame of mind where we don't give a damn where they send us just so it's somewhere.

I missed Elliott all around, and he is gone now. Rumor has it that he was assigned to an armored division, and I know he is singing the blues.

In the past, some of the boys have gone as close to home as Camp Chaffee, Ark., Camp Shelby, Miss., and Fort Worth, and if I should get one of those assignments by some stroke of luck…

We are just piddling around and marking time here. Everybody is on edge and ready to go almost anywhere to get away from here. This is not a pleasant spot, even if we weren't practically in jail.

Did I tell you that Mo, Hopper, Stobbart, and I are all living in a little cubby hole about the size of a pantry? We have to take turns about turning around. I'm afraid we'll all be scattered soon, but I hope some of us will get to go together. This is a good bunch, and incidentally the type of men from the 7th S.C. and generally from the western outfits is far above the rest of the men here. I hope I go with them.

The boys are beginning to get orders, and we will all be

gone by the time you get this. We are all being separated, and, judging by the grouping to date, the only one who may be with me is Estenson.

We have a big bull session going on - Mo, Stobbart, Hopper, and a couple of other guys, and Gossett just came in. Rumors are flying thick and fast, but nobody knows anything. Looks like Mo and Stobbart will get the cream of the assignments. It's all very confusing and prevents coherent writing. Zinsmaster just came in - worried about going to India - just another good rumor.

The bunch is being split all up. Hopper, Clark, Estenson, and one other are going with me, but only Estenson is in my group, which means we will be separated when we leave there. Stobbart and Mo Greevy are going to the Air Corps at Montgomery, Ala., as is Hecht, the lucky devils! Zinsmaster is going to California and thinks he is headed for India or Australia. The rest of them are scattered individually. I got a card from Elliott this morning; he is with an armored division in New York and not very happy.

They suddenly cut out about half the instruction we were supposed to get and cut our schedule from six weeks to three. Why they did so is a mystery, as they are going ahead with subsequent groups on a six-week basis.

We can't tell exactly where we are, but it is in the New York area. Of course nobody knows how long we will be here. We aren't too closely restricted as long as we are alerted and will probably be able to get out every other night, though I think I'll let the other boys catch up on their share of the passes. No telephone calls are allowed to be made from the post.

This is a very nice post, quite a contrast to the ones we have been on recently. We don't have much to do, and things are clean and orderly - really a change from the coal smoke and dirt of the past month. Most of the boys are well pleased.

I had a very enjoyable evening. There is an organization in New York which reserves blocks of seats for all the shows and gives them to service men <u>free</u>. As a result I had a $3.30 seat in the third row at the "Ice Follies" at Madison Square Garden. It was a wonderful show, graceful as only ice skating can be, and with beautiful costumes, lights, and music.

This morning I enjoyed sleeping late with no reveille, had breakfast at the Service Club.

Dear Dad,

Well, we are another step on our way. We didn't get much advance notice, finding out that we were to leave Camp Reynolds about five Tuesday afternoon, and leaving the same time next day. We had a rather uncomfortable overnight trip here, but are fixed up in a very good station in the metropolitan area. We can't tell exactly where we are and of course don't know how long we'll be here and couldn't tell if we did. I may see some of the bright lights, although I am not too much interested.

The Christmas issue of the Field came the day I left and made good reading on the way down on the train. I wish you would inquire whether I have to do anything to enable you to keep sending it. Also received the last bunch of World. I'm afraid you'll have to mail only clippings in the future.

There isn't any news. Write me about the dogs, and get in a bird hunt for me, as it looks like I'll have to do mine by correspondence.

Love to all.
Devotedly, Bud

Dearest Momma:

It certainly was good to hear all of your voices last night. The time flew by, as always, before we seemed to have started talking, but really the best part of the whole thing was just to hear you talk and to know that all of you are all right.

This morning I enjoyed sleeping late and then went to chapel, where I heard an unusually good Christmas sermon. It makes me a little blue to think about spending my first Christmas away from home at this ripe old age, and I certainly hope that when the next one rolls around I will be with you all again. I know you will be going to the cemetery, and I hope you will leave a special flower for me. But don't let it be a blue day for you. We have had many blessings and have many more to look forward to, and there are still many things to make us happy.

I think it is fine that dad made such a good sale of Marietta. Looks as if the horse business is moving towards the black side of the ledger. But aside from that it will give him room to develop his younger stock, and the place was a little overcrowded.

Yesterday was one of the most bitterly cold days I ever experienced, although the temperature got only about 15. In the morning there was a terrific wind, supposed to have reached 70 miles per hour, and you could hardly breathe in it. Fortunately we were able to spend most of the day inside, and the barracks were quite comfortable. Today is not unusually cold.

News is a rather limited commodity here, so I had better sign off.

Sorry I didn't get to say hello to Sister last night, but the minutes slipped by too fast.

Lots of love to all.
Devotedly, Bud

At sea

For several days we have been sailing peacefully over the Atlantic, and so far everything has been very pleasant. We were fortunate in sailing quite soon after boarding the ship, without a long delay in port. It was quite an interesting sight to see all the ships passing out of the harbor and to watch the convoy form.

We were not given our new A.P.O, so we don't know our exact destination, but are going where we anticipated when we left Reynolds.

The sea has been much calmer than I would ever have expected in these waters at this time of the year.

We have the run of the ship and are free to do almost anything we like, which doesn't mean, however, that we have a lot of entertainment. I got a lot of fun out of just walking up and down the deck, watching the sea and the other ships, and the sea air certainly makes one feel good. We don't have many duties, the principal one being standing watch two hours out of every ten. We all diligently look at the water without any particular idea of what we are supposed to look for. Also, we of course have boat drills, and some of us have been assigned to assist the gun crews. None of these things take up too much time, and we are left a good deal to our own devices.

A very interesting site was another {CENSORED}. We could see it all the way from the horizon until it fitted into our pattern.

An interesting angle to the travel is the bathing situation. We have to use cold shower of salt water, and since the soap won't lather in it under any circumstances, the whole deal is a bit discouraging.

Although I have occasionally wondered what Christmas might be like in distant places, it never before occurred to me to speculate what it would be on a {CENSORED} in the {CENSORED} Atlantic.

This morning one of the officers held a short non-sectarian service which was simple but quite effective and generally appreciated. Then we had an excellent turkey dinner, complete with table cloth and a decorated Christmas tree on the table. In the afternoon we had a little program, with a number of the boys doing songs and skits and everybody joining in Christmas carols. Afterwards there was candy and nuts, and Santa Claus appeared and passed around cloth bags designed for toilet articles, in which were a number of personal articles, I suppose the work of the Red Cross, USO, or some such. It was good entertainment and had everybody in good spirits.

Although we have had several rough days, the trip so far has been uneventful. At the moment we are rolling so that I have to hold on to the table to write, and every now and then the bench scoots out from under me. I am proud of not having been sick, although not too many of the boys have had trouble. We are beginning to speculate on when we will see land, and are hopeful of spending New Year's Eve ashore.

Chapter 6

Great Britain- Rear Eagle
30 December 1943 – 27 February 1944

We are now somewhere in England.

It's New Years Eve. After traveling nearly all afternoon and night to go about as far as from home to {CENSORED} in funny England's trains, and changing trains four times, we are now settled temporarily.

This is an old English Army post and looks like a college campus. It is said to be one of their better camps, which leads me to shudder in contemplation of their worse, and proves that among other achievements we build better Army posts. I am writing from the Red Cross Club, which is quite pleasant, good sized, and well fitted.

From limited observation I find England much like pictures and descriptions. The countryside is surprisingly green and both picturesque and pretty. The trains are dinky and ride very roughly. Although they make good time when running, it is amazing how many changes were required to go what seemed an insignificant distance.   Women and boys, as well as old men, are working everywhere, and it is apparent that these people are not fooling around about the war. I have seen none of the bombed areas, but you are immediately impressed with the seriousness of the war effort and its effects on everyone.

I would like very much to see something of the country. If we get passes they will be only at night, and then we won't be able to see anything for the blackout. That is really an experience, and on a cloudy night you can hardly see your hand in front of you.

My impressions of England are based on rather limited contact. However, I am convinced that the plumbing justifies all the jokes about it, and their soldiers must be a very short and very tough lot to endure the bunks. Much of the country that I can view from the camp is very pretty, with rolling, well-kept fields.

The camp is American-run, which I understand is fortunate. The food varies widely, from fair to awful, but they say it is much better than the British. I understand that on the outside liquor is practically gone, and beer, judging from samples on the post, is not worth the effort.

We had a comfortable train ride in daylight, and I enjoyed seeing the country. The fields all appear so regular with their little hedgerows, and they have some sort of winter grass that makes the fields look green. The houses are all gabled and brick, and look just like the pictures.

It is surprising how little trace there is of the bombings. You can see the places, but they just look as if old buildings had been torn down.

I am waiting to meet Hopper at the Red Cross Club. I have had a pass in London and have been able to see a few of the sights. There are shortages of everything, and people seem to get along without lots of things we would consider essential.

The blackout is quite an experience. You can't imagine how hard it is to get around a big city in complete darkness, and even in a camp it is a problem.

The Red Cross has a number of big service clubs in London, all of which do a rushing business. Apparently all of that sort of thing over here is in the hands of the Red Cross, and the USO operates elsewhere.

Soldiers are a dime a dozen over here, and you can pick almost any variety you like - American, British, Canadian, or a lot of off brands that are complete strangers to me. I never know whether some of these citizens are corporals or four star generals.

We were free yesterday and had a big time sightseeing. I was so impressed with Westminster Abbey that I went back yesterday afternoon to the services, which were both interesting and impressive. We have also seen Buckingham Palace, the Houses of Parliament, and any number of other places. Bulkley and I even visited the National Galleries.

St. Paul's Cathedral is also impressive and not greatly damaged although a bomb landed almost squarely over the altar. I have seen some extensive bombed areas, all old, but on the whole it is remarkable how much is left virtually untouched.

We have finally been advised of our assignments, and should soon be able to get started doing something. I believe mine is one of the more desirable jobs and am well pleased. I will cable also if I am permitted to do so.

Last night Dorsey, Bulkley, Arnold and I took in an old English play, Congreve's "Love for Love," which we enjoyed very much. It is a comedy, and some of the humor is pretty rough.

In my contacts with the British people I have found them courteous and anxious to be helpful. We have been quartered in old houses; they are really cold and clammy. We have no heat, but warm water. The houses have few fireplaces and no central heat, and from what I understand the English just stay cold, even in normal times.

At this time I don't know anything about my assignment except that it is in one of the branches generally considered desirable. Nick, Jovan, Brigham, McGrath, and several others of the original bunch are with me so far, but we have left some of the others whom I particularly like.

We are at our new station, which is located in a very pretty little town, cleaner and better kept than anything I have seen so far. We were met at the train by John Ryan who is the first sergeant of the detachment here.

We had a chance to sleep in good quarters last night, and it is remarkable how much one appreciates the little comforts that we always took as a matter of course - clean sheets, a shower with hot water, heating, and a dozen little things that we would think at home to be necessities. If this experience does nothing else for me, it will truly instill an appreciation of what home means.

Yesterday I cabled my address, which is AMEWAM PLATFORM. It is only necessary to give my name, serial number, and that address.

I got a letter off yesterday to the folks in Scotland in my very best-mannered style. I don't know what chance there will be of my seeing them, but may get work where I will have an opportunity to do so. I wrote the Dunshelt clan, as that appears to be the most numerous group.

We had the day off today, so Jovan and I and some of the others took a bus over to Stratford-on-Avon to see Shakespeare's birthplace. The country is pretty, every acre being utilized, and all the little fields neatly hedged off. Many of the houses are very old, a lot of them having thatched roofs, and the newer look just like the old ones. The roads are black-topped, but very crooked and narrow, and it must be a terrible problem finding your way around.

Stratford-on-Avon is a picturesque place, with many of the old buildings still in use. The town must look a good deal as it did in Shakespeare's time. We went through his home, where there were many interesting old documents, and also saw the new Memorial Theatre and the parish church where he is buried, as well as a number of other sights. The Avon is a beautiful little stream, flowing through a big park near the church and the theatre, and of course there were swans to complete the picture.

The chief vegetable over here is Brussels sprouts. I have actually seen whole box cars loaded with them.

British children are very appealing to me. Every time an American soldier walks down the street a bunch of kids appear, and invariably it's: "I sye, Yonk, have you any gom?" I don't know how they all developed such a taste for chewing gum, as it was never available to any great extent over here, but it seems to be the main thing they want.

The war is quite evident over here in a lot of little ways.

94

Women are at work everywhere - as railroad porters and agents, as bus conductors, driving delivery wagons, and in uniform everywhere. Rationing is real, and you notice the lack of sugar. The newspapers are of poor paper, only four or six pages, and the news is very stereotyped. Apparently the closer you get to the war, the less you know about what is going on. People really economize on coal and heat. And of course there is the blackout, which you must see to appreciate.

Last night I took in a movie at the Red Cross - one of Bob Hope's - which I fortunately hadn't seen. It had the additional virtue of being free. Bob Hope is a great favorite with the boys, and his broadcasts are quite an event.

We have learned where we are to work, and I am pleased with my district, particularly as it appears the most likely place to give me an opportunity to visit the folks.

This afternoon, Jovan and I went for a walk about town and looked over the local college. It is small, but quite pretty. The chapel was especially impressive, and reminded me considerably of Sewanee. The students all wear scholastic caps and look very dignified. Apparently the courses must take in some of our high school, as the boys looked very young.

In coming to our station we had an opportunity to see a new part of the country, and as usual our trip was quite interesting. Everywhere we saw picturesque little villages with old stone houses and peaked gables. The country was more rolling and hilly than any we have visited, and we saw a lot of pretty mountain streams with old stone bridges and quaint foot bridges. I am quite impressed with the land of my fore-bearers.

We will shortly be sent to the offices where we will work and I believe I am going to like the set-up. Nick will be with me, also Steinberg and Agnetta. I am glad to have Nick with me, although I hate to leave the other fellows.

I have gotten settled in my new quarters. I am living in the home of a very nice old couple who have three sons in the British Army. The home is very comfortable. I have the most comfortable bed that I have seen since leaving home. Mrs. Hannah is a very motherly old lady and is always worrying about seeing that we have everything possible. I get room and breakfast there, and if this morning was any sample, it is a vast improvement over the food I have become accustomed to.

There are three of us in the house, but I have a room to myself, which is a luxury in itself. You would be surprised at how little it costs, and we get tea and all sorts of little things extra. Mr. Hannah is in the insurance business here and is a very pleasant and quite intelligent man.

It certainly is a relief to get to unpack things out of my barracks bags after all these months, as well as unloading my pockets.

This looks like a very good deal, and I feel sure that I am going to be well pleased with the work and the set-up. It is interesting, and I wish I could tell you about it. The location is also not allowed to be published, but it is in the part of the Islands in which I am most interested.

Today marked my first real day of work. My job seems more like sight-seeing than the old pavement-pounding, but I am learning lots of things and believe I will soon get the swing of things.

You see lots of funny things over here, but I think one of the funniest was the other day when I bummed a ride in a jeep. It was driven by an old English woman with gray hair, wearing an American overseas cap, and driving down the wrong side of the road as unconcerned as you please.

There is very little news I can write, although I have had a rather interesting time and seen some new sides of the war effort.

I have received a letter from the cousins at Dunshelt. They of course asked me to come see them, and I hope I will soon get a chance. Apparently the whole tribe are within a few miles of each other in the neighborhood of Edinburgh. The station is Auchtermuchty, which sounds like a wonderful place to go.

The other day I had an opportunity to see a real kiltie band with bagpipes and a bass drummer with a flowing red mustache who was really quite a fair hand, flourishing the drumsticks and twirling them like a college boy - and he must have been past fifty. You know how I love the pipes, and this one was really good. It is surely wild music, if you can call it music, and there is something about it that makes your skin tingle.

It isn't usually cold, so I am not uncomfortable even without heat. The British say that heating rooms is the cause of having colds, and maybe they are right, because they don't seem to have them like we do. Anyway, they don't take any chances by exposing themselves to heat.

I don't know what to do with my spare time, but days get by in a hurry. Usually by the time I have come down town for supper, listened to the radio at the Red Cross for a while or read a paper, it is time to go home, as all transportation here ceases at eleven o'clock.

I spent yesterday, which was my day off, walking around the town to get myself located. These British cities have no system in the arrangement of the streets, and the only way to find any place is just to know where it is. In a sizable city, that is not always simple to learn. The streets are all crooked and winding, and to add to the complications, one will go along and suddenly for no apparent reason will have a new name. The numbering system is not uniform, and consecutive numbers may not be next door to each other.

Sunday night I had a very pleasant evening in the home of Jim Campbell, a man I met at church, a young fellow with an attractive wife and a 3 year old boy. They were very kind and insisted on feeding me more, I am sure, than was convenient with their rations. He is on some sort of traveling work, similar to the NYB and invited me to accompany him. If I can catch him on one of my days off, it will be a splendid chance to see the country in a car.

I was able to get a little news from Omaha, as well as from Mo. It seems that instead of being abolished the boys at Omaha have been fixed up for the duration.

I have written Capt. Frierson at Omaha and hope that I will be able to catch him wherever he is.

Loch Lomond from yon bonnie banks

Today was my day off. I decided after picking up the mail, to visit a lake, famous in song and story, not far from here, and it is one place which deserves its reputation. I made the trip by bus, and in spite of being close to a large city the place is as natural and untouched as it was a hundred years ago. It is a large lake - miles long - with crystal-clear water lying in a setting of hills. At the head is a sizable mountain with a little snow around its top. There are several fine country places around the shores, practically castles, with fine wooded grounds. There is one of the prettiest parks I have seen on a hill overlooking the shores - fine old trees, firs, beeches, oaks, and others, with an undergrowth resembling mountain laurel. The grounds are well kept, and in the center is an old place with towers and turrets, apparently the home of the person who donated the park. Birds were singing in the trees, squirrels played around, and it was hard to realize a place could be so quiet, peaceful, and beautiful so close to a dirty, busy, war-conscious city.

Did you know that no place over here, regardless of population, is classified as a city unless it has a cathedral?

Last night Nick and I went to a concert by the symphony orchestra. They played some light things that I could understand which were very pretty - "Hungarian Rhapsody No.1," "Londonderry Air," and "Tales from the Vienna Woods" - the latter especially lovely. Afterwards we went to the house of Mr. Campbell, and visited until nearly midnight. He had some excellent Vat 69.

They have no magazines over here to compare with our popular weeklies and monthlies, and sporting magazines seem to be unknown. While there is plenty of food here and it is nourishing enough, it is sadly lacking in variety. Meat is almost always ground and mixed with cereal or vegetables to stretch it. About the only fresh vegetables are cabbage and brussel sprouts, which are served daily. Fresh fruit is rare, although oranges are beginning to appear, and fresh eggs are priceless.

My friend Campbell has some sort of government job which allows him to travel in a car, which is unusual. He plans a fairly short trip, according to our standards, but it will take us through some beautiful and historic country which is not readily accessible.

Yesterday I had a wonderful trip to a town about ninety miles away. It turned out to be a very pretty day, and the scenery was excellent. We went up along the shore of a very famous and beautiful lake, the one I visited a couple weeks ago, for about twenty miles, then crossed over a mountain pass, down a very pretty valley and along the seashore for quite a distance to a very pretty seaside town. It is mostly a wild country with some fine forests.

Quite a lot of it is timbered, mostly small stuff planted about the time of the last war, but with some very fine trees, which they are being compelled to log now. It is noteworthy that there are quite extensive replanting along the hillsides, some of which must have been logged bare centuries ago. The timber line on the mountains here is quite low by our standards, probably not over two thousand feet, as compared with ten thousand in the Rockies, and the tops of the mountains are very bare and forbidding. The lower hills are also quite barren except where they have been forested. It is all very beautiful country, particularly along the lakes and sea.

Rhododendron grows wild in many places (I thought it was mountain laurel and mentioned it in one of my earlier letters as such) and some of the cultivated varieties in gardens are already blooming.

Campbell is an awfully nice fellow, and he made the trip even more interesting by his comments on historic spots and pointing out places of interest. The scenery compared favorably with any I have ever seen, and there were three of the King's pheasants along the way. My host was horrified when I told him that it was my custom at home to fire a barrage at such on sight. I guess I would be hung if I did a thing like that over here.

It has been a quiet day. I didn't get to go to church, as I was busy. Tonight I went to a symphony concert in honor of the Red Army, and suspected the audience of having a pinkish tinge, a feeling which left me definitely out of sympathy. However, the music was good.

Dear Dad,

The hunting news is welcome, as always, and I am interested in your trade. Looks like everybody wants to trade a pointer for a setter. Have you seen any of the Wally-Pride puppies in action? And how does our interest in that group stand? I have a notion the old master is not above turning up with all of them, or at least with the best, and I would very much like to have one broken to some extent for my return, preferably one of the bitches. It would be fine if Bobbitt could develop one of the litter. Wally is no longer a pup, and I would like her to visit Beau Essig before both get too old. I'm sorry you hit bad weather at the start of the trials and hope it turned out well. I wish I could be with you.

I have of course been interested in observing dogs over here, and was surprised to find that they are fairly numerous and invariably well fed. Apparently curs and strays have been eliminated, but pets are as numerous as ever and better fed than their owners. I have been trying to get a copy of the British kennel magazine "Our Dogs," but haven't found one. Noticed a column of advertisement in a paper, and prices were high. Retrievers were advertised - 2 months puppies $25 to $50 - but no setters! If you think of it, you might obtain from the Field the addresses of a couple of the better known fanciers, in case I should have a chance to visit them. Gordon setters are native in these parts, and I have seen a few, but mostly spaniels and terriers are the order. Dogs apparently are strictly pets here.

The country is wild enough to appeal to me, and very quiet and peaceful. There was a beautiful park on a hill overlooking the lake, and I walked until I was suddenly surprised to find myself quite tired. The banks are quite beautiful, arousing in me a desire to "stop and plug it." I enjoyed watching a bunch of ducks, coots being the only species I recognized. There was some remarkable submarine species; I watched a couple of them until they finally took wing, and when they did, a half dozen more suddenly bobbed up from nowhere and took off after them.

I will never get over looking at the country I pass through with a view to appraising it as bird cover, in which respect this was not too promising, but otherwise what I saw today was truly lovely. It surely did me good to be out, and of course getting mail didn't hurt any.

The other day I got into a conversation with a young naval officer and discovered that he was a Sewanee man. It developed that he was Colmore, the football player who starred on some of Sewanee's most disastrous teams and son of your old classmate, also a noted and a more successful player. We had quite a visit and called up some names I hadn't thought of in years.

I'm afraid I can't tell you much about my work, except that I am pleased with it. It may relieve you some to know that there is very little prospect that I will be called on to lead the invasion with a knife in my teeth and a tommy gun in each hand.

Everything is going nicely with me. Don't be alarmed over the recent air raid reports. I doubt that they have amounted to much, but anyway they are nowhere near me, and I haven't even been in an alert.

I finally got a little leave and had a chance to visit the folks. Two of them, Cousins Essie Walker and Mary Nicholson - met me at the station at Auchtermuchty, and we walked over to the little village of Dunshelt, about half a mile away. They live in a little cottage which is very unprepossessing from the front, but in back opens on a beautiful garden surrounded by a high hedge. It is quite nicely fixed up inside, very comfortable, and the garden is charming, with a fine view of the Loond mountains off in the distance.

They were awfully nice and apparently genuinely thrilled at seeing me. They talk a very pure English, much easier to understand than is common in Scotland, and kept me on my best behavior to demonstrate an equally pure brand of the speech. Their prize exhibit was a robin which comes up to take bread from their hands.

I was very much pleased with my relatives and with the Scotch people generally, whom I have found much more agreeable and friendly than the English and generally more desirable.

On the way I crossed the famous Firth of Forth bridge - a very impressive structure. The Firth is the name of the wide estuary where the River Forth runs into the sea, and must be well over a mile wide. The bridge runs from high hills on either side, and it is a dizzy height above the water. It was one of the first targets the Germans tried to bomb in the war, and the trains are still running without interruption.

If I can get a little more time, I hope to look up the rest of the family and also to visit St. Andrews, where my grandfather attended the famous old university and lived until he went to the States.

I learned something of the family history - notably about the university and that the uncle after whom you and I were named was a lawyer. Unfortunately they assumed that I knew all these things, and I had to proceed cautiously to keep from revealing my ignorance.

I was greatly pleased to find these relatives quite delightful people.

Love to all.
Devotedly, Bud

Chapter 7 -

Great Britain - Glasgow, Scotland
2 March – 30 April 1944

It is beautiful out today, with about six or eight inches of snow all over everything. It is a soft, sticky snow like we get at home and lies heavy on the trees and shrubs, so that everything looks like a Christmas card.

One of the boys got a package from home the other day, the first to arrive for anyone who came with me.

Last night Nick, Harry Steinberg, and I saw "Cry Havoc" at the movie. It is an old picture, just like "So Proudly We Hail" and is very good if you like war horror pictures, which I don't. The only pictures which are any good, as people here freely admit, are American, and they are all old. British acting is good, but their direction and technical work seems poor, probably because they don't spend money on the production.

Getting around by bus and train is quite a problem, and making arrangements ahead of time in my business is very uncertain, as I never know when I'll have something to do. Until you have to do without them, it's hard to realize how great a convenience it is to have a car to go places and a phone freely available to make arrangements. Getting a telephone call through over here, even a local one, is a great adventure, and from the number of buzzes, clicks, and miscellaneous roars involved I think they must route all of them through a foundry.

Yesterday I got off for church and then left the office a couple of hours early and went out to see my cousin Amy Low, who is stationed about twenty miles from here at a British hospital, where she is a laboratory technician, and also showed me through the hospital laboratory. She set a fancy pace in her walking. I stayed for tea and supper and caught the ten o'clock bus back.

I am enjoying my box thoroughly and rationing the contents, including the Fields. I don't know whether the nuts or the cake is better. Usually I enjoy listening to my landlady's chatter, but last night I was tempted to follow Elliott's famous example and tell her to shut up, while I read about Beau Essig's Don.

There is a very good article on our organization in the "Look" magazine of March 7, 1944, which gives an idea of some of our combat functions, of which I hope I will not have any. You might get a couple of copies to show our friends, as it says we are heroes, and that is about as close as I will ever come to being one.

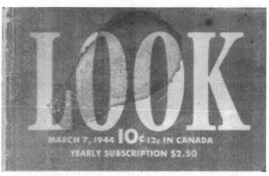

MARCH 7, 1944 10¢ 12¢ IN CANADA
YEARLY SUBSCRIPTION $2.50

Heroes Without Medals

Front-line detectives: the Counter Intelligence Corps

Second in a series on little-publicized Army units

Little known outside the Army, but highly important within it, are the men of the Counter Intelligence Corps. Specially selected, highly trained experts, they are, in effect, the Army's front-line investigators, their duties in the field in some ways approximating those of the FBI at home.

In an attack, the C.I.C. operates as close to the fighting lines as possible, one of its primary tasks being to press hard on the heels of a retreating enemy in order to obtain, by whatever means, revealing information left behind.

A day's work typical of this phase of Counter Intelligence ac-

tivity is recorded on these pages. The pictures were made during the Sicilian campaign by LOOK Photographer Bob Hansen, working on one of his last assignments before his own enrollment in the Army.

The six-man C.I.C. unit was headed by Lieutenant Rupert W. Guenther, of Bridgewater, S. D., and was attached to the G-2 (Intelligence) Section of the 10th Division during the island campaign. Typical of other C.I.C. units, the men in this one were all college-trained, two were lawyers, two were teachers, one spoke fluent Italian.

2 "The hard way" to determine whether a road has been mined is used, perforce, by Guenther's men, since theirs is the third jeep to travel over the route. Here a peasant describes the equipment of German troops he had seen; three pieces of heavy artillery, a dozen loaded troop-carrying trucks.

CONTINUED ON PAGE 66

1 Early in the morning, Lieutenant Guenther (wearing helmet) looks over orders from Divisional G-2. He will take two men, go into the town of Casteiverde, cleared of Nazi troops the night before but not yet occupied. The other men are assigned to check up on unfinished business in the rear.

3 **The village priest** of Castelverde (in round hat) speaks for the people of the town. Here, as in most cases, the Sicilians were vociferously glad to see U. S. soldiers, brought them gifts of fruit, wine and flowers. The priest offered a large bottle of wine, which the Americans tactfully refused.

4 **Initial courtesies** over, the people get down to business. Here they crowd around Cpl. Frank A. Messina, everyone trying to talk at the same time. The burden of their remarks: they wanted to hang the Mayor, not only because of his alleged maladministration, but because he was a Fascist.

5 **Speaking Sicilian Italian** as rapidly as any of the villagers, and twice as loudly, Corporal Messina lays down the law: there will be no rioting, no disturbance of the peace, no impromptu hangings of Fascist officials. C.I.C. operations are conducted with scrupulous regard for legal process.

CONTINUED ON PAGE 68

106

6 **City Hall and post office** is taken over by the C.I.C. as headquarters. Corporal Messina talks to the Mayor (left) and the Chief of Police, demands that they turn over all party records, undelivered mail, enemy documents. Mail can be particularly valuable, is forwarded after being censored.

7 **Desperately anxious** to resign, the Mayor explains that neither he nor the police can keep order in the town. Main reason for the people's anger was a reduction of rations two weeks before the German troops retreated. The reduction, demanded by the Germans, was firmly enforced by the Mayor.

8 **Solution:** Lieutenant Guenther informs the Mayor that Castelverde will be taken over by AMG and that the people may choose new officials. Seized documents were then piled into the jeep, rushed to Divisional G-2 headquarters—about 50 miles distant—and another exacting day's work was done.

END

By virtue of some very special arrangements I have obtained a few real eggs, and Mrs. Hannah has been fixing one for my breakfast every morning. You have no idea what a treat an egg with a shell on it is, that is, unless you have tried the powdered variety. At that, I am eating well, especially when I think that it might be Spam and K-ration.

Another Sunday has come and is almost past, a lot different from those good days we used to have all to ourselves. There isn't a thing to do here on Sunday, not even enough work, and it is even hard to get street cars and buses. This morning I went to church at the cathedral (Church of England) but didn't find the services particularly inspiring. It is rather high church and formal, with practically the whole service chanted, which is impressive when done right, but these ministers didn't seem to have much on the ball. The Church of England in these parts is considered Papist and isn't too well thought of by the Calvinist boys, and they may have something at that.

This afternoon I had some work to do out of town, but after trying for an hour to get on a bus I had to give it up in disgust.

I think that Sundays are the hardest days of all to be away from home.

We have a couple of lads here in the office who have got started talking about food, and it is very hard to concentrate on writing. Not that they are taking about anything very good, but they are maligning some of my favorite foods, like pecans and shrimp.

Sunday night I went to the Campbells' for the evening and had a very nice time, just sitting around the fireside talking. Mrs. Campbell had heard me tell about how fond we were of Scotch shortbread and had baked some for me. I find that the homemade variety is even better than the commercial tins that we used to get. I want to send some home, but this commercial shortbread is not nearly as good as it used to be on account of the shortage of sugar and butter. She says she will bake some for me to send home if I can get her the butter, so I am conducting some research into that problem. The evening also brought forth a good shot of Vat 69, and Mr. Campbell says he will look into the matter of getting me a little for my own use.

I have a nice trip to {censored} planned for Friday. It will combine business and pleasure, with business probably coming out in the customary position in the race. Nick and I are going together if everything works out as planned, and I think we will get to ride over with Mr. Campbell. I am looking forward to the trip very much, as it is said to be one of the prettiest cities in the isles, as well as historically important and interesting.

News is conspicuous by its absence. We have been pretty busy, though not overworked. I have suddenly developed into the senior man here, and with only a month to find my way around, there are lots of things I should know and don't. Things here are a whole lot different from sticking pins in my nice map in Omaha, and I don't have a swivel chair to get my feet on my desk.

Whenever you feel in the mood to send another box, this will be a request for it. Nuts are my favorite contents, as you know, but candy is also welcome, and you know how much I like the fruit cake. I am fixed all right for blades, etc., and have also discovered a source for sugar for Mrs. Hannah to feed me. I even discovered some eggs the other day – don't tell me I am not a super-sleuth. The salted nuts kept better than the fresh, though both were in excellent condition. You mentioned sending some smoked cheese, and I think it would be fine. The cheese over here is good, but like everything else it is rationed. Yes, I have come around to eating cabbage, also parsnips and turnips, but my enthusiasm for same can easily be contained.

The fact that I haven't mentioned other boys going on with me to places is not due so much to my going alone as the need for saving space. I would dearly love to have Elliott or Mc or some of the Denver bunch here, but they all seem to have settled down in the States or disappeared altogether.

We are very busy, and I have time for only a note.

At the last minute some important work came up, and I had to cancel my proposed trip to {censored}. It would have been a nice one, and I hated to miss it, but maybe I will get it next week.

One of the boys has turned up with a camera, which is fortunate, as we have never seen the GI ones we are supposed to have. He found some film a day or so ago and has promised to get some group pictures. I have heard that all the boys who were assigned to the Air Corps in the States have been recalled and sent across, as well as some who were left in the Service Command.

Sunday is just another day in the Army over here.

The mail brought a letter from Elliott, who seems to have come over to see me and promptly gone to the hospital with bronchitis or some such, which proves that he is really in the British Isles. I don't know where he is, but will try to arrange to meet him.

The long-awaited extra day off has arrived and I have got in most of my visiting. I have certainly had two very pleasant days. Wednesday morning I drove to Edinburgh and put in most of the day sight-seeing. I saw the castle, Holyrood Palace, the cathedral, the Royal Mile, the high court in session complete with wigs, and sundry minor attractions. I had time for only a few of the things I would like to see, as it is a most interesting city. The castle is a tremendous affair, with moat, drawbridge, and high walls on top of a hill overlooking the city. One of the features is Mary Queen of Scots' bedroom, where King James I was born and other interesting events are reputed to have occurred; it is a tiny place about the size of a bathroom. The Royal Mile was once a very fine street leading down from the castle to Holyrood Palace but is now somewhat down at the heel. The Palace could use a good cleaning or coat of paint and is a most unpleasant-looking place to live. The interior is largely a museum and would be quite interesting if you had a lot of time to spend. The cathedral is beautiful and imposing, and contains the Knights of the Thistle Chapel, which has exquisite carved wood fittings. Edinburgh is a fascinating place, and it would be easy to spend a week there. At the castle I ran into one of my classmates at Sewanee who hasn't done as well as the rest and is only a captain. We spent the morning and had lunch together.

Wednesday afternoon late I caught the train to Dundee and

crossed the Firth of Tay to Newport, where I spent the night with the Lows. They seem to have the family's money, and are awfully nice besides. Their present home is half of a large duplex house which looks out over the Tay, a beautiful view. The other half of the house is occupied by some more cousins. It is built on the side of a hill, and they have a beautiful rock garden. Heather, crocuses, jonquils, forsythia, and a number of other flowers were in bloom. They have another place, however, which was built by Mr. Low's father who died last year at the tender age of 92, and it is really something. It is at the other end of town on a wooded hill overlooking the river, with several acres of grounds, a keeper's and a gardener's cottage, a sunken garden, and a tremendous flower garden, including two greenhouses. The house is a great stone affair with fifteen rooms or so, including one bathroom, and a tower like a castle. At present it is unoccupied while they wait for the war to get over so they can modernize it. It is a tremendous barn of a place, and I wouldn't want it as a gift, but the grounds are lovely. All sorts of flowers were blooming on the grounds or in the greenhouse, which had some lovely azalea.

This morning turned out to be a beautiful day, and we took the bus down to St. Andrews. It is a lovely town more or less untouched, with the university looking out over the sea. The beach is quite pretty, and the golf course is one of the most famous in the world. On the way down we passed Balmullo, where my grandfather was born, and Leuchars, where we saw the old church, to which the family strolled a couple of miles.

Mr. Low cemented the family relationship, as far as I am concerned, by presenting me with one of Haig's Dimple Bottles, containing a fluid which is almost priceless hereabouts. I continue to be well impressed with family, even those who have no bottles.

I have become quite gadabout and last night stayed up until one-thirty. Did you ever hear of anything so devilish? Yesterday afternoon Jim Campbell called me and said he was going out in the country a way and asked me to go with him. He made a little drive out east of the city, and it was quite pleasant.

After we got back from the ride, I had supper at the Campbells', and afterwards we started out to go to the symphony concert. However, he had to stop by the home of a friend (strangely enough named McDonald, the traditional blood enemies of the Campbells). Anyway, McDonald came up with a couple of bottles, and bitterly against our will compelled us to remain and drink the nasty stuff. McDonald is dean of the Law Faculty of the local university, which is some five hundred years old and regarded as one of the best on this side. He is a young fellow, about thirty-five or so, and has a very attractive wife and three small children. He is quite a brilliant man but very entertaining, and you would never take him for a college professor. We talked for quite a while and wound up playing bridge until the small hours of the morning.

In the evening I fell onto a real genuine American steak from a highly confidential source, took it out to the Campbells, and cooked it for them. The Old Master hasn't entirely lost his touch, and was it good! You should have seen how they appreciated it. I visited with them a while and then went with him down to the police station – he is an auxiliary policeman two nights a week – and wound up playing cards with the law.

You asked about my days off. We are on seven day duty, but take a day during the week if not busy. Then on Sunday we can always get time for church unless we have something special. As a matter of fact we get quite a little spare time, and I have been fortunate in getting to see a lot of interesting places.

As long as I am going and doing things, I enjoy my time over here. People are almost universally kind and hospitable, and they as well as the country are interesting. It is only when I am alone or have nothing to do that time drags.

Have you heard any more from Mc? He owes me a letter, which I suppose I will receive in due course. Rumors reach me that a lot of those boys who got the good jobs in the States have been recalled to Baltimore and sent back to the wars, and I wonder if he was one of them. From what I hear, I think it is just as well that I came on over and got it done, because there must be no peace back there. Those poor fellows must shiver every time they see the postman coming, and the suspense is probably worse than the event.

Every day I meet fellows who have been over here a year or more, and I wonder how they stand being away from home that long. Though every day brings us that much nearer the end of this mess.

It would amaze you if I could tell you all the things the Campbells have done for me, and they are equally willing to entertain the whole detachment if they had the means. I have never met more hospitable people, and anyone who says the Scots are tight have never visited them at home. Southern hospitality has nothing on what I have encountered.

This morning I went to church, though it required quite an effort to brave the weather. A small potted palm was the sole evidence of Palm Sunday, and it was probably nipped by the cold.

Sunday night I went up to the Campbells', and had a very pleasant evening. We had finnan haddie for supper, which is smoked fish and very tasty. Last night I stayed in and read.

The thought of getting back to you is the one thing that seems sane in all this crazy mess over here, and whenever it seems like an endless job sweating out this war, I think of that and know it is worthwhile no matter how long it takes. One day it will all be over and we can be together again with no Army to come between us, and that day will mark the beginning of wonderful times.

Last night Nick, Harry, and I went to the concert of the Orpheus Choir, and I believe it was the best choral music I ever heard. They had wonderful harmony, and the whole choir seemed to be under prefect control. The leader seemed to play on them as he would an instrument. Most of the numbers were folk songs of local origin, and a number were religious. It was truly beautiful and impressive, and I thoroughly enjoyed it.

We have a new kind of time here, "double summer time." They already had daylight saving time, so they added another hour the first of April, and are having the best time you can imagine fooling themselves into thinking they are not getting up early. You never saw such people as these for liking to sleep. My landlord calls his "early morning" the one each week when he has to be in his office by nine o'clock. None of the shops are open before nine, and lots of them not that early. They all take an hour and a half for lunch, and most people go home for lunch, unless it is too far. Then about four o'clock they take time out for tea, and close about five-thirty. Days are very long here in the summer, and even now with this new time it isn't dark until after nine at night and is light by seven in the morning. They say that in midsummer it is not dark until midnight and doesn't get really dark at all.

About the last place I would ever have expected to attend service on Easter would be a Presbyterian church three thousand odd miles from home, but that is just what I did today. It was a very pleasant service, and there was a little odor in the church with a few flowers and people a little more dressed up than usual. However, five years of rationing have done pretty rough things to Easter costumes hereabouts, and even a pressing job was unable to make my uniform look less G.I. The day is dark and gloomy and not well suited for an Easter parade. Still, the service began with "Jesus Christ is Risen Today," as all Easter services should, on the old familiar tune, and I thought of you and everyone else at home, with a prayer that before long we will all be together again. When that time comes, no bad weather can make Easter or any other day gloomy.

The major just read an excerpt from a letter he is writing home. He says he wants to go where he can be waited on, where he won't have to get up early seven days a week, where there is sunshine and blackout is just a word, where eggs come out of shells and meat in pieces instead of shreds, where food doesn't taste of tin. He passed over the heating and plumbing as minor annoyances, and about the only thing I even think he might have added to the list is a place where there never would be another damned uniform.

Easter is observed over here as more of a holiday time than it is at home. Many places close from Good Friday over the weekend, and Easter Monday is a general holiday, when every-thing closes (except the American Army). As a matter of fact,

114

they seem to take their holidays pretty seriously here. We heard a lot of stuff at home about how hard they work at the war and all that, but as well as I can see they don't work as hard as we do at home, though they are more totally mobilized as far as having women at work and everyone in the war industries. They have just as much trouble with strikes as we do, and in spite of all they say they don't take the war any more seriously.

Last night I had a very pleasant evening. Jim Campbell took me around to visit Superintendent Smith of the local police, whom I had previously met, and who had invited me to look at his saddles. He and his brother, both old bachelors and rather gay ones, live in a nice old house with beautiful furniture that seems somehow to go with their tweeds. Believe it or not, they need to have a butler named Fotheringham, but unfortunately he got drafted, so I was denied the opportunity to meet a real live butler named Fotheringham. The place was quite horsey, and he showed me pictures of steeplechases and some rather good hunting prints, as well as his scarlet hunting coat – ah, me! I am afraid I went down in his estimation when he found that I am not a fence-jumping fox hunter, but none can deny the love of a fox hound in cry. He is no longer riding and his saddles need care, but they are beautiful jobs, and I think I got some pointers for Dad. Maybe I'll be able to get the saddle he wants.

Tonight I went to see Betty Grable in "Sweet Rosie O'Grady" and thoroughly enjoyed it. What a chassis!

I am enclosing a little souvenir of my recent furlough, showing you what intellectual entertainment I go in for. I went with one of the boys from the office to a matinée performance of "Faust," and enjoyed it very much. It was the first time I had ever seen that opera, and the company was very good. Of course, the Jewel Song is hard to beat, and the Soldiers Chorus has been one of my favorites since I was a small boy. I used to sing it at the top of my voice as I walked down the hill coming home from hunting, and as I recall the effects they must have been pretty gruesome.

Jim introduced us to a friend of his, and ex-sergeant pilot invalided out of the RAF, and he was quite a lad. He must have spent his entire Army career learning risqué songs.

I went up to Stirling with Jim and spent an evening there. The country on the way up is very pretty, particularly at this time of the year with the first green of spring appearing on the countryside. It is a wide rolling valley with fertile-looking well-kept fields and farms. The hedges are turning green with the new leaves, trees are budding, and flowers are blooming everywhere. Stirling is an old town, the scene of battles from about 1200 on, as it seems to be there that the Scots periodically got tired of running away and chased the English back to England. The Battle of Bannockburn was fought there, and another at Stirling Bridge. In fact, you are supposed to be able to see five battlefields from Stirling Castle, but the town has grown up on some of them. The Castle is on top of a high hill right in the middle of the town, and there is a magnificent view from there. Off on a hill in the distance there is a tower erected as monument to Wallace. The castle is in good shape and is still in use to some extent, so I couldn't get in at the hour when I was there. All around it there is a big cemetery, I suppose for the citizens who tried to get over the walls, as it looked to me like that would be something of a job. The whole hill top used to have some sort of citadel wall around it, and the ruins are still there. The town is very old and has picturesque winding streets, which are very fine to look at, but I am glad I don't have to drive down them or live on them. It is definitely something from the Old World and one of the most picturesque spots I have seen.

Just to show you that I am not starving to death and that rationing does not conquer all, I will tell you what I had for two meals yesterday. For dinner I had radishes and ripe olives, fruit cocktail (canned but good), soup, roast capon with potatoes, lettuce and tomato salad, and peach pie a la mode. For supper I had celery and green olives, split pea soup, a delicious pork chop, head lettuce with thousand island dressing, and bread pudding. Where I got it is a military secret and I'm not going to tell because the censor would probably be there when I got back, but anyhow I'll bet you didn't have any better and can't get much better.

In the morning I had some things to attend to at the office

before church. After lunch I made a talk at the University Settlement project to a bunch of student social workers on the subject of American schools and colleges. Jim Campbell had to get up the program and asked me to do it, and I rather enjoyed it. After I finished talking, the meeting, which was only a small group, broke up into a round table discussion, and I answered numerous questions. That took all afternoon, and I spent the afternoon at Jim's apartment, so it was a rather full day.

On my recent furlough we had an opportunity to spend a very interesting day down in the "Burns country," Ayrshire. We passed through Kilmarnock, where Johnnie Walker is made but, unfortunately, not sold, and spent quite a while in Ayr, the birthplace and home of Robert Burns. I picked up a few post cards there, which I am enclosing.

It was a beautiful day, and Nick and I spent some time sitting in the sun in one of the parks. We were able to soak up enough to make us faintly pink, and it sure felt good. That is a rolling country, looking like middle Tennessee or Kentucky, and is principally used for pasture and cattle and sheep raising, the Ayrshire cattle being quite famous. It was very pretty, with everything showing the fresh green of early spring, trees budding and fruit trees blooming, and lots of flowers. Ayr is on the coast, and we traveled quite a distance along the shore. It was a little hazy and the off-shore view was not too good, but there are some islands in the distance which are beautiful and must be especially so on a bright day. The fields, with their orderly hedges and stone fences are quite a lovely view. The cottage in the post card is quite typical of the buildings in the small villages, though you don't see thatched rooves much now.

Tonight I have tickets for a Strauss show, The Waltz Dream. All of us are having supper together and then going to the show. It is said to be very pretty, and it's more in my line than opera.

Last night I sat by the fire and finished reading my Fields, then wrapped them up to send off to Elliott. Wasn't that heroic of me? I hope some more will come, because I don't even have the old ones to look over now. However, I'm still looking forward to your next box with interest, and maybe there will be some more mental food as well as physical there.

Mac wrote me about some fellow who had returned from North Africa and is now in Denver, and I was just getting ready to cable and ask how he did it when I read on that he had accomplished it by getting shot up and sent home. While I am almost anxious enough to see you to consider that, I would want to pick the spot where they were going to do the shooting, and I don't think they have worked out the necessary arrangements with the Germans yet.

Chapter 8

Great Britain – England & North Wales
3 May – 14 July 1944

The Fields were particularly welcome, in as much as one of them reported the National Free-for-All trials, which I had been unable to get previously. Apparently your boy Bobbitt is still too tight to hire a scout and lost one dog in record time as a result. Beau Essig's Don seems to have some sort of record for running in bad luck as far as weather is concerned, if Wally will respond to your advances and bring us one as good as he is, we ought to have something.

Today is Mother's Day, though it is not observed in this heathen land. Contrary to my custom of many years, I was not able to go to church today, as some work came up that could not be postponed. However, I have been thinking of you all day, and if I had no red rose for my lapel, at least I felt all that the rose could have signified. Long ago I realized that if every day were Mother's Day there still couldn't be time enough to express my appreciation of the wonderful mother with whom God blessed me, and no words I can ever master are able to do it. If this says a small part of what I want to convey, I will be happy, but I am sure you will know that I am thinking of you now and always with a heart full of love. May it be the last Mother's Day we will have to spend apart.

Tomorrow the fishing season will open at home, and I could spend my time much more pleasantly and just about as profitably for all concerned if I were at Bear Creek or Storm Creek. Which reminds me - have you heard whether Henry Gregory ever got joined to the Army? He isn't a very military figure, and I had some doubts about his passing the physical if he has been called. However, I suppose you have to be a professional football player or a big league baseball player to be 4F.

I talked to Keigley over the phone today, and he advises

that Captain Frierson is now Major Frierson and still fighting the battle of Omaha, which I would say is getting along very nicely. However, he has more sense than all his superiors there combined, so I guess it is proper that he should be promoted, and anyhow I am glad he got it.

It is a bit annoying, though to see good men frozen in grade over here and promotions going on regularly back there. Some of the boys are still there, notably Clark, who was over in Des Moines with Keigley and is the source of this information.

I was interrupted in the middle of yesterday's letter by one of these rush jobs, which, like all those I used to go on, failed to justify the rush. I did get a nice Sunday afternoon drive down the country out of it, however, and things are certainly pretty now. There are flowers everywhere, and they seem to be trying to make up for the drabness of the city.

Walking back to the offices after church I saw something that I'll bet you never saw. It was a man and a woman riding along on a bicycle built for two, and attached to the side was a little yellow sidecar, glass-enclosed, with a little boy about a year old bouncing along in it. He looked as if he would bounce through the roof at any minute, but he seemed happy enough about the whole thing.

I continue to be as busy as a one-legged man at a tap dancing contest, which isn't as bad as it might be, because it at least keeps me from being bored. It would be nice to be back in my peaceful office in Omaha, though, with everything nicely systematized and nothing to do that I didn't know about. Here I never know when somebody is going to turn up with some problem or something to do that I never heard of before. To do this job you need to be a walking Encyclopedia Britannica (!) and know all about everything except your own business.

It looks as if I will be reduced to writing you on my own time, as Uncle has got into a foolish idea of making me work on his. I have been busy all day, so I'll put the evening to better use.

I think I have seen everything now after two cases I have worked in the past two days. I thought I had about covered the field in the way of doing foolish and unnecessary things, but there's always something new. After this war I will have some choice stories to tell you. However, they were entertaining, if nothing else, and I shouldn't complain if that is what your Army wants me to do. If the G-2 has as much fun out of reading about my doings as I have doing them, we will at least keep up our morale.

Tonight I went again with Jack Little to hear Barbirolli's orchestra and enjoyed it very much. I don't really appreciate symphonic music, but I listen to it all relaxed and think about days with you, those past and those to come, and my dogs and field trials, and a fly dropping just exactly right in the spot where a big bass lives. The music doesn't mean much, but there must be something fine about it when it makes me think of such good things. And everybody sits quiet without bothering me and just leaves me to my thoughts.

I read the other day that the American Army is the most homesick Army in the world, and I don't doubt that it is so. We have so much more than anyone else to go home to, and I think that the sole interest any of us have in post-war plans is to get home. That is plan enough for me, because I know that I have everything there that I want, and these people can keep Europe or throw it to the hogs for all I care.

News is very scarce. I haven't heard from any of the boys in a long time, and assume they are all pretty busy. I had hopes that Elliott would write me whether he got the Fields, as I have some more to send him. He is usually a pretty good correspondent, so I guess he is tied up. Even Hopper has failed me, and I haven't heard from Tub in a long time. I owe Mo a letter and have been wondering if he is still around. I guess he is on needles and pins about now; he'll really be the original proud papa. Frierson is definitely on my blacklist, as he failed to answer two letters.

You should have seen me Thursday night over at Prof. Mc-Donald's. I went there with Jim and found him trying to repair a fly rod which he had pulled loose at the joint. He was making a terrible job of it and was all tangled up in thread, so I undertook to wind it for him. It was the first time I had tried to wind a rod in fifteen years and I never was much good at it, but I think I made a better job than he was making. It did me good to have the feel of a rod in my hands again, even if it was a long way from using one.

I listened to the King's speech and the invasion broadcasts while enjoying a couple of good drinks of Scotch. He told me all about his fishing trip, and they must have really had a nice one. Four of them caught about sixty trout in one afternoon and the next morning, which isn't bad at all. One of these days maybe I can go fishing again.

I had a letter from Hopper today, written before the invasion. He seemed to be more or less resigned to being a part of it, though I don't know whether he was or is. He had seen a number of the boys, including Charlie Meadows, the infantry expert. Judging from the tone of the letter, he had been preparing himself spiritually for the attack and seemed to be very happy about the whole thing. I don't know how he felt when the spirits ran out.

Last night I went home early after seeing Keigley off and

got a good night's sleep - about ten hours - which was very beneficial to me. Today I am just back from seeing Little off, which was a bad day, as I thought him the most likable of the lads we had here. However, I guess the war has to go on, and it can't be fought here any more than it could be in Omaha, though this is one of the places like Omaha which are very handy for the purpose of fighting it. If somebody is going to fight it here - or there - I would just as soon be the one, but I have a notion that I may run out of luck here as I did there.

I guess the Army Postal System is like the Canadian Mounties or the CIC - they may take time but they get their man. At least they got me.

Last night I stayed in and read. Mrs. McDonald gave me the book "Assignment in Brittany," written by a college mate of hers, who must be quite a babe from all accounts. It's a pretty fair spy yarn, and was made into a movie with Joan Crawford. Tonight I think I'll finish it.

I ran into a boy who went to the University of Arkansas with me, Charles Whiteside, who is now some sort of naval officer. We had a little visit but unfortunately were heading in opposite directions.

Last night I had a very interesting evening. Steinberg had met some people by the name of McDonald, and he is the assistant prosecuting attorney for the county here.

This morning at McDonald's invitation we went down to listen to a case he was presenting. The court system here is different from any I have run across, the judge being called the Sheriff and the prosecutor the Procurator Fiscal. Lawyers are known as agents. The judge wears a robe and a wig, the latter being a most ridiculous looking affair, and the attorneys wear robes but no wigs. In the higher courts all of them were wigged. The procedure seemed to be very similar to ours. They were trying some citizens for stealing a barrel of whiskey, which I consider a very laudable undertaking and nothing to blame a man for. I was quite interested in the proceedings and was glad to have the opportunity to go.

Last night was pretty and after supper I walked up through the park, taking the long way home. They have an outdoor dancing place there with some sort of glazed concrete surface and a loudspeaker attachment broadcasting records. I thought I had seen everything, but my education still had not included a man in full dress dancing in a park with the sun shining on him, that is, not until yesterday. There was a tremendous crowd assembled watching the dancing and a good number on the "floor." The music sounded much better across the park than it did close at hand, but the whole thing gave the appearance of a lovely peaceful evening. You would never have thought that the war is reaching its climax a few hundred miles away.

This will be just a note to advise you of a new address. Write me in the future at: CIC DETACHMENT, HIRAEL BEACH CAMP, AP.O. 515-a, c/o POSTMASTER, NEW YORK, N.Y. This is not a move off to the wars or anything like that. It may mean quite a period of GI life, but I have taken that before and can take it again. I have been anticipating this change for some time, so it is no surprise. It is not a danger area, and I do not think that it means moving into any dangerous territory, at least not in the immediate future. Although I don't think the change promises anything pleasant, it just means military life for a while, and that is nothing that millions of others are not enduring. I am supposed to continue in the same type of work I am doing now, which is generally regarded as the best work we have over here.

I have arrived at my new station. The set-up here is not bad at all. We have only our own boys here, so it is more pleasant than being in a regular camp. It is a beautiful place, right on the seashore, with very pretty mountain rising in the background. The neighborhood is considered a resort area, and the towns are picturesque and lovely. Our quarters are quite comfortable.

We are serving under our own officers for the first time since I became a soldier again, and in consequence are getting much more decent treatment than at any other stage of our travels. I think I am going to have a very good setup for my future operations and am more optimistic than I have been at any time since I found I would have to leave my last station.

This is a beautiful place, and we have had very good weather. Night before last the officers obtained the use of the cow pasture of the local big shot and threw a beer bust and fish fry for all the boys. Of course, it rained in torrents, but a good time was nevertheless had by all.

There was an excellent view of Lord Plushbottom's castle, a most imposing edifice. He has half the country under fence for the grounds and is altogether quite a large operator. People here haven't seen many Americans and seem to be very friendly, though I haven't had a chance to meet any of them.

The delay in writing was caused by a trip which I took, some seven hundred odd miles between Friday night and Sunday night. That is quite some traveling, even in the good old days when we were touring the West, and I was not driving a nice comfortable Chevrolet sedan, either, but instead a ¾ ton truck with much the same riding qualities as Dad's Ford. It was a very interesting trip, and I volunteered for the job to get to see some of the country which I had missed previously. I would have enjoyed it very much if it hadn't been so strenuous. Driving all night isn't much of an obstacle to seeing the country, as it is only dark about four hours and not real black then. I first went through some beautiful mountain country near here, then into a fertile rolling farming country which looks like a miniature Iowa, with good wheat crops and lots of cattle and sheep. Further on there was a flatter farming country, and then more hills and finally bleak moors, which remind you of Wyoming, except for the fog and dripping continual drizzle. A long the way there are the interesting English villages and some famous old cities, and in many places old castles in various stages of ruin or use. I got back here last night a little before eleven and had every intention of writing you, but by the time I had got my stuff straightened out and cleaned up a bit, I was just too tired to make it.

There isn't much news. It is not unpleasant here in a worthless GI way, and the fresh air and a little exercise are probably doing me good. Gradually the picture of what we can expect in the immediate future is becoming a little clearer, and I don't think the job will be bad.

George Jovan is here in the room with me, crying about not getting home until God knows when, and any number of other things. Brigham has been around too, and I am seeing lots of fellows I have run across before, including several of the boys from Omaha who were in the office as typists while waiting for the school. I didn't remember them too well, but they seemed like old friends. I have a nice bunch of boys, including Nick, on my team, and am well satisfied with the outlook. I am the senior man, with a lieutenant as my C.O. who seems to be a decent sort.

I have been pretty busy, though not overworked. This is not a bad place, and it would be easy to loaf away the war here. I haven't met any of the local people, but they seem about as friendly and well disposed towards Americans as any I have run across. Crowds of kids wait around the gate all the time and march with us to and from the mess hall. Their motives are not altogether altruistic, but they seem to enjoy the procedure even aside from the prospect of "gum, chum." On the trip I made the other day there were kids all along the road, holding up their fingers in the V sign and hollering for gum as we passed. Of course, they are democratic and will take candy, cookies, souvenirs, or anything else of value, if gum is not available. I believe they are worse about begging here than in Scotland, though there are plenty of them there too.

Yesterday marked my first Fourth of July outside the U.S., and we made a bit of an occasion of it. We had a formal Retreat formation, the first I have stood in many moons. Retreat is in my mind the most impressive ceremony in the Army and will give you a bit of a thrill under any conditions, but this one really made a little lump come in my throat. The captain made a little talk which was rather to the point, and everybody felt almost like a soldier. The boys gave a dance last night, and as I had no better sense than to mention the fact that I was not particularly interested in attending, I wound up with the delightful duty of guarding the door while the more sociable lads tripped the light fantastic within. I did get in on the refreshments, which consisted of real ice cream and cake, a rare delicacy in the ETO.

Tonight the USO put on a show for us, and it was quite enjoyable - a good pianist, three American dancers and singers with pretty legs, a juggler, and a master of ceremonies who did some very clever imitations. It was nothing remarkable, but worthwhile entertainment and the more enjoyable because this is a rather out-of-the-way spot where entertainment of any kind is rare. The day before we had really big doings, when none other than S/Sgt. Joe Louis honored us with his presence. He did not engage in any warfare for our benefit, though he put on an exhibition somewhere in this neighborhood that night. He did appear and spoke a few words, and I should say that he would do better to stick to fighting, as he does not talk a very good game.

The camp has a mascot, a black sheep named Confusion. He has CIC painted right over his tail and corporal's stripes on his sides. He is a magnificent animal and well selected. The only incongruous thing about him is that he seems to be the only one on the post who is entirely sure what he wants to do and perfectly satisfied with his lot in life.

Time seems to get by in a hurry. I am busy, but am not having a hard time in any sense.

Tonight I went down with a bunch of the boys to a little pub in the village and stayed until closing time - the devilish hour of nine o'clock. These are nice people, and they seem to have the most widespread and genuine like for Americans of any people I have run across. They got a singing session started, though it was mostly mental stimulation, as the beer was about like drinking water. It is funny, but the songs that seem to appeal to them most are the American western songs, the cowboy numbers.

This afternoon I made a trip of about twenty miles up the coast to get my finances straightened out with the Army, and it was a lovely drive. The road winds along the side of the mountain overlooking the sea, and it is all very pretty. There are a number of estates of the local big shots, all with fancy houses, and one real live castle, which is quite impressive, especially from a distance.

There is a lot to be seen around here, and I would like to spend days just wandering around the countryside. A few miles away there is a very lovely cascade, which I passed on the trip I made last week.

I have made another hop and am now in a new camp, which is not at all bad. It was a rather tiresome trip by jeep, but quite interesting, as it was through new country, and almost everywhere over here is pretty if you stay out of the cities. This is a prosperous looking farming section, and we are situated out in the country on the estate of one of the big shots, but he has apparently moved on. I don't know whether Lord Drizzlepuss is a sportsman or it's a general condition, but the place seems to be full of game. I never saw so many rabbits, and have seen several of the big gray partridges. Yesterday just outside the camp I saw a covey of Hungarian Partridges, squeaking all over the place. There were a couple of old ones and about a dozen young ones about the size of quail, just learning to fly.

The villages are typically old English and have many cottages with thatched rooves.

I am getting along fine and rather enjoying the change. I see lots of new things and find a lot to interest me. The food here has been good; we have only our own boys here, even the cooks, and are quite proud of them for taking over the kitchen. I am greatly pleased that the cooks are on my team and will be with me permanently, so I guess that angle is provided for.

I thought when I left Scotland and moved south I would hit better weather, but can't see any improvement. Natives say this is the worst summer in 40 years, but I guess that's just an alibi. I am sleeping under three blankets, and wearing the top of my winter underwear. Some of the boys wear the full long boys and still complain of being cold. I don't see how anything grows here, but everything is very green and pretty.

This is all very interesting and I wish I could tell you about it. Every day there are new sights and new experiences, as I am seeing a part of the country and the Army which I have previously missed.

DAILY JOURNAL
CIC CRT 4 - CONQUER

The Mission:
Operation Over-Lord

Code Words
I N D E X

HOLIDAY -- 28th Infantry Division
CADET -- 7th Army
LATITUDE -- 29th Infantry Division
HICKORY -- XV Corps
WORKSHOP -- 7th Armored Division
DISCUS -- 78th Infantry Division
COBRA -- 3rd Infantry Division
CHLORIDE -- 137th Signal Radio Intelligence Company
CLOFAX -- XVL Corps
CONTROL -- XIII Corps
BLACKBIRD -- 83RD Infantry Division Artillery
EAGLE and REAR EAGLE -- 12th Army Group (TUSAG)
POWER HOUSE -- 2nd Armored Division
CONQUER -- 4th Army
ADSCZ -- Advance Section Communication Zone
VICTOR -- 5th Corp
MONARCH -- 7th Corp
LUCKY -- 3rd Army
ARMOR -- 19th Corp
MASTER -- 1st Army

THE MISSION

Invasion plans, which the Army had worked on night and day for almost 2 1/2 years, were reaching their finishing points when most CIC agents reached the European Theater of Operations. It was obvious to the enemy that we were pouring men and material into England at a prodigious rate, late in 1943 and early in 1944. It was well known that the invasion was to come in 1944 and we made no denial, in fact all sorts of propaganda emanated from Army Headquarters concerning the invasion, done deliberately to keep the Germans in a constant state of turmoil. It became necessary therefore to keep only 2 things from the enemy:

1. The date of invasion
2. The landing areas selected

In order to protect information leaks from coming out of the loading zones, debarkation camps, and other loading zones, it was necessary to set up some sort of an Intelligence Organization to cover the security of Over-Lord. CIC was selected for this task.

THE ACCOMPLISHMENT

Scattered throughout southern England, the Army had established camps where troops from the northern training areas were to be funneled and sealed off prior to the actual embarkation.

CIC Agents, working in small groups, acted as S-2's for the camp commanders advising upon Security precautions to be taken and recommending measures to be instituted. The work was undertaken under the usual difficulties attending such a vast undertaking and such improvising and "on the spot" action was accomplished. The men worked hard and long through the exercising (up through and including Overlord, there being several practice exercises or dry runs which preceded the actual one).

The mission was accomplished. It was generally conceded through First Army Intelligence Circles following the invasion, that the elaborate plans laid out completely fooled the Germans and they clearly were outwitted and guessed wrong both as to the date of the invasion and the location of the beaches we could use for our main effort. Considering that hundreds of persons knew the invasion plans, and at the last few days thousands did, the security accomplishment was considered remarkable.

By now you have no doubt received some written after D-Day and know that I did not go storming up the beach with a tommy gun in each hand and a dagger between my teeth.

These are very uncertain times, and almost anything may happen in the interests of security. No doubt a lot of us will be moved sooner or later to places where we can do more good than here, and if I am one of them, mail might be interrupted for a while.

In the forward areas they are much stricter about what can be said in letters than here, so if I should get there I probably couldn't tell you anything about my duties, even to say that they were safe. So don't be concerned about things, and just grin and bear it. Maybe it won't be too long now.

Chapter 9

France - Brittany
July - August 1944

Tonight it looks as if I have practically gone to war. I have just been looking out over one of the beachheads, a very busy but not too warlike place. In the distance I can hear the big guns like a far-away thundershower on a summer evening, but here it is quiet enough, though everybody is busy.

We had a very nice crossing. The sea was quite calm, and I was amazed at the absence of any signs of trouble.

This evening I stood watching swarms of pursuit planes circling the beaches, for all the world like bunches of mallards circling across Porter's Lake late in the evening. Tomorrow I hope to get some information as to our location.

I am sitting under one of the famous apple trees of Normandy in a scene which is quite peaceful except for numerous GI's, of whom I have never seen so many. We are not located yet, and life is a bit rugged, though not bad. Last night I slept under this same tree in the grass, looking up at the stars, since I was too lazy to put up my pup tent. Toward morning some English weather blew over, but fortunately it didn't get damp enough to make me move.

Yesterday we moved through some of the area covered by the campaign. In general there is less sign of the conflict than I expected, but at some of the places where there was strong resistance the destruction is appalling. The country is rather pretty and has more woods and thickets than England. I am quite safe, though I can occasionally hear the faint rumble of guns in the distance.

My address is: CIC Detachment, G-2 Section, Headquarters F.E. Comm. Z, A.P.O. 350, c/o Postmaster, New York, N.Y. I am addressed as a civilian but certainly not living as one.

Food is not bad, and my pup tent does as well as could be expected. We are waiting to be assigned our territory, so I spent the morning washing. It was quite an arduous process, hauling a bucket of water up the hill from the pump, boiling it and washing the clothes in an old gas can, and repeating the process for the rinse. The water is harder than that at Omaha, which I always thought had the record.

This isn't bad, and I am rather enjoying my camping trip - at least there's plenty of fresh air.

My apple orchard is beginning to have all the comforts of home, and I now have a portable to cuss, showing that one never knows when he is well off. You may think you have seen everything, but you have missed one of the choice sights of our times in not seeing me yesterday at my bath. When you are sitting in your warm tub, think of me standing just as I came into the world out in the middle of an apple orchard in the bright sunshine, taking a bath out of a helmet.

I have done a little traveling around the country and have now covered most of the highways which it is safe to travel, that being a fairly short journey. I have seen Cherbourg, as well as some of the other towns which you have been reading about. In many places there is very little sign of the fighting, and the country as a whole shows it less than you would expect, but now and then you hit a place which looks like nothing so much as the track of a real full grown tornado. Some towns have scarcely a whole building in them, while others which apparently were just as much in the path seem to have little damage. However, the people seem to have returned to them and to be going about their business in as normal a way as possible. I have tried out my French to some extent and in simple conversations I have pretty good luck at making myself understood and am even able to understand the general drift of what they say to me. How I will get along when we start talking business is something else.

There has been no mail so far, and I am not too hopeful of getting any soon. We are supposed to have some forwarded from London, where I should have quite an accumulation, and I hope it will find us before long. However, I will consider it a minor miracle if it does locate us. We certainly occupy a very small area in the midst of a great number of soldiers.

For the past two days I have been learning what boys in the late war meant when they cussed "sunny France." It has been raining cats and dogs, and I never saw mud develop so fast. Fortunately I have a good pup tent and it stayed dry, but living in tents in the rain is not much fun.

We have been assigned to the place where we are to work and expect to get located there shortly. Today I have been out with the lieutenant looking over the situation, and it looks like it might be a pretty good deal. I don't think we will work ourselves to death by any means, and the prospects are that we will at least have some sort of house to live in, maybe even with furniture. We should have enough to keep us busy, and the change in working conditions will be very interesting. I tried my French out again today, and it will take quite a bit of improvement before I will be able to carry on any conversation beyond the simple amenities. It is easy to make purchases or ask directions, but when you get into more involved matters, it is something else.

You see lots of interesting sights in driving around over here. People here are rural, and you see all the picturesque customs that you have seen in the movies and pictures - people riding in funny high-wheeled carts with folding tops like buggies, and donkeys pulling other little carts. A lot of the women wear peasant costumes, or part of them, and all the men wear black berets. There are hedges around all the fields and along all the roads; this is said to have been one of the great difficulties in the advance, and it is easy to see why.

We are near some stables which were formerly used by the German officers, and they must have had quite a few horses, judging by the extent of the stables. The grounds are fixed up with hurdles, water jumps, and all sorts of devices to entertain the boys. One of the boys who came in early said that they left behind a lot of the horses and that they are magnificent animals, very stylish and well gaited. He said the French peasants have appropriated

134

them and put them to work pulling carts.

This life is not too bad, but it is just an existence.

Yesterday I missed out on your Sunday letter because I was busy all day inspecting and arranging our new home, and when I got back in the evening there was a free movie which I could not afford to miss.   Today I was back again supervising the cleaning of our mansion, and tomorrow we will move into it. Being very aristocratic as well as lazy, we preferred to hire a bunch of French refugee women to clean our establishment, which they did better and with much less complaint than we would have done it. Our home once was quite an establishment, a very nice hotel looking out over the little harbor where we will perform some part of our duties. It evidently was rather a fashionable place for these parts, but some years ago the Germans occupied it and then moved out and left it vacant. Between the Germans, the weather, kids' slingshots, and various other causes the windows are practically non-existent, and the place was a mess generally. However, it has a roof, which is something, and good floors, and does not look too bad now that we have got it clean. We will at least have a room with a view, and not much glass to obstruct the view.

I am seated in my seaside villa looking out over the bonnie shores of Normandy, with the sunshine showing on a point in the distance, the sea very blue, and a fine summer breeze blowing right in the window. This is a very fine view and must have been a lovely hotel when all of it was here.

My French is still my major problem. However, already I find it easier to pick up the drift of conversation, and as my vocabulary comes back to me it should not be too difficult. There are so many little everyday words that I never had any occasion to learn in studying literature. The other day we had a bunch of women cleaning up, and I could hardly think of any of the words I needed to tell them what I wanted done, though I could have talked about more elegant matters with less trouble. The people really chatter fast, and we all have to keep telling them to slow down.

I am feeling fine and am as comfortable as could be expected. Food at the moment is something of a problem, but we have been managing at least one warm meal a day, and when we get all our arrangements made, we will probably dine at least as well if not better than the general Army mess. In the meantime, there is always K-ration.

These last few days have given us all the feeling that we may not have too long to wait until this is over and we can be with those we love.

I ran across Hopper's trail today and just missed him by a couple of hours. I know where he is now, and will try to catch him again. He may be able to pick up some information about Elliott, who is rumored to be here now. I also saw John Ryan - it is amazing how many people one can run across in the course of a day of wandering around. However, there isn't a whole lot of country here, and there are a lot of the boys around. As you might know, Hopper has got himself set up in the choicest spot available. However, we don't take off our hats to many people as far as quarters go now. We have moved from our open-air villa into a large house in town, which is not quite as beautifully situated but has windows, running water, and plumbing of a sort.

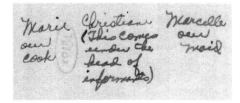

The electric lights were sabotaged by the Germans, but we are not suffering too much, as it doesn't get dark until time to go to bed. We have our own kitchen with two French women to do the cooking and cleaning up, and to date the meals have been exceptional. We are gradually accumulating a little furniture, tables and chairs, but beds are a bit scarce. Although this seems a little like the height of luxury, I would readily exchange it for my small room at home. Still, we are very lucky indeed to have as good a set-up as we have.

There aren't too many things that I need here, so don't worry about it.

That was bad news about losing Wally and particularly that litter of puppies. Maybe I won't be as overstocked on dogs when I get home as I thought I would be. She was nice, besides being a darned good one. I will write Dad to keep Freckles if he hasn't already sold her, and I can start over on the same lines. Poor Elliott - now he will find that he has won the war for nothing, but maybe this is his punishment for not getting over here and getting it finished instead of leaving the job to me.

This sheet of paper is a present from the Germans. I understand it is their best grade, and if they are down to calling this paper, they must be about whipped. However, the boys who were here ahead of us got one of their typewriters, and it is plenty good - I hope this portable will get jealous!

Yesterday I went around to call on the port commander, and was a bit taken back when he called me by my first name. I roomed right down the hall from him for three years at Sewanee. He is only a lieutenant colonel, so he isn't getting along as well in the Army as I. He was quite cordial, and I shall go back and see him again. He was one of the few track men I could outrun.

I am in the office most of the time and have to interview numerous French people who come in. There ensues much waving of arms and very little understanding, but eventually we decide that we know what is intended to be conveyed both ways. I have an idea that neither party to the conversation has any idea what the other intended to say, but each goes his way rejoicing at having made his point. I am getting so that I understand it a little better, but have a terrible time talking. After a while I think I will do fairly well, but I hope the war doesn't last as long as it will take for me to become fluent.

Work over here is much more interesting than what we were doing in the States and shows some sign of being what we were trained to do. Some of the boys have done some really valuable work. We are probably going some day to a more important place than this and should have a chance to see some of the really interesting jobs. Meanwhile we are enjoying a quiet life in the country and have few complaints.

Last night I got my first taste of the famous vin rouge which everyone reported to be so common over here. It is not common at all, and besides being pretty expensive is hard to get, as most of the towns are closely restricted and there are very few places to spend any money. What I got last night was fairly good, but nothing to get excited about. I had a little cognac a week or so ago, and it is powerful stuff but very hard to find. It is quite similar to the grapejack I used to drink when I was a reckless college boy. The most common drink around here is cider, which is mildly hard but tastes like vinegar and has very little authority. It costs about eight cents a quart and is bringing its full value at that price. The grape country is further south and east, and maybe I will have better luck one of these days.

I am glad you received the package with the records and were pleased with the brooch. Jim and Mrs. Hannah had to pay some duty on those packages, but it only amounted to about 25 cents. The Skye Boat Song is also one of the typical Highland airs and a rather famous one; to help you get the drift of it, it is about the trip Bonnie Prince Charles made when he was rowed to the Isle of Skye as a fugitive after he had lost the Battle of Culloden and all his hopes of restoring the Stuart kings to the throne of Scotland and England. That also marked the end of the clan system in Scotland, so far as the power of the chiefs was concerned.

Yesterday I was down in one of the areas where supplies are being moved forward, and every time I see it I marvel again at the terrific activity. Everywhere you look there are trucks and dust and GI's, all seeming to be in endless confusion but getting a tremendous job done in spite of it all. Seeing endless traffic jams in these sleepy-looking French towns and Americans all over the place is certainly a strange site.

News of the amazing process the boys are making in Brittany comes back to us rather slowly, and you probably hear it before we do. Nevertheless, it is a big boost to us, and we actually have some hopes of getting home much sooner than we had dared hope two months ago. It seems too good to be true that we could get home this year, and I am not getting my hopes up too much, but it is nice to think about it.

I can think of lots of ways that I have spent Sunday more profitably than this one, though there could be lots of worse ways too. It would be much nicer to be driving with you up to Echo Lake or Evergreen, or even lying out on the sand at Merritt's Beach. In fact, I can think of lots of nice Sunday afternoons sitting quietly in our apartment, with perhaps a beer or two or maybe some ice cream - just think of beer and ice cream now! When I look back on them, it is the little things which seemed commonplace and not at all remarkable that I miss most. The occasions which we think are remarkable really don't mean a whole lot, but the ordinary everyday events are the big things after all. At least, they are the ones that you remember and miss when you don't have them.

This will have to be more or less of a note, as I am trying to write it by the light of a gasoline lantern, which seems to get more light in my eyes than on the page. Days are getting noticeably shorter now, and the Germans neglected to leave us any electric lights, though I am sure this was just an oversight caused by their hasty departure.

Tonight the Army provided us with a movie, "See Here, Private Hargrove," which I thought very good entertainment. One thing about these affairs - they are all on the Army, as are cigarettes and such candy and gum as we get. Unfortunately, I don't smoke the cigarettes, but there is nothing like them to improve relations with civilians.

Two of the boys were invited out to dinner tonight in this starving land, and this is the menu, as well as I can recall it: soup, shrimp, a whole lobster each, a fried fish course, roast beef, potatoes, green beans, butter, chocolate pudding, cider, wine, and cognac. I don't suppose they eat that way every night, but it certainly isn't starvation. The Army is at great pains to preserve the civilian food supply, and it is against the law to buy meals, so I haven't tried the special variety of French cooking which is reported to be so good, as I am not yet on inviting terms with any of them. However, we have a French cook preparing our meals, and she does a very good job.

Although the Germans are responsible for the necessity of my corresponding with you instead of talking to you, they seem to be trying to make up for it. They left us this nice paper to use, and one of them left with a Frenchman the enclosed trinket off his hat, just so I could send it to you. The Frenchman did not tell me whether the German still needed a hat, though I suspect that he probably didn't. Anyhow, it is something very valuable, and now you can wonder what to do with it instead of me.

You see how times have changed in the way I spend my Saturday nights - no more night spots and whoopee juice, damn it! The towns are all off limits to soldiers, and though that doesn't entirely keep me from going for one reason or another, it isn't too good an idea to overdo the privilege if I don't have some more or less legitimate reason. I'll bet I haven't spent five dollars since I've been over here, and at that rate I ought to make money even faster than I did at Glasgow.

This is one of those intensely bright days with warm sunshine that is meant for nothing other than lying on the beach. At the moment the tide is out, and the sea is about a mile away, but later in the day I may take advantage of the opportunity. The sea is a brilliant blue that reminds me of the Gulf of Mexico, and I would really love to be on the Gulf about now. Some days ago a fisherman offered to take me out with him, and I have a notion to go one of these days.

Everybody is dressed up in his Sunday best today and out for the "promenade." A lot of them have saved clothes back and are better dressed than you would expect. French women pay more attention to their clothes than the English, and when they dress up usually contrive to appear neat even in old clothes. Most of the time, however, they clump around in wooden shoes, and today you could notice that a lot of them felt awkward in their high heels and looked as if they were about to fall on their faces, as Paul Mohr would say. It is quite a sight to see them riding along the road in a cart with a buggy top and great high wheels as high as your head, all of them quite dressed up - I often wonder how they get in those things with their good clothes.

Your letters sound as if you are worried about me, and there is no reason why you should be. As my letters have probably already indicated to you, I am in a very secure place, as indeed almost any place over here is when it is out of immediate artillery range. None of the boys are doing anything very hazardous; that is, none of the boys with me - those with the divisions have a plenty rough go. The chance of a stray German plane drifting over here and lowering a bomb on me is considerably less than that of being run over by a bus or a street car in Glasgow or Omaha - there are a darned sight less German planes, and they are more careful with their bombs than most of the bus drivers I have seen. I am quite comfortable, eating well, and getting along all right in every respect, so don't worry any more about me.

You asked about my civilian clothes. I still have them with me, and there is a remote chance that I might use them at some time, though hardly as a permanent change. The "Mr." is very confusing to all concerned, that being the policy and practice of the CIC, but anyhow to carry out the effect and add to the confusion we wear what is called the civilian uniform, such as is worn by all war correspondents and such. It is the GI uniform with no insignia and US on each collar. That makes some of the boys feel like big shots indeed, so they are happy, and it seems to do nobody any harm.

In addition to the letters, yesterday brought an American Field and a great bundle of Helena Worlds, all of which gave me some fine reading matter. Incidentally, I am enjoying the Reader's Digest which came in the package and will appreciate your sending others, as they are very scarce, like all other literature.

141

Last night I went out to dinner with a French family (at least my French is good enough to understand a dinner invitation). It was really a spread and lasted over two hours: an excellent aperitif to start off with, a wine fortified with several concoctions which gave it an excellent flavor and plenty of authority. The name of it is Byrrh, and if you ever see any in your wandering around the bootleggers, be sure to swing onto it. Then there was a really good soup, followed by a course of hard boiled eggs in a sort of potato salad with vinegar dressing; then very good tender lamb with green beans which were fresh, tender, and devoid of strings; lettuce salad with real French dressing, rice pudding and cake. With the dinner we had cider, which was different from the variety I had previously seen in that it was sweet and had a little sparkle and life to it; after the dinner there was red wine and then coffee. It was a real feast, and as a result I didn't get home until after the blackout.

Today I have been very busy. I had to make a trip down to one of the big beaches, and it was a long, tiresome drive with the traffic and dust something awful. Every time I go down there I marvel at the tremendous amount of work they turn out. Otherwise I haven't done anything very remarkable.
P.S. -In case this ferocious-looking address has worried you, "Com Zone" means "Communications Zone," and the forward part (FE - Forward Echelon) doesn't mean anything except that it is on this side of the channel.

There isn't much news. I have been busy the past two days getting up last week's report, which is practically all the paper work for the whole group and quite a lot of trouble. I work in style, however, dictating my reports to our clerk (male), who is named Junior. I wish I had a dollar for every line of reports I have written since this war started, not to mention all of them I have read. It's a good thing the Army found out my eyes were OK.

I am on the move again and have just finished a very hard day's driving. Of course, after three weeks of beautiful weather it had to start raining, and it was definitely not a pleasant day. However, there was a pleasant ending. Instead of the pup tent on the wet ground which I had anticipated, I find myself in a private room with electric light and running water in it, the best bed I've had in France, and a steak dinner. Not bad, what - and, oh yes, a pillow, the first I've had since I left Glasgow. We are quartered in what used to be a dormitory of a girls' college and was subsequently the Headquarters of our friends, the Gestapo. It is a very good modern building. Unfortunately, this is only a temporary stop, and we are moving on. However, we are being sent to a nice town, and I anticipate a satisfactory setup there.

It was very interesting to pass from the area where the slow infantry battles were fought into the "blitzed" area. Around Constances and Avrances, where the going was tough, there has been terrible destruction, but further on, where they really got rolling, there is scarcely a sign of the war except wrecked German vehicles now and then. People seem very enthusiastic and even in the rain were standing everywhere along the road to wave at convoys. This part of the country looks more fertile and more prosperous than where we were.

I was busy packing most of the day, but late in the afternoon decided I ought to go tell the port commander goodbye. He had a major visiting him and in honor of the occasion dug out a bottle of Seagram's V.O., which I reluctantly sampled. It developed that he had also arranged a lobster dinner, and he insisted that I join the party. There was more than one a piece for the half dozen or so officers (somebody got the idea that I was a captain, so they weren't disgraced by eating with me) and the lobsters were delicious. They had also dug up a couple of bottles of Calvados, the local name for Applejack, so it was a fine affair. As I was returning, I met a couple of the boys who informed me that I was expected at the house of the local resistance leader. He broke out some wine and capped the evening with his last bottle of champagne, which was excellent. I told him it was nearly a year since I had champagne.

We have arrived at our new station, and it is certainly nice. It is a resort town, very pretty and clean and undamaged by the war. The buildings are more modern than in the places where we have been, and there is a beautiful view of the sea. There is also a fine beach which I have not had time to try. Have only seen it from a distance and don't know whether it is being used by the civilians or not, though I know that there is some beach around here where they go. The beach is one of the principal attractions, but it may be that some of it was mined.

We are located in a house which would be considered better than average even at home. Some of the furniture is left and is very good. There is an excellent bath room which even has lukewarm water occasionally, and the lights burn a few hours every night, which is sufficient to operate the radio.

The enthusiasm of the people around here is amazing and a bit embarrassing. Everywhere we go a crowd gathers around, and all the streets and roads where convoys pass are lined with people. I have nearly waved my arms off. In many cases they have wine, cider, cognac, eggs, and vegetables which they hold up as the cars pass - some of them free but mostly in the hope of promoting a trade for chocolate, cigarettes, or gasoline, the latter being as precious as gold. They don't want money, which is about the least valuable thing you can have around here. This thing of being hailed as a conquering hero makes me feel a little ashamed, as I certainly haven't conquered anything. At any rate, there is very little doubt that the local citizenry consider that they made a good deal in swapping the Germans for us.

I continue to be amazed at the friendliness of these people. This afternoon I went up to look up an old lady who owns a garage where we wanted to keep our jeeps. It involved the necessity of her walking half across town to open it up for us and was a transaction from which she stood to gain very little if anything. Yet before the transaction could be completed she had served us a drink of old cognac liqueur which would bring no small price on the market, a piece of apple pie with a glass of Beaujolais wine which was real vintage quality, and a small clear liqueur afterwards which was also of excellent quality, according to my small knowledge. I told the lieutenant afterwards that the doorbell-ringing business was never like that at home.

These people are great ones for shaking hands, and even the kids when they come up must shake hands with everybody very solemnly. When anyone comes in the office, it is necessary to shake hands with everyone in the room, an affair which greatly delays getting down to business if there happens to be a half dozen of us standing around. Then when they leave, it is necessary to go through the whole business again, even though the people are perfect strangers and calling on some routine matter. No matter how well you may be acquainted with a person, there seems to be a great handshaking when you meet, even though you have just seen him an hour ago. If I am riding, I nearly wring my hand off waving and making the V sign, and if I am afoot I wear it out shaking hands, so it looks as if I will get a CDD because of being one armed.

Last night the old gentleman who lives across the street brought us over a couple of bottles of champagne-type wine (it is the same as champagne only it can't be called that because it does not come from the right part of the country) and a bottle of sparkling cider, also like champagne. Yesterday I went out to work in the next town, and the fellow on whom I called to obtain my information insisted on taking me to dinner and buying me a bottle of vintage wine - can't you hear me screaming in protest? I think we were the second American group that ever stopped there more than a few minutes, and everyone was greatly excited. The mayor was a typical politician and practically made a speech to the two of us - if there had just been a couple more around I am sure he would have come up with an oration. On the way back in we obtained two and a half dozen eggs and about a pint of Calvados, in return for a couple of packages of cigarettes, a couple of bars of chocolate, some biscuits out of K rations, and a few matches. Each party went off thinking how badly they had gypped the other, and as a matter of fact we could have got all of it for less but our conscience wouldn't let us. This is a very interesting and sometimes amusing life.

I think I will try to get out of the office more from now on and see more of the field work. I enjoy getting out and meeting the people, particularly when they are so enthusiastic. They do all our work for us, and all we have to do is tell them what we want. It is really difficult to keep in as close touch with what is going on as we need to, because they want to do everything and ask us only for suggestions. It is really pay day for those who worked with the Germans, and these people are not kidding about it.

These Free French look like a bunch of Villa's bandits, in all sorts of uniforms and carrying guns, knives, pistols, tommy guns, and every kind of weapon you can think of. They are just about as rugged as a bunch of cowboys on Saturday night, and I am just about as happy that they are on our side.

I have been pretty busy liberating the countryside. It is a wonderful occupation, this being one of the conquerors. Yesterday we went to a little village, mostly to get some eggs, and it developed that we were the first Americans there. The whole place turned out, and nothing would do but we must have a drink. We left our egg box to pick up on our return trip, and when we got back discovered that the farmer's daughter had baked cakes for us all afternoon. They acted as if we were doing them a favor to come in and eat them. The farmer had bees, and he served us a most unusual wine called Hydromel made from honey, as well as a liqueur made from the wine.

Last night two of us were invited to dinner with a local family. It consisted of a tomato, onion and beet salad course, a course of two kinds of a spiced sausage like salami, steak with French beans, an omelet, a dessert made of whipped cream or sweet cottage cheese and two huge cream puffs, accompanied by three different wines and champagne and a liqueur. I nearly foundered.

This week I have been getting out of the office and doing field work, which is most pleasant, but today my sins found me out. I had to work all day setting up a filing system and writing reports and only finished dictating the latter at ten tonight. I even had to write some myself. When I'm in hell I'll probably be writing up reports in triplicate on the loyalty and discretion of the devil. Anyhow, I'm sure that the guys that require these things will be there.

It's almost time for the midnight news, and I think I'll take it in. Last night the announcer was so pepped up he almost cheered. We may get through here before cold weather after all.

But whether the time is short or not, it can't be short enough for me.

This is a beautiful night with a full moon. Two of us spent the evening with a French family, and it was quite pleasant.

The past few days have been quite busy. I am trying to set up a filing system and am doing my best to recall how we did it in Omaha. Just when I think I have everything provided for, something turns up that I didn't think of. Probably the main thing I haven't thought of was to bring along a dolly who would know how to set one up, as that is the only way I ever saw it done right. Anyhow, it is much more fun to go dashing around the country-side being the Army of Liberation.

News is amazingly good - I have just heard the midnight broadcast, and we are half-way across Belgium already. Tomorrow we may hear that they are in Germany. Surely this must be over before long.

According to recent information on the subject, it is now permitted to mention towns you have visited, so I will tell you about a few. I believe that I wrote you I had been in Cherbourg a couple of times. It is a dirty place and horribly crowded and busy, though not greatly damaged except in the dock section, which was a holy mess. It is now overrun with big shots, and I am glad I wasn't stationed there. Another interesting spot is the little fishing port of St. Vaast on the north side of the peninsula. Rennes is a much more modern city, with very impressive buildings for numerous government departments. It is cleaner and brighter than any of the towns I saw in Normandy, and of course has suffered much less damage than most of them. One of the prettiest and most pleasant towns I have seen in France is St. Brieuc, a resort town on the north shore of Brittany. It, too, is quite modern and very pretty.

I have been quite busy all day and will have several more active days this week. We are now getting our feet on the ground and find out more of what is going on. It is interesting to see how casually we dispose of cases that would have been three star sensations at home. Of course, there is nothing to most of them, but the very possibility of having a real live spy around would have brought out all the big shots in the organization back in Omaha. I am meeting some very interesting people and finding out a lot about the French people. My French still leaves a lot to be desired, but I am beginning to have pretty good luck at understanding it. I will never really be fluent at speaking it, but I manage to make myself pretty well understood most of the time. You would have died laughing the other day if you could have heard me arguing in French with a Hungarian about whether or not he should go to jail. Both of us spoke very poor French of different varieties, and it was most edifying to our interpreter and a couple of French officers who took in the show. I don't know whether it was my superior French, but anyhow he went to jail and I didn't, so I guess I won that round of the argument.

This has been a most hectic day, but I will try to pull my thoughts together and get off a letter to you. All day there has been a steady stream of people coming in and talking to me in French when I was trying to think in English, or asking questions about work when I was trying to think of what I had to say in French. I have been out of the office for a couple of days and was trying to get caught up on the routine matters, and I don't think I ever had so many annoying interruptions. Of course, when I had finished it all, I couldn't look back at a single constructive accomplishment, and I was completely worn out too. You know what days like that are.

I have been very busy and promise to be for several days to come, though to what purpose I can't say. It seems that all I do is run in circles, and I don't know what good it does to worry about things, as I think the war will be over just about the same time in any event. I hope that is soon.

According to General Patton, I shouldn't have too much longer to wait - at least on his part of the job. I hope he's right.

Chapter 10

France - St. Germain Report & Paris
September - October 1944

DAILY JOURNAL
CIC CRT 4 - CONQUER

ST. Germain Report
COUNTER INTELLIGENCE CORPS
ACTIVITY REPORT
September 1 and 2, 1944 at St. Germain-En-Lay

On September 1, 1944 this detachment (CRT4 – CONQUER) commenced operation in St. Germain. At 10:00 AM a conference was held at the Bureau of Securite Militaire and included representation by Lt. Pomerat, Chief of SM, Major Berillot, M. le Commissaire Blandignieres, Commissariat De Police, Captain Marceau, Chief of the Regional Bureau of the Gendarmerie, FFI, Lt. Gagnon, Civil Affairs and Agents Gikas and Farris, CIC.

The following matters were established at the conference:

1. Hours of curfew to remain at 2400 to 0500 as already established inasmuch as there has been no difficulty in this city and people are generally off the streets after dark.

2. General Koenig's order that no travel permitted into Paris to be enforced by Gendarmerie and Gendarmes to man post at Mantes, Etanipes and Rambouillet from 0700 to 2100 hours.

3. Telephone communications restricted to intracity calls with the exception of Lt. Pomerat, Chief of SM, Mayor Barillot, Commissaire Blandignieres

149

and Captain Marceau who are to be permitted to call Paris Headquarters for official and military matters.

4. Civilian mail service suspended except for intra-city business by French authorities to be permitted to function for the convenience of local business men.

5. All prisoners of war and suspicious persons apprehended by French authorities to be turned over to American military authorities through CIC.

6. The newspaper "Ce Soir" printed in Paris permitted to be sold in St. Germain.

7. Travel restriction proclamations to be posted and screening hitherto conducted solely by CIC was set up as follows

- All persons requesting passes to travel beyond the 6km restriction directed to present themselves to the mayor.
- After being screened at the mayor's office to present themselves to Bureau of Securite Militaire to be placed on security records, and possibly for further screening.
- If the person is not locally identified or there are any suspicious circumstances surrounding him, or his request he is to be conducted to the CIC office.
- Person then to go to Civil Affairs to procure his pass.

This has been my busiest week since arriving in the ETO. Last night I was up until one o'clock and up again at daylight this morning, both of which are decidedly not my favorite practices, and this afternoon I worked until seven-thirty. You would think that with all that I had no doubt practically won the war single-handed, but I can't say that I really accomplished anything sensational. Most of it was my old sport of report writing, which goes unabated, and in fact in a more vicious form than ever. I was up another night at midnight on a wild goose chase, and otherwise have managed to keep myself well occupied at all times. I can think of very few times in my career when I have found it so hard to get things straightened out and work systematically on what I had to do.

Last night I had a very pleasant surprise when a knock came on the door and there stood Ralph Harden. He didn't know I was here and was merely passing through with his captain and major and looking for a place to spend the night. Contrary to what I had heard, he has not been in Omaha since shortly after I left. He is with one of the Army groups, and though he has not been over here very long, has apparently had a rather rough go of it, sleeping on the ground and eating K-ration. We fixed him up with a comfortable bed and served him a breakfast of fresh bacon and eggs in bed, a luxury we don't enjoy ourselves. He went off after a hot bath and a full night's sleep with a fair impression of our hospitality, if not our rugged GI life.

A couple of days ago I was invited over to luncheon with a bunch of French regular Army officers who were entertaining in honor of their visiting boss. (How they would have suffered if they had known my rank!) It was a noon meal, supposedly during duty hours, but I finally staggered home at four o'clock in the afternoon, leaving some of them still at "luncheon." I procured a copy of the menu and will send it to you with my air mail letter tomorrow. It was one of the finest spreads to which I have ever seated myself, not to mention the wines.

Last night I wrote you I would send you a copy of the menu of the party I attended several days ago, and it is enclosed, with appropriate translations. In case this arrives before the V-mail, this was a "luncheon" in honor of a visiting big shot (Charles D'Gaulle), and it lasted from noon until four o'clock, as you might well guess. It was quite an affair, and the old liberator really enjoyed it. No wonder the French lost the war, but can they ever set a table.

In spite of the prospects of an early end to all this mess, I don't see too much prospect that I will be home very soon. The demobilization plan doesn't seem to have my picture painted on the front page.

XIᵉ RÉGION MILITAIRE

SUBDIVISION
DE SAINT-BRIEUC

MENU DU 7 SEPTEMBRE 1944

Mixed Hors d' Oeuvres ⎰ *Small oysters or clams*
⎱ *Tomatoes + onions*
⎱ *Sardines*

HORS D'OEUVRES VARIES

-:-:-:-:-:-:-:-:-:-:-:-

Brook trout fried in butter

TRUITE MEUNIERE

-:-:-:-:-:-:-:-:-:-

Fricaseed chicken in gravy

POULARDE MARENGO

-:-:-:-:-:-:-:-:-:-

Roast lamb

GIGOT DE PRE SALE MARENGO

-:-:-:-:-:-:-:-:-:-:-

Green beans and Boston beans

HARICOTS PANACHES

-:-:-:-:-:-:-:-:-:-

Lettuce + dressing

SALADE

-:-:-:-:-:-:-:-:-:-

Crisp short cakes with sauce like egg nog

CREPES DENTELLES CREME ANGLAISE

-:-:-:-:-:-:-:-:-:-:-:-:-:-:-

Souffle pudding

SOUFFLE AU RHUM

-:-:-:-:-:-:-:-:-

MUSCADET *white wine*

SAINT EMILION *Bordeaux (red)*

CAFE *coffee*

-:-:-:-:-:-:-:-:-:-:-

LIQUEURS

De'Gaulle's Return Luncheon Menu

I put in about one hundred twenty-five miles or more in a jeep today, and feel like I had been run through a meat grinder. They certainly constitute a rough way of travel. I visited our Headquarters, which is a good thing to do, as one is likely to forget his blessings if he doesn't do something like that again. Whenever I begin to lose confidence in my own ability I have only to see some

152

of my superiors, and I know then that I haven't slipped as far as I might.

I have recently seen a couple of real live Gestapo agents, somewhat the worse for wear, it's true, but still all in one piece. I must say that I am not greatly impressed, and have come to the conclusion that they put on their pants one leg at a time just like everyone else. From what the French say about them, they are not nearly what they were cracked up to be as far as investigators are concerned, though there seems to be no way of exaggerating their meanness. It is noticeable that in almost every case they are tied up with a lot of women of one sort or another, mostly tramps. If we had just one or two of these cases, we could have more fun than a three ring circus, but as it is all you have to do is walk down to the nearest jail and it will be full of people who are either Gestapo or have somebody mad at them who has said they are. I figure that when the French that are left get through killing off those the Germans didn't kill there won't be more than two or three Frenchmen left, but anyhow they are having more fun than a bunch of drunk cowboys with plenty of six guns.

For the past ten days or so I have been very busy, and at most unpredictable times, so that my correspondence has suffered no end. I have been having some rather interesting experiences, but mostly have been occupied with routine matters and endless interruptions that keep me from accomplishing anything before I have to start something else. Being an orderly soul and more systematic than you might suspect, that sort of thing is no end of an annoyance to me.

I had planned to take the day for the purpose of catching up on my neglected reports, filing, and other troubles, while the French were "promenading" and not disposed to worry me. They all dress up in their best, and the whole family goes for a walk on Sunday afternoon. If you go out in the country a little way, you can see the traditional costumes, and the fancy hairdresses for which this section is famous, each covered with its particular kind of little white cap or bonnet.

After breakfast, after a few minor interruptions, I was qui-

153

etly composing myself and trying to figure out what I should worry with first, when who should drive up by the colonel in charge of the whole section. He is just such a guy as Col. Fitzpatrick, and the lieutenant had gone to church, so after that I didn't need to think about what to worry about - that was taken care of. Not the least of my worries was how to get rid of the champagne bottle that a visiting captain had left on the mantle piece in my room the night before, but I at least accomplished that. It wouldn't have been so bad if I had more of the champagne. When the colonel left, he carried off the wrong set of papers, and I had to chase him down the road and get them back. It seems that life is always like that. By that time I was in no mood to write reports, file, or do anything else, but after adjourning to the kitchen and consulting a bottle of cognac for a few minutes I became more tranquil. By the time this war is over I will probably be like Paul Mohr; anyhow I see how he got that way.

I think the past week has been one of the busiest I have spent in the Army, and as I look back on it I can see very little that is done and finished. If we were at home, they would have special squads out working on every case we have, and all we have got is a few guys that can't even talk to the people whose doorbells they ring.

There isn't any news. I haven't been doing anything but working all day and stewing around. I like the investigation work over here and could have a swell time if I were free to devote my whole time to it, but the office work nearly runs me crazy. There is always something coming up to keep you from accomplishing whatever you start out to do, and everything stays confused. I don't know why I worry about things like that instead of just saying to hell with it, but I hate to do a half-way job of anything. If I take off to do a little investigation, when I get back I have twice as much to do to catch up, and if I stay in to do the office work, something always interrupts and I don't get it done anyhow. Ah, well, pretty soon the war will be over, though I am not at all sure what good that will do me.

This isn't a very cheerful letter, in spite of the fact that I have many things to be thankful for. At least I am not crawling through the Siegfried line or laying Bangalore torpedoes to knock a hole in the walls of the next house at Brest. In fact, I am entirely comfortable, eating well, getting a drink of good cognac when I need it, and generally having what is the best of things in the Army. As one of the dock guards remarked one day in Scotland, if General Eisenhower knew the kind of job I have, he would kick me out and take it himself.

I have just refreshed the fount of inspiration with a glass of very good cognac which is a present from our friends the Germans weighing themselves down with a lot of useless, unpleasant, and heavy guns and things. Unfortunately, the warehouse was not still full when we arrived, but there was a little left. That is one of the bad things about arriving a little later at the liberation. The Germans are certainly a stupid lot of citizens; they not only start a war, which is very silly, but then they don't know when to stop, which is sillier, and to top it all off they go and leave their drinking whisky. It's no wonder we can't understand such people.

This couple who helped me on the last transaction are very fine people, school teachers at a little town near here. The husband was one of the leaders in the resistance movement, and he seems to be one of the few who are not trying to feather their own nests out of it. He comes up and puts in a whole day's work with us several times a week, and is most welcome, as he speaks excellent English, is very well informed, and is intelligent enough to understand what we want.

It has been a beautiful day, clear and bright with a snap in the air that makes you think of football. If I were home I would probably be celebrating Arkansas beating Missouri, which news I just heard over the radio. It helps some here, in as much as there are a couple of Missourians with me.

I have hardly been out of the house all day, though there is no particular reason why I could not have been, as business was not that pressing. It would have been good for me to go for a long walk, and I may do it after supper, but I didn't have the ambition. For no particular reason I am feeling fed up and generally worthless. Being homesick is a continuous condition with all of us, but it seems to come in waves and to be contagious. When things are going good and everybody is interested, it isn't so bad, but now and then all of us lose interest in everything, and we seem to be having one of those spells now.

I had a very interesting day today, more or less on the hush-hush side, but one of these days I will tell you about it. It may have been one of the few times that I have been of any use in this war, and at least it was one of those affairs that you read about in the manual or they told about at Chicago.

While I was at lunch today, on the sidewalk outside a hotel, a fine-looking old setter dog came up, sat down and offered her paw in the best French manner, and proceeded to beg me out of part of my steak. I guess she could tell when she had a sucker. It was my first experience with a sidewalk café, though I have seen a few, and it dished up a very nice meal. Unfortunately, it was during duty hours and in a very public place, so I had to confine my sampling to the cuisine and pass up the wine list.

Tonight for some reason the menu issued by the Army was turkey - maybe Mr. Roosevelt has moved Thanksgiving up again. Anyhow, they sent us plenty of them, much to our delight, and it was really good. There was celery too, and you know how I hated that. We had a good soup, turkey with dressing, celery salad, and apples fried in a sort of batter that was really good. We had white wine with the dinner and vodka for a liqueur.

In your letter you asked about the boys you knew. Nick is still with me, the only one of those you knew, although another one of the boys, Bill Ens, used to be in the Bismark office with Paul Mohr. I have no idea where Hopper is - the last time I heard from him, he was still in Normandy, but I feel sure his outfit must have moved far forward. I haven't seen Jack Hay since shortly after I got over, but I understand that he was quite sick for a while. I saw John Ryan the other day. Elliott is no doubt up where the war is. He owes me a letter, but the last time I heard from him he was complaining that I hadn't written, though he should have a couple of letters from me. I suppose his service is even worse than mine.

156

Yesterday the mail man was back in his usual form, and there was not a single letter, which is very bad for my morale. The situation is so serious that the lieutenant and I are going up to Paris tomorrow to see if something can't be done about it. Of course, there are other reasons for going, but we would probably struggle along if it were not for the mail. We will probably be there over-night and come back the next day. I suppose everyone should see Paris while there is an opportunity, but I would have been a whole lot more interested in the prospect ten years ago. This war is a place for young single men, not old married citizens who want only to get home to their ever-loving wives.

I am back at my house again after a most strenuous trip. I went to Paris Monday, started back yesterday afternoon, and got here a little after noon today. It is a long, hard, all-day drive, and the past two days have not been at all pleasant for that sort of thing. Yesterday and today it has been raining, and the chill goes right through you. Fortunately, when I got back there was some hot water, and a good hot bath helped the situation a lot. I feel like I had been beaten with a club, and I am ready to stay put for some time to come.

The trip was interesting, though I wasn't in Paris long enough to see much. We got in about seven in the evening, and after we had got something to eat and got located there wasn't time for anything else, even if we hadn't been too tired. The Army is set up in great style in the finest hotels available, and all the big shots who were formerly in London have arrived and set themselves up in a very fancy operation. All the rest of the Army is in field uniform but there it is Class A, officers in pinks, and spit and polish on all sides, with everybody saluting everybody else with both hands. We were busy until after lunch and then struck out for home, stopping to spend the night at a little hotel about half way.

Paris is a beautiful city - I think the most beautiful I have ever seen. The streets are wide, quite in contrast to most European cities, and are arranged with some plan. The public buildings are quite as pretty as they are supposed to be, and are not as dirty and soiled as in most large cities.

The enthusiasm of the liberation has worn off a bit, but the city seems to be still celebrating. At least it seemed like celebration to me, having all the aspects of a Saturday night in a college town after a big football game, but maybe that is the way it is all the time. Our hotel was out in the Montmartre district, where all the night spots are located, and they were whooping and hollering up and down the street far into the morning.

One of the principal items of business on our trip was to get the mail straightened out, and we accomplished that to the tune of a great bag full. I got six air mails and three V-mails from you, the most recent being your air mail of Sept. 21st, which isn't too bad. I also got your and Mamma's birthday boxes, and appreciate both the candy and the Reader's Digests.

There are a lot of the boys in Paris, and of course one of the first I saw was Hopper. He seems to be enjoying life in the big city and offered to take the afternoon off and show me the sights. I imagine he could have done a swell job of it, and an even better one in the evening, but fortunately for your peace of mind I had to leave. About Elliott. The last Stars and Stripes said that his outfit, the 5th Armored Division, is in Germany somewhere around Luxembourg, after taking an active part in the drive across France.

You certainly have a lot of difficulty with your mail, and you seem to scream about it almost as much as I do about mine. I hope it has been coming through better. All you need to do is start crying about not getting a promotion, and I will think that you are in the CIC. That is the principal way of distinguishing the members of the Corps - when they quit cussing the mail, it is the promotions.

I haven't done anything interesting, except that last night I went to a French movie. It was a British propaganda film about the RAF and probably wouldn't have been any good if I could have understood it, which I could not. I think I will give up on French and start learning German anyhow.

With that exception I have done nothing except shuffle papers around and grow progressively worse-tempered. This is report time, and I am well aggravated with the Army in general.

After preparing reports of my own all day I have been typing those of others tonight in order to have them ready to get off by tomorrow's courier, and I am about fed up.

We have managed to obtain a little coal and our house has a furnace, so we are much better off than most citizens. I do not look forward to the approach of winter with any joy, however. The other day I had breakfast with a company of engineers who were sleeping on the ground with two blankets and no overcoats, and was I proud of the day when I left Leonard Wood!

While I was coming back from Paris the other day, in two separate places I saw a big old cock pheasant sitting out in the field. It really made me homesick for the good old days when we were riding around with one eye always peeled for a pheasant in range. They were certainly better times.

Monday I have to go back to Paris for a couple of days, and I am not too happy at the thought. Traveling in a jeep isn't my idea of fun at best, and the cooler it gets the less fun there is in it. That long a trip in one is just about like twice as long in a car, and with roads getting rough from heavy traffic it is just a beating. I hope to get to see something of the city this time, though. Jordie Lambert was certainly right when he told me I was too old to get any fun out of the Army. If I were ten years younger, the trip wouldn't mean anything, and would I see the town! It is probably just as well that I have become a respectable married citizen and outgrown my youthful ideas, as there is no telling what I might have got into if I had reined in there about the time I got out of school.

Junior just brought me in a nice shot of cognac which is one of the little presents the Germans sent us. It makes the evening very pleasant, but the evaporation is something awful. I guess we will have to chase after the Germans and get some more. This area has got so civilized that people wear ties, and that is not for an old combat soldier like me. By the way - did I tell you that I am authorized to wear a campaign star on my ETO ribbon. It's for the Battle of Western Europe, and it gives me something to laugh about whenever things seem a bit gloomy.

You won't be getting a letter for the next day or so, and that is about the only reason I have for writing tonight, except that it's Sunday and you should always have a letter on Sunday. I will be taking off for Paris tomorrow morning bright and early and probably won't get back until Wednesday, so I'll miss a day or so writing. Unless I find more news than I have had lately, you won't miss much.

I got back from Paris this afternoon after a rather stormy trip home. We left there right after lunch yesterday, but after getting lost and going around in a circle for sixty miles we hit a rain and gave it up for the night about half way home. I know that sounds pretty bad, but I assure you that it was a honest mistake, involving a whole lot of "red ball" one way highways going the wrong way, and other complications.

While I was in Paris, I picked up our mail. I got an American Field there and found three more here when I got back, so I am fixed up with reading matter for a long time. I received a letter from Jack Little with two enclosed pictures, taken in Edinburgh on the second trip I made there. The tall thin fellow is Jim Campbell.

The tall building in the background, which is rather hazy as if the camera too had been having a few, is one of the Scottish national monuments to some worthy cause.

We had a very nice trip to Paris and managed to see more of the city than on the first round. I saw the Notre Dame Cathedral, which is a most impressive sight; the detail of the carving and the thousands of figures are amazing, as well as the size of the place. The Louvre's Palace and grounds are most impressive, and the Tuileries Garden, though part of them is being used for a motor park, are still beautiful. I have never seen a city with such pretty buildings and streets, and all the avenues are lined with trees which are now in fall colors. We finished our business Tuesday afternoon, and that night Bill Ens and I undertook to see some of the bright lights. Unfortunately Hopper wasn't there, so we lacked an expert guide. We went out to the Montmartre District to see the night clubs, but the hot spot to which we had been recommended was closed and the other places we went were nothing to get excited about. They were very much like American clubs, as well as I could observe - high prices and not much for the money. After spending about five bucks each for some cognac which wasn't as good as what we had been getting for nothing, listening to some entertainment which wasn't as good as you can hear on the radio, and observing that the best looking girl we saw was an American Red Cross worker whom an Air Corps Captain was guarding, we gave it up and retired for the evening. I observed the next morning, however, that the cognac would provide as good a headache as the best.

I didn't see as many fellows whom I knew this time as I did last. I saw a couple of fellows from Elliott's outfit, and they have had a very rough go - in some real fighting and right up front. One of them said he had been eight miles into the Siegfried line - don't you know how Hugh loved that? He said Hugh was enjoying a cold in the hospital the last time he saw him but was otherwise all right.

This damned business will be over one of these days, and though I am afraid that will not do me too much good immediately, at least we will be on our way then, and it can't be too much longer. There has been too much talk at home about getting people out of the Army, and it has got everyone to thinking that as soon as Germany surrenders the whole Army will arrive home the next day. Unfortunately, a lot of us will have to stay and finish the job, and I don't think anybody is going to get home as quick as the politicians would have everyone believe.

I have been reading away on the American Fields I accumulated and having a fine time. I have four weeks in succession from July 8 through August 5, and though the summer issues are the least interesting ones they publish I still find lots to amuse me. Maybe they will come through better now, and the next ones will have reports of the trials in them.

Headquarters is sixty miles away, and the weather is not fit for man nor beast. Fall is on us in a big way, and it is most peculiar weather. The sun will shine very nicely for a few minutes, and then it suddenly begins to rain. It may pour for a few minutes, and the sun will come out before it has even stopped. Today has been very windy, and when the rain squalls come it is most unpleasant. Every day like this makes me more thankful I am not a combat soldier and sorrier for the poor devils who are. Those who survive pneumonia will certainly deserve their supposed priority going home.

I continue to do nothing which would make the least bit of interesting reading. However, whenever I think it is getting a bit monotonous here, I remember how much more pleasant this is than the places which are perhaps livelier. Even Paris would not be too good a change, because it is overrun with the big brass, who always manage to make things unpleasant.

It doesn't seem possible that it is only a year ago that I was at Ritchie. There have been so many things that have happened since then that it seems more like ten years than one. Still, the time has passed quickly, too, and it is hard to realize that summer has passed and winter is almost here again. It will be over none too soon, I'll be home some day, and then we can look back on all this as a bad dream.

Received a couple of air mails from Mamma, a letter with some Helena Worlds, and two letters from Elliott. He has been having a rough go, as his outfit, the 5th Armored Division, recently was written up in the Stars and Stripes for its part in the big drive through France, and CIC was used pretty roughly in that bunch. However, he says that he still has not acquired the Purple Heart, and he is talking about his Beau Essig pup, undaunted by losing Wally.

I am leaving tomorrow for Paris on a permanent transfer. Nick and Bill Ens are going with me, and it may be something good. I will write you more about it later.

Tonight for the first time in nearly three years I am a civilian. It seems strange, and I never thought that if I once got out of the Army they would ever catch me again, but tomorrow I will be back in again. However, there will be a difference, as you have perhaps observed from the cover. I intend to cable you if possible, so you probably will have heard by the time you get this. Anyhow, now it is 2nd Lt. George D. Walker, ASN 0-1997934, CIC, Headquarters Com Zone ETOUSA, APO 887.

I have been working on this for a couple of months, but never had too much confidence in the prospect, so I didn't say anything to you about it in order to avoid disappointment. Now it looks as if it is really through. The discharge was written up this afternoon, I had my final physical and turned in my GI stuff, and technically I am now a civilian, though they hang on to the discharge until I am safely back in the fold again. Naturally I am quite pleased, not so much because I have any burning desire to be an officer as because it constitutes recognition after a long time, and receiving it direct in France makes up to some extent for not having got one sooner. At least I avoided the misery of OCS, and I feel as if I earned a commission the hard way after proving I was entitled to it.

There are, of course, a number of angles to be considered, and I have tried to look at all of them. This will undoubtedly mean staying over here a while, but as well as I can tell we are stuck for that anyhow, so it might as well be as an officer. That seemed about the only chance of getting ahead, and being a T/Sgt was getting a bit old after 23 months. I don't believe I will be here any longer this way than I would have been in any event.

Several of the boys are getting commissions, including Nick and Brigham, and Don McGrath was before the board today.

I have seen Charlie Meadows, who is just out of the hospital after a month or more, and he looks bad. He came in on D-Day with the 1st Division, one of the toughest, and had very rough going. After going through the fighting safely, he cut his eye opening a can, and was very fortunate to have only a slight impairment of vision. He has had it pretty tough and doesn't seem like the old Charlie.

Did I write you that I have heard from Elliott? He also has had a rough go, but seems okay. He has finally made T/Sgt.

I don't know whether I will get a section of my own or will work a while as a junior officer in another section. Should find out in a day or so.

Well the dirty deed is done, and I am back in the Army again. At one o'clock this afternoon I became a gentleman, and I am still wondering if somebody isn't going to come along and say it's all a mistake. I have a 50 franc note autographed as a souvenir of my first salute by a lad to whom I presented a perfectly good dollar, making it a rather expensive performance, and I will send it to you along with my discharge certificate by registered mail.

This is not exactly the way you expect to spend an evening in Paris. Most of the other boys are out night clubbing, but I can't work up much enthusiasm for it. So Paris is just wasted on me. I might as well be out in the woods accumulating meanness for the Germans.

I don't know how much longer I'll be here or where I'll go, but don't imagine I will be around very long. I would like to write McGreevy. I would also like to smile quietly at Jim Hall and Seminara sweating out that MP OCS.

A few more days, and another duck season will roll around - one more of the good things in life wasted on account of this miserable war. Now I am just speculating whether I will make the next one.

We are living in a nice hotel and eating well enough, but this does not compare with our house in our former quarters, nor with the cuisine. Food for civilians is said to be scarce, though I see no signs of starvation. There is, however, a thriving black market in everything. As far as food is concerned, there was plenty in Brittany, but transportation is difficult.

Tonight I wanted to go to the opera or the USO show, which is supposed to be the best entertainment in Paris, but I couldn't get tickets, so I settled for a GI movie, Lana Turner in "Marriage is a Private Affair." It was better than anything I ever saw her do, and the show really had comfortable seats, besides all of which it was free.

Today I discovered that they were holding steeplechase races at Autevil Course and that it is within walking distance from our quarters, so this afternoon Bill Ens and I went out. It is a tremendous course, and it was a beautiful day, with the Bois de Boulogne, a famous wooded park, making a background which was particularly pretty with the fall colors. There was a big crowd, and a very good entry in the races. The horses looked rather like plugs, but they could run and jump fences, which seemed to be the object.

AUTEUIL

PROGRAMME : DEUX FRANCS
DIMANCHE 29 OCTOBRE 1944

1re Course. — A 13 H. 30. — PRIX DE LA FLÈCHE (Course de Haies. — A Vendre aux Enchères)

80,000 fr. au 1er; 12,000 fr. au 2e; 6,000 fr. au 3e; 3,000 fr. au 4e. En outre, 9,000 fr. à l'éleveur du 1er et 4,500 fr. à celui du 2e. Entrée : 100 fr.; forfait, 40 fr. s'il a été déclaré. Pour tous poulains et pouliches de 3 ans, à vendre sur les mises à prix de 250,000 fr., 200,000 fr. ou 150,000 fr. Poids : 66 kil. Tout poulain ou pouliche mis à vendre sur la mise à prix de 200,000 fr. recevra 3 kil.; de 150,000 fr., 6 kil. Distance : 3,500 m. environ. — Parcours F. — 28 engagements. — 4 forfaits à 40 fr.

Départ adossé à la haie du talus en terre. — Corde à droite jusqu'à l'intersection des pistes.

A. F. Chevalier	1 Mistouflette, 250,000 F. b. 3/66	Taj Akbar et Mistenflûte	Charles Bekejen	1 Cer. gris et violet, m. violettes, t. grise.
Roger Coureaud	2 Margot, 250,000 F. bb. 3/66	Le Chatelet et Margaret	Roger Coureaud	2 Jaune, cr. de S-A. violette, t. blanche.
Mme M. Anguenot	3 Braco, 250,000 M. al. 3/66	Bracken et La Montagne	Maxime Saias	3 Bleu-clair, m.cer.rouge&bleu-clair, t.bl-cl.
Raymond Dubus	4 Hallebarde, 250,000 F. b. 3/66	Brûledur et Hallebie	Raymond Dubus	4 Jaune, m. et t. vertes.
E. L. Dupont	5 Le Capelin, 250,000 M. b. 3/66	Trapolin et La Belle Capucine	Jean Sanz	5 Marron, t. jaune.
Jean Fugier	6 Mon Prince IV, 250,000 M. gr. 3/66	Birbi et Cailla	Noël Pelat	6 Mi-rouge, mi-bleu, m. et t. marron.
R. Pillot-Beauretour	7 Lydia, 250,000 F. b. 3/66	Le Val d'Enfer et La Huppée	William Adelis	7 Cer. blanc et vert, m. vertes, t. noire.
Comte de Rivaud	8 Oakuse, 250,000 M. b. 2/66	Motrico et Ebaluka	N. d'Ahuyian	8 Rouge, ceint. rose, t. rouge.
Comte de Rivaud	9 Oreste, 250,000 M. bb. 3/66	Motrico et Résina	Valère Perstld	9 Rouge, ceint. rose, t. rouge.
François Scacchi	10 Drake Lodge 200,000 M. bb. 3/63	Admiral Drake et Lo Jinks	Roger Coureaud	10 Cer. blanc et vert, m. blanches, t. jaune.
E. A. Toulemonde	11 Apparition, 200,000 F. b. 3/63	Le Grand Cyrus et Avalanche	Robert Wallon	11 Noire, ceint. verte, t. grenat.
Edmond Ferdeau	12 Roseraline, 200,000 F. b. 3/63	Prince Rose et Maxeina	Joseph Migeon	12 Bleue, pois blancs, m. bleues, t. blanche.
Joseph Migeon	13 Pivolo, 200,000 M. al. 3/63	Foxnor et X. P	Joseph Migeon	13 Bleue, croix et m. rouges, t. blanche.
Antoine Monnat	14 Quitorario, 200,000 F. b. 3/63	Fiterari et Queen of Bactra	Antoine Monnat	14 Bleue, une étoile et t. blanches.
L. G. Perrin	15 Princesse Monarch 200,000 F. b. 3/63	Monarch et Charming Girl	William Bates	15 Bleue, bret., m. et t. blanches.
Frank Gillis	16 Maurienne, 200,000 F. bb. 3/63	Van et Reine de Savoie	Arthur Bates	16 Verte, cr. de S-A. rose, t. verte.
Roger Guesdry	17 Ouvira, 200,000 F. gr. 3/63	Motrico et Neuvirenne	Antoine Kennat	17 Rouge, une étoile et m. blanches, t. rouge
Edouard Balzan	18 Modérée, 200,000 F. b. 3/63	Vatellor et La Mode	Sylvain Lafarge	18 Gros-bleu, m.ray.rouge&gros-bleu,t.gr.-bl.
Marcel Brasseur	19 Lambin, 200,000 M. b. 3/63	Camilon et Lauterkaria	Antoine Kennat	19 Grenat, cr. de S-A., brass. et t. bleu-clair
Fernand Burat	20 Maknas, 200,000 F. b. 3/63	Dadji et Mireille	Georges Lacombe	20 Noire, bande jaune, t. noire.
Marius Delavaranne	21 Seras, 150,000 H. b. 3/60	Lovelace et Servisol	M. Delavaranne	21 Marron, brass. et t. verte.
R.Despbs de Porpessac	22 Berlingot, 150,000 M. b. 3/60	Sultan Mahomed&Belle France	Désiré Kalley	22 Verte, m. ray. orange et vert, t. orange.
André Manni	23 En Cas, 150,000 M. gr. 3/60	Rienzo et Estelle	William Bates	23 Marron, m. vertes, t. marron.
Bernard Valette	24 Topinamdor, 150,000 M. b. 3/60	Milan d'Or et Guinefaugères	Georges Gigant	24 Blanche, cr. de S-A. et t. orange.

For the first five races we couldn't hit a thing and the Walker family jewels looked to be in danger, but on the last two we caught winners, with the result that we left about $1.50 each ahead. I really enjoyed the afternoon.

However, just to show you that I am not entirely lost, this morning I went to church for the first time since I've been in France. I hunted up a Protestant church, no small trick in France, and found the service interesting, though I didn't have much luck at following it. Some of the hymns were familiar, and the choir was fine.

You asked in one of your letters about a remark I made indicating I would be over here a while. I guess you understand from what I have written since that I anticipate being in the Army of occupation for a while at least. That part of CIC in the scheme of things is not public, and I don't know too much about it myself. Some of the boys are talking about bringing their families over, but that remains to be seen.

Tonight I am just back from the GI movie. Coming back I walked up the Champs Elysees in bright full moonlight, and it was really beautiful. It is a great wide street lined with trees and with sidewalks nearly as wide as the street, along which are what used to be fine shops when they had the stock. The street leads up a long gentle slope to the Arc de Triomphe, which is a magnificent sight at any time and especially in the moonlight. There is something different and attractive about Paris, even with all its chiselers, and it must be a wonderful spot in peace time when the lights are on and the shops are full.

I am making a little trip, and when I get back I should get my assignment. I don't know what the deal will be, but it will be just as well to get back to work, as I feel a bit useless around here.

Tomorrow I will mail this from Paris, but tonight I am almost in Belgium. I thought I was close to the war, but they tell me here that it is still quite a way. I drove one of the boys up here to his outfit, and when I get back should have some news about mine.

We left Paris in clear, bright sunshine, a beautiful fall day, though a little frosty. However, before we had gone far a nasty fog settled down, and jeep riding is just as cold as ever. The country up this way is entirely different from that on the other side of Paris. Here it is a flat prairie country with large open fields like you see out west, and no hedgerows. Occasionally there is a large wood, as there are all over France, but mostly it is quite open. The architecture too is different. The houses here are mostly brick instead of stone and plaster, as they are in the south. The towns do not seem to have been shot up too badly, but some of them still show the ruins from the battles in the early part of the war. I passed right through some of the famous battlefields of World War I.

Most of the boys I knew well have gone, and I find it a bit lonesome, though I have no complaints at remaining here. I still don't know what I'm going to do, beyond some vague hints that it's something good. I hope that's not just a rumor.

This morning I went to services at the American Episcopal Cathedral and was delighted that I had found it. It is a beautiful church, and I heard an excellent sermon by the Bishop of Southern Ohio. Also it was Communion Sunday, the first opportunity to attend I have had in a long time.

I caught the Red Cross tour and took in some of the famous sights. I had already seen most of them, but I learned the correct names and something of history of each. It was interesting and thoroughly enjoyable, and I consider it an afternoon well spent. I picked up a pack of postcards showing most of the places I saw and have made notes on each to pass on my newly-acquired learning. They are arranged in the order of our tour.

I walked down the Rue de la Paix, saw the Ritz Hotel and one of the sundry monuments to Napoleon, and went along the Tuileries Gardens and through the Louvres Gardens, which are beautiful.

The more I see of Paris, the more I am impressed with its beauty, but I would gladly trade it for Helena, Arkansas, and particularly would be glad to trade my hotel for a house with some heat. I am not looking forward to a second winter in coal-less Europe. I am coming to adopt the French view that the way to solve the German problem is to kill all of them, which would be very speedy and simple and would get us home sooner, the most desirable part.

A very famous and beautiful church, which I haven't seen. The part of Montmartre I saw was all night clubs, and I am afraid my wife will beat me if I go back.

Tomb of the Unknown Soldier under the Arc de Triomphe.

I also have some cards of Rennes which I have been intending to get off; I consider it a very pretty place.

Tonight I drew my first liquor ration, that being one of the several privileges enjoyed only by officers for some reason which eludes me. I had already laid in a little stock, and I now have three bottles of champagne, three of cognac, one of Benedictine, and one of Cointreau - and they still owe me a bottle of Scotch and a pint of gin. Goodness knows what I'll do with the stuff, but maybe you can guess.

Last night Brigham and I saw Gary Cooper in "Casanova Brown" at the GI movie, and it was a riot.

Tonight I am on night duty, a pleasant little job of sitting in the office all night waiting for nothing to happen. However, it's my first contribution to the war effort in some days.

Yesterday I located Jack Little, who has recently been sent to Paris on duty, and had a nice visit with him. He is one of the nicest fellows I have worked with, and it was good to see him. I find it a bit lonely here, because there aren't many boys here whom I have known before and most of them have different interests. A lot of them devote most of their leisure to having one hell-roaring big time.

I haven't moved far from the one room in the hotel with a fire in the fireplace. It isn't really cold, but the dampness makes it penetrate. How miserable it must be up front! I certainly don't look forward to this winter, except that it will bring us that much nearer the end.

Yesterday afternoon, being bored and needing fresh air and exercise, I decided to take advantage of the pretty day and go for a walk in the Bois de Boulgone, which is not far from my quarters. I enjoyed it so much that I went back again this afternoon and walked for over an hour. It is an enormous wooded park, and though it is a little late for the prettiest colors, the trees are still beautiful. There is a good-sized lake there, and I was greatly pleased to find a flock of mallards in it. They turned out to be tame, but there were a few wild ducks of a species I didn't know. When I heard those old hens calling, it made it seem very much like the kind of afternoon I might be spending if I were home now.

171

Last night there were a couple of visiting firemen in from the provinces, and of course they wanted to go to one of the wild, wicked spots, so I went with them to a night club noted for its floor shows and $12 a bottle champagne. I am enclosing a program and a pin which is a souvenir of something - looks like a EN fraternity pin. The show was really good, and for a wonder we had seats almost close enough to do Sloppy Miller's act. There was an excellent ballroom dancing act, and some very good and really funny comic tumblers and jugglers, and of course the dollies. Unfortunately there seems to be a brassiere shortage here, which must be very embarrassing to the poor girls, because the bad old Germans or somebody stole their skirts. However, the show must go on, so they did the best they could without any. Isn't it awful?

Tonight I was more conservative and went to the GI movie, Don Ameche, Carmen Miranda, and some new babe in a musical show which was very ordinary except for a pretty concerto arrangement of "Whispering," which was the theme song of the whole affair.

Out in the wood yesterday I saw a man go by with a beautiful trotting horse hitched to a little two-wheeled buggy. They are quite common here with gas out of the reach of ordinary people, and the only taxis are horse-drawn cabs. There are also bicycle taxis - a man on a bicycle pulling a little closed cab which rides right on the ground but had a surprising amount of room once you get in.

This morning I went to services at the American Cathedral and again enjoyed it very much. I realized that it was a beautiful place, but this morning the bishop who preached referred to it as one of the most beautiful examples of modern Gothic art in Europe. It could easily be, and as far as real beauty is concerned it compares favorably with the older and more famous cathedrals. However, it hasn't much on the one in Denver, not even in getting your feet cold.   It takes real religion to go to church in Europe, as they are not heated, and it would be quite an undertaking to heat some of these tremendous places.

I am enjoying the luxury of a fire in my room tonight,

and it is something fine. I can't even see my breath as I sit here writing. This miracle was accomplished by bribing the maid with cigarettes to bring some coal, and attacking with a boy scout axe (pardon me - axe, entrenching, M-I) an empty champagne crate which I found in a store room. The room is only about ten feet square, and a little blaze improves it in a hurry.

Yesterday the French celebrated Armistice Day for the first time in four years, and they made quite an event of it. There was a parade and Winston Churchill was there, but I was too lazy to fight the crowd to see. All day yesterday and all day today there have been great crowds around the Arc de Triomphe, standing in line for hours just to file by the Tomb of the Unknown Soldier.

This afternoon I decided to walk down and visit the Aquarium at the Trocaders, just a comfortable stroll from here. The only things of great interest were some big trout which would have gone very well either on a fly rod or in the frying pan, and some curious eels, which were very slimy and shivery looking affairs.

This afternoon I went down and had my picture made. I don't have too much confidence in the outcome, but as I look the same as I always did, the uniform is the important feature, and I guess it should photograph reasonably well.

I still have no assignment, and I'm certainly glad that I am sitting here without one and not in some miserable hole.

174

Chapter 11

France – TUSAG/Verdun
November - December 1944

NOV. 9, 1944

Dear Dad,

I see by the press that you have re-elected your personal president, no doubt out of admiration for his charming wife. It looks as if when the Army of Liberation has finished its job here, it will have to return home and do the trick for the poor Republicans and anti-New Dealers. Anyhow, the good Deomcracks can rest assured that they won't have to go to work for another four years.

I guess by the time you get this another bird season will have rolled around, and I will be looking forward to hearing how my menagerie is shaping up as bird dogs. If you have not had some luck in disposing of some of them, maybe it would be better to cut them in with Earl Wells' hounds and train them to hunt in a pack. My thoughts at the time of the break-through in France about getting home for a hunt this year were definitely inspired by ignorance, and now I am beginning to wonder about next season. I would hate to bet much money on it.

Lots of love to all.
Devotedly,
Bud

I noted in yesterday's Stars and Stripes that Arkansas had polished off Rice. The only other scores I have seen were victories over Missouri, Ole Miss, and Texas Aggies, which add up to the best season they have had in many years, regardless of other results. You can also imagine my tears at the light trouncing Army dealt Notre Dame, even though I have no great love for West Point.

I still have nothing to do, and will soon be too lazy to do it when I get something. I guess that is training to instill the officer attitude, since I haven't the advantage of OCS or West Point and will have to learn how to be a heel on my own initiative. However, I am in no hurry to leave here, as this is no weather to be farther north, and it will doubtless improve for the worse from now on.

Tonight Brigham, McGrath, and a few others of us are going to the Follies Bergere. I always had an idea that it was strictly burlesque, but the fellows who have seen it say that it is a high class production, comparable to the best Broadway musicals. I'll tell you about it tomorrow.

It looks as if my show-going days are about over, though. I have an assignment and will leave in a couple of days. I don't know much about it yet, but think it will be all right.

I am reporting near where Hopper is, but don't know where I'll be stationed.

Even if I liked everything else about the Army - or anything about it - I would still find it a pain in the neck because I always have to pack up and move.

All this is brought on by the fact that I leave in the morning for my new assignment. I don't know enough about it to know whether it's good or bad, but I shall confidently expect the worst, so that any change will be for the better. While I am glad to get something to do, I hate to leave Paris.

Last night I finally got to see the Follies Bergere, and it is a wonderful show; I am enclosing a program. I always had an idea that it was like our burlesque, but it is a much higher class performance. The scenery and lighting effects were splendid, and there were some beautiful costumes, as well as some beautiful places when there were no costumes. Apparently Civil Affairs hasn't got those brassiere factories going yet, because the poor girls didn't have any in some of the scenes. However, it's not true that they are out of pants too, though some of them are apparently wearing ones they had when they were very small. Really, though, it is a beautiful show, and some of the comics were screamingly funny even when you couldn't follow the conversation. Of course, 95% of the audience were Americans, and they even made announcements in English. I made several noble efforts to get to the Opera or the Opera Comique, but could never get a seat, so I suppose that will have to await my next visit to Paris.

I have arrived at my new station. I am in a big Headquarters, stationed in an old French barracks, where I will be reasonably comfortable, in spite of beaucoup mud.

I will take over command of a small detachment. It doesn't appear that I will be too busy for a while, which is fortunate, as it will give me time to get oriented and accustomed to the new job. The boys seem to be a high type, and I don't think I will have any trouble.

The trip up was the usual cold affair in a jeep, in the usual miserable weather. We came through some of the famous battlefields of World War I, of which little trace remains. There aren't too many signs of the present job - a few wrecked houses, German vehicles burned out along the roads occasionally, and most of the important bridges blasted and replaced by temporary jobs. Otherwise, things are near normal, and there is little sign of the war. I am now in an interesting place with a famous history, about which I will tell you later.

Last night there was nothing to do except sit around with the fellows in the room and destroy our respective liquor rations, which is entertaining in a medium sort of way. I am in a room with the chaplain, the Judge Advocate, and a bunch of medics, so my conduct should be well regulated.

This is not a bad set-up, except that there is nothing to do. We are comfortable enough, though not as well fixed as CIC usually does for itself. We are safe enough, and in this weather it means a lot to be in a good place. I guess until the Army moves some we will not have much to do and should be glad of it.

We have an exceptionally nice bunch of fellows here, though they are suffering severely from boredom at present, having nothing to do but wait. I am beginning to study a little German and hope I will have perseverance enough to learn a little, perhaps enough to enable me at least to use an interpreter intelligently. I have found that if you can't keep up with the conversation to some extent, interpreters are liable to take charge of the whole conversation and tell you what they think you ought to know, which is not always a very happy solution.

The past two days have shown some improvement in the weather, and with a couple more maybe the mud would dry up. Coming up here I noticed that the rivers were bank-ful or out of their banks, so I take it that the weather has been unusually bad even for this season, which is supposed to be rainy. We are up in the region which the boys used to refer to rather bitterly in the last war as "Sunny France," and I see what they meant. It seems to develop with unusual speed into a particularly sloppy variety of mud. Fortunately I don't have to do much more than look at it and get my shoes in it.

Thanksgiving will be here Thursday - my third away from home. I still have many things to be thankful for, notably that I have such a fine home to return to. When one sees what will greet some of these poor French devils when they return "home" after four or five years of imprisonment, it makes him realize how very fortunate we are to be spared that. Fighting a war a long way from home is the best place if it has to be done. Still, three Thanksgivings away is enough for anybody. I think if anyone had told me when I went over to Camp Robinson that I would wind up drawing extra pay for over three years service, they would have had to send the FBI after me.

Last night the colonel in command of this CIC detachment gave a party for all the boys in the vicinity at a local hotel, the big item being a wild boar which he had killed on a hunt up in Belgium. It was a very small boar, and in fact there was some doubt as to whether it was a gentleman or a lady boar, but it made very good eating. It seems that he saw this ferocious animal at some fifty or sixty yards and only shot one full carbine clip, 15 shots, with which he actually hit it twice. We had a very nice party and some good red wine. Maybe by the time I have been over here long enough to get to be a colonel I will get invited to a hunt.

Today I am so busy that I could only spend all morning playing solitaire with one of the boys - the old game of Canfield where one buys the deck for fifty-two cents and the other pays him five cents for each card he is able to play up. It is not the fastest sport in the world, but it proved quite profitable to me, to the extent of some five bucks.

The weather has been too bad to get out and see anything, and it's hardly worth the trouble anyhow. This place was one of the famous battlefields of the last war, but they just look like fields now. No doubt there are beaucoup monuments like those at Chattanooga, stating that at this spot Gen. Whoosit and the xtyxth Infantry stood up to their necks in mud for two or three years. That I can well believe, because mud is evidently the chief product of these parts. Recently it hasn't been as cold as it was when I got here, but that is just an excuse for more rain.

I am living in a French barracks, apparently a fairly modern one, and from my observations of those I have seen here and in England I cannot help but be amazed at the contempt European nations have for the comfort of their soldiers. Of course, the English don't know anything about comfort for themselves, so that is not too surprising, but the French are a luxury-loving lot. These barracks must have been built since the World War, as everything around here was razed then. Yet they have no toilet facilities of any kind, and the running water has no means of heating it and no place where you can sit a helmet to wash out of it, nothing but a few taps. It is necessary to walk half-way across the camp to take a shower, and then most of the facilities are those the Americans have provided. That is to be expected in the field, but this place was provided for a peace-time garrison. If American soldiers were put in such a place at home, there would be more investigating congressmen there than soldiers.

What you thought was AOS was AUS in my stylish hand, and it stands for Army of the United States, as distinguished from the United States Army, which is the regular Army. The AUS is the temporary war-time Army in which all commissions are now given, and since I am not assigned to any of the regular services in which commissions are given, I am just 2nd Lt. AUS.

Today I took over my new command and the personnel is presently engaged largely in a very secret mission of bunk fatigue and writing letters home, to which they will apparently be assigned indefinitely. However, it is a command, and I never had one before. One of the boys fought the Battle of Minneapolis with Paul Mohr, but he doesn't know any more about his present whereabouts than I do.

Today I have a lot of things to be thankful for. It is no small matter to be alive, well, and reasonably comfortable in a world where so many in the past year have found themselves otherwise. When I think how much better off I am than so many others, I am ashamed that sometimes I complain and fail to appreciate my blessings.

In war time we cannot wear our own insignia, so I am to all outward appearances an infantryman, a profession which currently receives more honor than it did in early days of the war, but is still just as undesirable. Fortunately, wearing the insignia is the extent of my connection with the duties of that unhappy branch. As for promotions - don't hold your breath.

This morning I went over to a little Thanksgiving Communion service that the Chaplain held in his office. It was rather a peculiar place for such a service, a little barren room in a barracks with some old bookcases that the Germans had left still showing their German labels. He had fixed a portable altar up and being apparently an Episcopalian, had his vestments and read the Episcopal Communion service. It was surprisingly well attended, and made the day seem a little more like Thanksgiving. Tonight we are having the big dinner about which the Army has been putting out much conversation. I will be thinking of all of you, as I have been all day. It is now about three o'clock, and about this time (really about six hours from now) all of you will be feeling very stuffed indeed. I am conscious of many blessings - anyone who sees what is going on over here must be - and I will have the greatest of all on the day when I am back with all of you again.

I am enclosing a menu, which I would translate only I don't know some of the words. I am also enclosing the program of a play I went to last night, put on by one of the outfits on the post. It was quite an elaborate production, and the boys must have gone to a lot of trouble in getting up the costumes and painting scenery with the materials at hand. It was a typical GI show, with burlesques of everything, the officers they didn't like, all the silly things they were required to do from time to time, and of course the GI chorus girls. It was very good, and parts of it were really funny.

I forgot to mention it, but in Elliott's letter he says Hopper is supposed to be commissioned soon. Also said that he had recently seen Parker, who is worrying already about how to get the Mrs. over. Elliott seemed in good spirits in spite of the unhappy outcome of the election and prospects of a nice visit to Germany, but he always was happiest when he could complain and put out philosophy at the same time.

Another day of fine, driving rain - it's been this way all week. God knows how the poor GI's in the lines keep going in this kind of stuff, but they seem to be doing a pretty fair job. The Lt. who pulled out took our radio, it being his, and we just guess at what is going on now. However, I have confidence in our scroungers to come up with another without too much delay. Given the opportunity, it is amazing what CIC accomplishes in that way, but our boys here are somewhat handicapped by not having enough opportunity to get out and circulate.

I am trying to learn German, but don't really have the ambition to pitch in and study it the way I would have to do to get anywhere. It is a horrible language, but I guess I might as well make up my mind to do the dirty job. If I couldn't learn French any better than I did in four years, I don't know how I am going to learn German in a few weeks.

I went out to an ordnance place where there had been quite a bit of traffic, and it amazes me that the Army is able to move at all in this mess.

I would like to get out and see some of the World War I battlefields and forts, but the weather has been too unpleasant to make it interesting.

Last night before dinner the chaplain brought out a bottle of Burgundy wine which somebody had given him, and said he was afraid it wouldn't keep after he opened it, so we had to help him out. It was delicious - I think Burgundy is my choice of the French wines, maybe even over champagne. The chaplain is a mighty nice fellow, thoroughly human and easy to get along with, and still of high principles. He enjoys a drink as much as anyone, but never takes over one or two, with the result that his ration is a big boon to all his neighbors.

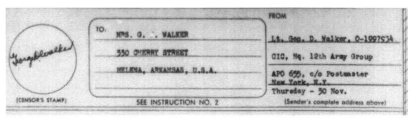

There still isn't any news, for the very good reason that I have no place to go and nothing to do, so my life is neither interesting nor exciting. I guess I should be thankful, as I am well fed, comfortable enough in a repulsive sort of way, and quite safe, whereas there are lots of people who are none of the three. One good thing - though this is one of the highest Headquarters in the Army and overrun with big brass, it is not too GI, and we don't have to worry too much about spit and polish. That constitutes my particular horror of warfare, and as long as I avoid that all is not lost. That's one good thing about being out in a mud hole - there's no way to look good, so we don't have to try.

I am following my usual occupation of hugging our little pot-bellied stove, which I love dearly. That is the only desirable spot in France, and it's only less undesirable than the rest of them.

This morning I went to services and heard the chaplain's usual good sermon. He made major last week and brought out a couple of bottles of Mr. Pommerey's excellent champagne in honor of the occasion - a wonderful fluid which goes off with the prettiest pop and has the loveliest little bubbles in it. And guess what happened - the JAG captain who lives at our house came up with a bottle of Canadian Club! What a wonderful liquid that is! I hadn't seen any since some months before I left the States; in fact, we long since got too poor to drink such, even before it got too hard to get. I am certainly in favor of more promotions.

It is no wonder that people over here are crazy and want to fight all the time. Living in this kind of climate is enough to make anyone blow his top, and they certainly haven't anything to lose by getting killed. At least it will be warm where they are going, and it never is here.

There isn't anything to fill this letter, but perhaps you will want to know that the old gentleman is still around and in good health, as well as enjoying exemplary conduct through no particular virtue of his own. This is about the most place to do nothing that I ever saw. The weather doesn't even change to give a new topic of conversation there, and I might add that almost any change would be for the better.

No mail ever comes, either, so I don't have any letters to answer. I have read everything on the place except some western storybooks, and I am even beginning to eye them. I study German sometimes but don't seem to make any progress at learning the damned stuff. Either I am not as smart as I was in school, or I need somebody to make me study harder. I am convinced that the aversion which prevented me from studying it in college was well founded, because it seems to be a hell of a way for people to communicate with each other.

Last night I played bridge and lost for the third straight time. I don't remember ever losing even once before when I played for legal tender, and this isn't because the other guys are better players. The coin involved is a very small item, but my pride is damaged.

I have been sitting here for half an hour looking out the window and it isn't a pretty view - trying to think of something to write about, but no luck. I heard about a fellow who got a discharge because he just sat all day and looked out the window, so maybe it will be good practice.

There isn't any news. I have nothing to do and do it all the time. This is certainly the Headquarters of mud and monotony. This morning I had occasion to go out to an ordnance depot where they handle a lot of wrecked vehicles and all sorts of junk - you would love the place - and I never saw such mud. You couldn't get out of a car without getting in mud to your ankles, and if you were not careful it would be the knees. There is a miserable little creek running through the town, one of the famous rivers over which they fought for months, or maybe years, in the last war. Ordinarily you could probably spit across it, but now it looks like a river at home in the spring. I noticed a valley out of town where it must have been spread out nearly a mile.

I have been trying to devote part of my spare time to learning German, but I find that the principal result of my studies is much the same as that of a large dose of morphine. It is certainly a sleep producer. If I couldn't learn French any better than I did with four years of expert instruction, I don't know how I am going to learn German all by myself in a few weeks, but maybe I will learn enough to be able to guess whether the interpreters are double-crossing me. One thing I have learned beyond all doubt - it is certainly a horrible language.

Yesterday I received your letter of 28 Oct. enclosing clippings of the Pheasant Futurity. Both letter and clippings were greatly appreciated, and I passed the latter on to my friend Elliott, who is fighting a more rugged variety of the war with the armored forces. I am sure he will get great benefit from them, as he is, if possible, an even more ardent setter and field trial lover than I. He is the one to whom I have promised the long-delayed Beau Essig puppy on the condition that his armored Army get the war over in time for us to get home before it is an all-age.

I thought about you yesterday and hoped that you were getting some decent weather and an opportunity to open the season in the proper style. I have seen some birds which look like squeakies and may be either the Hungarian or Gray European Partridge, if they are not the same; they are in coveys like quail and appear about the same in flight from the distance that I have seen them. I wouldn't mind having a go at them, except that I have no shotgun, no dog, and no desire to walk on any mines. I am certainly glad that people in our part of the world have better sense than to go around filling all the bird fields up with mines.

I will have to do my hunting vicariously through you, so I will look forward to your reports of same.

It is just a year ago today that I sailed out of New York harbor. It seems like some date in the remote past. Still, time gets by remarkably fast over here, even stuck in a mud hole like this with nothing to do. If we can just make as much progress in the next year as in the past, maybe it will all be behind us. I have few hopes of getting home quickly, but do hope it won't be as bad as some think. I hope that Morgenthau and those who want to occupy Germany for a generation will come over here and do it. We will have a tremendous job to do there, but I believe that if we are allowed to operate properly we can get it over with, and then I am ready to get out.

It doesn't seem possible that it is just ten days until Christmas and that I will spend it in this fantastic place, which is almost as bad as the innards of that freighter where I spent the last one. I hope I don't spend the next one in a castle on the Rhine. This should reach you about that time and will perhaps say Merry Christmas!

Yesterday yours and Dad's letters of Nov. 30 came in and the day before Dad's of Nov. 27, not greatly delayed by having the wrong A.P.O. The 12th Army Group is Gen. Bradley's personal property and hence reasonably well known, as the A.P.O. didn't make too much difference. Incidentally, lest you get an erroneous impression, Harry Neblett and I are at the same place, but it isn't Luxembourg; if he was there, he isn't now, which may be unfortunate, as it is reputed to be a very nice place.

This afternoon I went out for a long walk with one of the boys. Walked out from town and up a high hill to look at one of the old forts that stopped the Germans in World War I. There was a fine view of the surrounding country.

Christmas is only five days away. Headquarters threw in a bit of cheer today when they announced a special ration of two bottles of champagne and a bottle of cognac. That should help the occasion some.

Last night I just read a while and went to bed early, which didn't do any good, as I couldn't go to sleep. I need exercise and am getting fat from sitting around doing nothing. The food is good here, and I don't even have enough responsibilities to make me worry.

I hate to write these miserable excuses for letters that I have been getting off lately, but there just isn't anything to write about. I don't go anywhere, do anything, or see anybody.

Chapter 12

France, Belgium, Holland & Germany
24 – 31 December 1944

DAILY JOURNAL – CIC CRT 4 – CONQUER
C. H. Meyersberg investigating parked car, 1934 Chevrolet, in front of Austen's, Heek C 22. Vehicle being used by Captain Van Walt Van Praag, liaison officer for displaced persons affairs to Supreme Headquarters G-5. Driver of the vehicle; Jan Guerten. Car had broken down. Mr. Fransen of the police department assisted in the investigation. Gross and Meyersberg conducting investigations - Valkenburg.

I hope that this will be as they all say the last big effort and will result in getting this business wound up. Until that happens, I can't even get started on what I have got to get done to go home.

I thought today that we were about to have a white Christmas, as we had a heavy snowfall this morning. Some of the boys got up a party for the French children yesterday. The mammas enjoyed it as much as the kids, and took a large hand in the carry-off. You should see the French in operation.

Captain Hancock to Ordinance and to military police Headquarters. The following were brought in for questioning and then turned over to the N.B.T. as travel violators, MULLENDERS, Pieter Hubertus, Maastricht, Meerssenrweg 47: KONING, Petrus Everardus L., St. Antonius Gloyster, Bleyrheide: PRICK, Franciscous Paulus H., St. Antonius Gloyster, Bleyheide: VRANCKEN, Laurentius, Galeen. Gross conducting investigations in Valkenberg. Conochan, Mendoza, and Peisak out as one team. Stewart and Fisher out as another team. Capt. Hancock and Meyersberg operating office. An EM from 3965 AM Truck Co. came with request for CIC help on walkie talkie scare - Meyersberg dispatched with him. Lt. S. W. Wiskowaty, S-2 of 538th Ord., at Simpelveld came in reported that civilian (name withheld) reported to him this date that there was a nazi symphathizer in Bocholtz. Told him a check would be made. Mr. Leufkens Hubert Nicolas Josef Heerlerweg brought in a travel violator of no CI interest, turned over to N.T.B. Mr. Johan Josef Hanneman, of the same address were brought in as travel violators, of no CI interest, were turned over to N.B.T.

I couldn't for the life of me remember Sprat Parker's name, but on consulting Headquarters I find it is Olan - no wonder I couldn't remember it. I suppose that Anita is in Jonesboro, and I am sure that a letter to her there would reach her. I forgot to ask, but I am under the impression that he is a Jr. I know that his folks are old residents of Jonesboro, and I am sure a letter would be forwarded to her if she is not there.

It is a beautiful day - a truly rare occasion in these parts - and I hope that the Air Corps will do their stuff and polish off the German offensive. A few days like this would be the best Christmas present we could get. It would be just right to be starting out bird hunting - what a waste of everything war is!

Paine in hospital. Corps Headquarters in Herleen. Conohan, Meyersberg, Mendoza out in investigation. Gross checking hotels in Valkenburg. Kinch to Maastricht with messages for Maj. Ault and Lt. Slaughter, plus mail, plus recovered signal corps Equipment (walkie-talkie) for delivery to CONQUER CIC for disposition. Miller and Mendoza to Geleen - investigation. Gross, Meyersberg, and Capt. Hancock at office. Stewart and Fisher out on investigations - southern part of territory (Ulpen and vicinity). Conohan and Peisak cleaning up other section of territory. Conohan contacting MP's (Valkenberg). Capt. Fleck and Capt. Sawyer of CRENSHAW visited office. Requested check on civilians at Hotel Princess-Juliana. We advised them this would be done at once and they would be advised if anyone there was believed a menace to security. Gross on OD, they have a girl with German camera we will interrogate. T/5 from Ordinance Unit in Hotel DeKroon reported suspicions re-visitor to hotel to see owners daughter. Stewart and Peisak investigation, subject left at 2050 before arrival of agents.

We got one real Christmas present - good weather for the second day in succession, and everyday we can get like that now cuts weeks off the time we will have to worry with this damned war. The air corps is out doing its stuff for the second day in succession, and I will even forgive those miserable scoundrels who used to devote their time to stealing my true love if they are out there polishing off some heinies. I have hopes that we are not only stopping the German attack but fighting the final big battle of the war.

This morning I went to the Christmas services, and you can't imagine a stranger setting. Up in the front on a platform with the choir was a fair sized Christmas tree, looking very much out of place and decorated with paper ornaments and tape; there was also a smaller one with some real tinsel on it. Everyone was in field uniform and carrying arms, which added the final bizarre touch. However, the choir was good, and there is one thing about a soldier's service: everybody sings and the old carols really sounded good. The chaplain always has a good sermon, and I enjoyed the service in spite of almost freezing. It was surprising what a good crowd there was.   Tomorrow there is a Communion service, and I think I will go.

Mail is still the main thing I don't get. I guess it is because they have something more important to do with transportation, but it is certainly bad for my morale. I guess Santa Claus ran out of gas for his jeep, or maybe he stopped for a light cognac.

There isn't any news. Of course, the big interest is in the German drive, which I am glad to say is headed the other way, but you probably know more about what is happening than we do. It looks like our inning is coming up, and maybe they'll wish they had stayed in Germany. They certainly created a furor by coming out.

Stewart and Fisher checking road blocks in Gulpen territory. Kinch placing new CIC sign up on road intersection Valkenburg. Conohan, Mendoza, and Peisak checking road blocks through northern part of territory, also with MP's at Valkenburg. Mrs. Maria Hubertina L. Ensinck-Mawhin, of Schinnen were questioned and turned over to the N.B.T. as travel violators.

Merry Christmas! Last night I left the office without a sign of Christmas, but when I got back about eight o'clock the boys had brought in a beautiful fir tree about six feet high and had it decorated with packages, cotton, scraps of paper, and cards. There were other sprigs of pine and fir around the room, and it really looked nice. There was enough food to supply an Army, and I contributed my Christmas ration of two bottles of champagne, so we had a very nice party.

We are getting the Christmas present we need most - good weather. It is a beautiful, though cold day, and the windows rattle with the vibration of plane motors. It's tough on those boys to have to go out today, but they are doing wonders.

May God bless all of you and keep you well and safe.
It seems the situation growing out of the counter attack is more or less in hand.

It seems strange that Christmas has passed already. Now after a few days to get over the indigestion and eat up all the surplus food, we should be able to get on with the war.

Today is another of those beautiful days... Days like this are meant for bird hunting.....

Capt. Hancock, Kinch and Gross arrive at Aachen. Moved in with Armor CIC. Gross working with ARMOR CIC. Capt Hancock and Kinch to Maastracht to get billet requisition completed. Major Ault visited office. Capt. Hancock met with T force IPW personnel in evening.

One of the fellows around here who started cutting the tongues out of the shoes of all the people he didn't like; he is making it home on the strength of that, and I am kicking myself for not thinking up some good original idea along the same lines.

Major Jensen of CONQUER CIB visited office. From him Captain Hancock requested return of all team personnel now at Checkmate, the T force personnel be allowed to remain with this team indefinitely. Kinch cleaning up building. Capt. Hancock visited MP Headquarters and City Prison. Conohan and Meyersberg to Laurensberg. Gross and Kinch supervising hauling of coal by PW's. Capt. Hancock to MG Headquarters. Capt. Hancock going over records left by Jayhawk. Armor has conducted no investigations whatsoever since they took over from Jayhawk and have not been able to get records in any semblance of condition. Entire takeover in terrible state due to Jayhawk's hurried departure. In evening Capt. Hancock had two hour conference with T. force IPW people.

Visited by Major Jones of MG who requested screening of all household employees of MG. Conohan and Meyersberg screening Red Cross civilian employees for Col. Goodwin, Special Service Officer, Armor Rear. Lt. Peine in hospital.

There isn't any news, but I may not get a chance to write for a day or so, and I'll get off a note to let you know I'm thinking of you. I am going up to work with Harold Hancock for a few days, possibly a couple of weeks, on account of some guy with him got sick. This should be a chance to do something for a change and to see another part of the country. I am supposed to come back here as soon as they get somebody to take my place, so I won't change my address. It will probably mean another mail delay, but the service could hardly be any worse than it is now.

Stewart and interpreter Charles Snijders moved in from Valkenburg. Major Gagan of ARMOR CIC visited office and was here for dinner. Lt. Peine returned from hospital.

Lt. Fisher and Meyersberg working with Lt. Mendel at museum. Lt George Walker, of Eagle arrived and reported in for work. Col. Clements of CONQUER CIB advises that Walker is to replace Peine.

Chapter 13

Germany – Aachen & Muchen-Gladbach
1 January – 1 April 1945

Happy New Year from Germany! I started the last year off in a strange new country, England, and it looks as if I am doing the same thing again. Well, the last one didn't turn out too badly, so we will hope for the best from this one.

This appears to be a captured German typewriter, and among other peculiarities has the Z and the Y reversed, so don't be too surprised if you get some strange results. I can't make out whether the I is defective or this is another peculiarity.

I spent yesterday and the day before getting here, and was in four countries in all in the two days, France, Belgium, Holland, and Germany. Since I got here it has been very nice, though plenty cold. Nevertheless, it was a very interesting trip, with new people, new country, and lots of famous places where important events have happened and are happening.

We are in what was once a beautiful old city, but it now has scarcely a whole building left in it. By a strange coincidence, the CIC has installed itself in one of the few that is largely undamaged. It was once a rather pretentious residence, and the windows, plumbing, light fixtures, and some of the furniture are still intact. Also, it has central heat, and the Germans are furnishing us coal, though I feel sure that such was not their intention. We are far enough back to be out of artillery range and too close for the buzz bombs, so it appears to be a very desirable location.

I am going to remain here, so address my mail to CIC Detachment, G-2 Section, Hq. 9th Army, A/P/O 339, c/o PM, New York. I think it is a break to get here. There is plenty of interesting work to do here, and I don't think it is dangerous. It will give me a chance to get used to operations in Germany before the rest of them get here, and I will have a much better idea of the job.

The Rathaus in Aachen. This was one of the most famous and beautiful public buildings in Eurpoe and probably a small idea of its former beauty can be gathered from this picture. When we were in Aachen debris was piled around this building as high as the top of the steps leading to the entrance. At the upper right can be seen the toppled steel framework of the tower which evidently was an artillery target.

Also, the men in the Headquarters here are much better type both in personality and ability than those I worked under before. Hancock, as always, takes everything, including himself, very seriously, but he is a worker and conscientiously tries to do things the way they should be done. I think I am going to be well pleased with the change.

I saw Ralph Harden this afternoon. He is hobbling around with his foot in a cast as a result of dropping a jeep or some part thereof on it, but otherwise seemed in good health and spirits. Elliot doesn't seem to be in this part of Germany.

I now have in my pocket Belgium, Dutch, and French money, none of which is any good here, and I haven't any idea what the former two are worth.

I haven't been here long enough to observe very much,

but here are some impressions. People in Germany passing you, ducked heads and avoiding meeting your eye. Kids in Holland with red faces, looking cheerful, carrying skates down to the pond. But the part of Holland I saw is hilly and has no canals. I saw a couple of dog-fights, the first time I ever saw a German plane out in the daytime. They aren't like the movies - no acrobatics, nobody falling in flames, just going round and around, firing a few shots now and then, until finally the Germans duck in a cloud and disappear. Funny how they couldn't find them again, though it was not a big cloud. Maybe it wasn't a good dogfight.

There is an old saying that whatever you do on the first day of the year you will do all the year...

The Cathedral in Aachen. Miller, Gross, Gikas and Conohan attended Mass at this Cathedral on News Years Day 1945. Because of the battered condition of the structure services were held at one of the side altars. This church will be remembered because most of the windows were shattered, however, the sections of the leaded glass windows that were not broken were beautiful examples of stained glass windows.

Mendoza and Lt. Peine left for Eagle.

This is a good night for V-mail, as I haven't much to write about. I have got started to work, and it is good to be doing something again, though I feel a little out of place and strange. Things here are quite a bit different from France, and it is a nuisance not to be able to speak even a little of the language or to rely on people for help. I am out of touch with the procedure here and things seem strange, but I will be better oriented in a little while. It seems strange to be on a team and not run it, as I had gotten quite used to doing even before I had my commission.

By great good luck I fell heir to an extra liquor ration today, almost got two, but couldn't quite swing it. I just sampled one of the bottles of champagne with a couple of the boys - Pommerey '37 - would you like a sip? It's really not a bit bad. There is another bottle of that, which I shall save for some special occasion, and a bottle of Martel's cognac, also something special.

I swapped jobs with an officer here who got sick, and one of the boys drove him down to my former post today.

Life with the field soldiers isn't so bad. We have electric lights, steam heat, running water, table cloths and napkins, beds, and would have had sheets if they hadn't been too small for the bed. The house was shot up some and had a few bullet holes in the walls and round about, but the windows are all repaired, and we are living in style fit for kings. In fact, judging by the samples of his houses that I saw last winter, the king doesn't live nearly as warmly. I like this much better than Verdun.

I am getting down to work, and believe it is going to be very interesting. There is plenty to do, and at present we are a little like fish out of water for want of someone to trust. However, it appears that the people here are passive rather than really hostile. They don't seem to care much about us or anything else. I guess that is a natural result of being gone over as thoroughly as they have been here. You can't imagine the destruction here. There doesn't seem to be a building without some damage, and most of them are so torn up that you don't see how the people have any place to live.

This is a good-sized place, and though most of the people

seem to have gone, you wonder how the rest live....

Lt. Badger of Jayhawk CIC stopped for a brief visit at 1600 en-route to ARMOR CIC.

We are just getting organized in our work here, and there is a lot to do and probably there will continue to be. It seems strange to be working where it is just a matter of course for people to be Nazis and nothing is done about it unless they are big shots in the Nazi business. When I think of all the fuss we used to make over some small fry who maybe had a picture of Hitler in his desk, I wonder how we get along with dozens of Heinies all around who freely admit being Nazis and lots more who lie about it. It is all very interesting and gives me some hope that maybe some day I will earn my pay.

No mail. The war is now more or less between me and my mail.

Sunday here is truly just another day in the Army, and I have been working all day. There were services this morning, but I wasn't able to get away. The cathedral here is not damaged, or not much, and I would like to go to services there sometime, as it is very famous. However, the services are Catholic, and I have an idea that I would not be too welcome, as they would doubtless believe I was there to spy on them. (As if I would have any idea what was said.)

I drove down into Holland a couple of days ago, the first time I had been out of the city in several days. The fir trees on the hills looked like Christmas cards. In Holland there was a peculiar cold mist which froze to everything it hit, and it was beautiful on the trees, though not so nice on the windshield. It is not good weather for my version of the Fresh Air Taxi Company, which doesn't have a top.

I also received a very nice letter from McGreevy; he writes good letters and always has all the gossip about the boys. It is surprising how many of them are still in the states, but it looks like their luck is beginning to run out, from what he said and what I have heard here. Mc says they have to go back to Richie for eight weeks, and I think I would rather be here.

No letters came today, but one of your Christmas packages came, bringing a little belated Santa Claus. It had the can of walnut fudge, which was in excellent shape with the walnuts just as fresh as the day they were picked. I set the olives aside for a special occasion - the can I opened at Verdun was excellent, and I really enjoyed them. Gum is always welcome; in France I used to give it away to the kids but here that is out. Somehow, though, I can't get very mad at the kids and can't work up much enthusiasm for the war on them. The other day I was walking up the street, which was ankle-deep with new snow, when a funny-looking little girl with long pig-tails picked up a snowball, grinned, and looked like she would give anything to heave it. Her mother said something to her, doubtless to the effect that I would boil her in oil, and she subsided. I have an idea that a stick of gum there would have undone about five years of Nazi schooling.

The house stays warm, and enough people come in to keep me busy. In fact, the past two days have been rather hectic, with things piling on each other, all demanding to be attended to at once. Somebody is constantly dragging in some miserable-looking bum, announcing that he is a fierce Nazi, but mostly they are a very ordinary-looking lot.

It doesn't seem possible, but I have been here almost two weeks. Time gets by much better and more pleasantly when you're busy.

Visited in A.M. by Capt. Paul Mellon, P&PW of Eagle - working in Master Territory - here to contact two civilians, Erich Kunz and Oswald Taffel.

I am sorry that you and the folks have both apparently been upset because you thought I was caught in the war. I never was in Luxembourg, but the city of Luxembourg was never reached anyway, so I would have been safe anyhow. It is never too good for those at home to know where we are for that very reason. I drove around the end of salient when I came up here, but aside from hearing artillery in the distance and seeing a line of prisoners about half a mile long, saw little evidence of the fighting. It is a pretty good bet that the CIC will not get caught in any breakthrough unless it reaches the proportions of a disaster, so don't worry about me. I am very nicely situated here, and this is as good a place to be as any.

I haven't heard from Elliot since I got here. Thought he was somewhere in this vicinity but can't find any trace of his outfit. I haven't heard of it being involved in any of the recent fighting, though it may have been. He has one of the worst assignments in CIC over here, his particular division being notorious for having a bad set-up, and I have no doubt that he finds it plenty rough.

There isn't much news; it has snowed again and is plenty deep outside, where I don't go. Haven't been out of the house for two days, but my super-sleuths go out and track down their victims in the snow. The American Gestapo is doing all right with its German counterpart. The Germans say we are polite and friendly and not at all like the Gestapo, but it all winds up the same way anyhow - they get thrown in jail....

13 Jan 45
"Somewhere in Luxembourg"

Dear Dave,

Your letter was quite correct in your analysis of our situation. We did not have as much amusement as you think and we had no intention of deserting our very comfortable set up. The Germans couldn't budge us but as you might guess the Army did. Brass ousted us without a struggle.

So we moved up even further sat down to figure out how the hell Com Z. troops do it. When we moved into our present abode there were no windows, electricity, water or comfort. Now we are only shy of running water so we are doing pretty good once more.

I also managed a little jeep accident. The roads as

you know have been very icy. I slid a jeep into a tree and escaped with a few bruises. However, I spent a day and a night in a Belgium farm house waiting for help. I should have known better. The farmer had four children and four cats so I didn't escape Scot free from the accident.

Incidentally, I heard that you had passed through Namur on your way to your new assignment. I should imagine you will like it better as at least you might find a little something to do. Right now, speaking frankly, our team is not doing a damn thing worth while.

I heard from Sexton not so long ago. Team S. is really scattered. Sexton apparently was in the hospital for a while. However, while Sexton was moaning a little apparently he also has a swell deal as he says it is better than St. Brieuc. The team is all split up. Underwood is in the hospital and Sexton said he would probably be sent home.

I haven't heard any new rumors lately. I'm just living from day to day, being as comfortable as possible and taking it as it comes. Right now the Germans are still showing a lot of life and the end seems pretty far off but I keep my fingers crossed. And just to make me feel good my friends wrote of quail hunting back home.

Well, Dave, that's all for now. Write when you find time and let me hear how things are going on your front.

Good luck,
Bill

This letter is being written under some difficulties, as the lights have gone out, and I am using a gasoline lantern, which seems to get a lot of light in my eyes and not much anywhere else.

I have been very busy all day, and continued my record of not getting out of the house - this is the fourth day. It is bitterly cold, but today was clear. Those who venture out tell me that the hills and woods around the city are beautiful. There is often a fog which blows in from the North Sea and freezes onto every-thing, and it has the fir trees, which are very numerous around here, looking like the white Christmas trees which you have seen fixed up with great trouble. The snow is quite deep, and I don't go in for that sort of thing.

I have lots to do, and it appears that I am just getting into the beginning of it. As we begin to find people who will tell us things, we dig up more work every day. Also, most of these Germans lack any sense of loyalty to their comrades, and will tell anything if they think it will save their own hides. They don't seem to have any of the American feeling toward "squealers." We are getting to do real CIC work, what we were told we would be doing, and here we have it to ourselves for the first time, without a lot of people butting in.

The Stars and Stripes today says that the mail service is being delayed some on account of the offensive, and I think that may be taken as a true statement.

Speaking of true statements, I am reminded - I don't know why - of an article which I read tonight, clipped from the December "American," entitled "G-Men in Khaki." Strangely enough, it is about the CIC, and it is a little more factual than any similar effort I have seen. Be sure to find a copy and read it, or at least show it to all my acquaintances so they will be properly impressed. Most of the cases that are referred to have actually happened, but they are definitely not routine. Anyhow, it is interesting reading, and should be preserved so our six boys will know what a hot shot their papa was in his young days.

I am more or less at the tail of the dog up here as far as news is concerned and don't ever see or hear of anyone I know. Now and then a visiting fireman stops by. By now I suppose I know in one way or another about half the men in the outfit, but there are only a few whom I know well enough to have any curios-ity about them. I haven't heard from Elliott since before Christ-mas and can't figure out where he is. I thought I was coming right up in back of him, but nobody here has even heard of his outfit. I will write him again as soon as I have some clippings from the field to send him.

Visited by Capt. Jay R. Dunlap was from CIB Section of Gangway. Visited by Lt. Michael James, P&PW Eagle. Visited by War Correspondent with CONQUER, Henry George Wales, Noncombatant... Was asking re CIC operations. Referred him to CONQUER CIC Headquarters. Visited by George Joseph Hart, Royal Air Force, says he is working for Co. Sutherland of CONQUER. Visited by Capt. Josendale of CONQUER OSS with Cheif of Belgium Int. Service. Gikas delivering Farris to Checkmate. Visited by Capt. Riddle of VICTOR CIC. Meeting held in afternoon of Detachment Commanders headed by Major Ault and Col. Clements from CONQUER.

I had another lucky break today. Two fellows from Elliott's detachment showed up at the office, and I found out that he is only about fifteen miles from here. To us that seems like right across the street, but around these parts it is quite a distance.

Nothing exciting is going on. I stay busy, and prospects are that I will get more so. I find Hancock a nice fellow to work with; he has put me in complete charge of our most important job, and he does not interfere but is always cooperative when I want anything. He drives himself awfully hard, being one of those fellows who doesn't know how to take it easy, and he doesn't look too well as a result.

Yesterday the weather let up a little and I ventured out and walked about a half a mile to a civilian barber shop to get a haircut. That is quite an experience. I have known barbers before who I thought might cut my throat by accident, but this was my first experience with one who might do it on purpose. However, he was a good honest kraut and did not cut it even slightly, and charged only a dime.

In just two weeks I will have worked out my "fogy" - three years in the Army - and get a five cent extra pay. That is one ambition I never had, but the extra $7.50 is some consolation anyhow.

It seems like a hundred years ago that we were spending those last few nights before I was dragged away screaming to Camp Robinson. Still it is hard to realize that it has been three whole years. How I wish the next one were behind me - maybe I could at least be to the place where I could see some chance of getting home.

I haven't sent you much money lately, so I am enclosing some that will help keep the wolf from the door. This will show you what inflation does to your money. Note the ten cent piece has shrunk, and how light the franc is. The ten cent piece is Dutch and is worth not quite four cents, and the francs were issued by the Petain government of France; they are supposed to be worth two cents but probably are worth much less. Also, I sent you yesterday a fancy umbrella. It is a gift from one of my informants, a very dubious character whom I shall doubtless have in jail if I stay around here long enough, but such is war.

Days go by much as usual, with lots of work, not too much accomplished, and more to do all the time. The situation is very interesting and very complicated. Every day it becomes clearer that the occupation of Germany will be one continuous problem with no ready solution. I wish some of the people at home who are so quick to put forward plans could be here and see what they have to contend with. I don't mean by that that the people are hostile so much as that they are confused. If anybody knew what the answer was, it would be easier for all concerned, but we are all wondering what comes next. All I know is that it is a tremendous problem, and most of the people who venture to say they know the answer don't even know what the question is. Whatever they decide to do with Germany, I hope they will send somebody with some sense to do it; it isn't a job for broken down politicians, nor the New Deal type of day dreamers.

But enough with philosophy of government - you never did like for me to talk politics anyhow.

It is a wintry world around here, and the snow is plenty deep. I am tempted to go out in the country just to see how pretty it is, but I manage to resist the temptation. We have had several more inches of snow in the past couple of days, after a slight thaw.

The natives say this is one of the worst winters in years, but natives always say such things. I want to drive down to see Elliott, but can't get too enthusiastic about jeeping on the icy roads or in the icy air.

Nothing very exciting is taking place, and I go in the even, or uneven, tenor of my ways. I have given up trying to plan what I am going to do, as every time I think I have it all figured out, somebody comes in and talks all morning. Usually I find that the terrible Nazi or spy he is denouncing is somebody to whom he owes a couple of hundred dollars or whose wife he is courting, or vice versa, or some other high-minded ideal, but I have to listen to all of them. I will not be happy until I get all the Germans in jail, throw away the key, and go on home and leave them there. That is my solution for the German problem, and I defy anyone to find anything wrong with it.

Yesterday I finally got away and went to see Elliott. It is only about half an hours drive, but it is really a cold one. The country is beautiful under nearly a foot of snow, and along the way I saw some skiers, tho' at the time I saw them the skis were up in the air. That is no kind of weather to be riding around in a jeep without even a top on it, but it was too far to walk. He was most surprised to see me and really pleased, by all signs. I had only a couple of hours to visit with him while one of my boys was working on a case there, but in the course of that time he brought out a bottle of cognac, which we polished it off with little assistance. That caused the trip back to be more comfortable and also me to have a headache today.

Elliott seemed to be much of his old self, complaining about everything, but looking very well. I took him the copy of the Field I got the other day and the clippings. It was interesting to observe that after showing me pictures of his dog he came up with a couple of snapshots of a "St. Louis redhead," hitherto not referred to, and spoke vaguely of making her an honest woman some day. Judging by the pictures, it should be a worthwhile enterprise. However, he did not devote too much time to his love life and soon settled down to talking dogs, between spells of cussing the Army. His outfit has been off the line for some time after getting pretty well gone over in the course of the drive into Germany, and he has got to take a good rest. Says it is the first time he has lived in a house since last August; he picked a good time to move in.

We got a shipment of oranges in our rations a couple of days ago, and I had not realized how much I wanted one. We get lots of juice in cans, but it isn't like the real thing, though I suppose it is just as healthy.

It must be getting near time for us to move, as we have finally got a plumber to fix up the hot water system so we can have baths. One of our colleagues of the Gestapo had his basement nicely filled with coal and coke which the loving citizens had provided for him, so we have no worries on that score.

It seems strange that I can go along about half way contented in this kind of life. I hardly ever get out of the house. I scarcely do anything except think about catching nastys. That doesn't seem like much of a life, and it isn't.

I am awfully low on news tonight, so I think I will dash off this and get upstairs for a bath in our newly completed hot water system. Isn't it a hell of a life when getting a bath is a noteworthy event? Second only in importance to getting a shipment of oranges last week. I think I got three whole ones, and they were really good.

I shudder to think of Brother Tub, John, and Bill reunioning in England, and I imagine the country will never be the same again. If only I could have been there, I am sure that the old island would not have been able to stand it. V-bombs are not the only horrors of war in those parts, it seems.

It is too bad that you missed out on New Year's Eve. I have become such a connoisseur of champagne that I probably will not enjoy it unless we can get Paul Roget '29 or Veuve Cliquot or Peiper Heidsick in one of the vintage years, but I will bear up bravely under a substitute. I have come to the conclusion that champagne consists of 95% of the atmosphere in which you drink it, and that if you want to do some plain business-like drinking to get your head charged it is better to stick to something more authoritative. Nevertheless, I love it plenty, and when we can be together and use our long-stemmed glasses, and have table cloths and maybe soft lights and music, there is nothing like it.

As usual, there is no news except that my morale is greatly improved by all the mail. I have had a rather hectic day, as we had a meeting here of all the CIC officers from surrounding units, and I had to try to run my business with visiting firemen and brass swarming all over the place and getting in the way generally.

Elliott is here visiting me, and we will have some elbow work to do. He is now enjoying the luxuries of our shower and hot water, so I will fill the interim with this note...

As he promised, Elliott came through with our bottle of genuine Parisian perfume, which I am instructed to deliver to you. Just now he is complaining that the water isn't as hot as I guaranteed. He is having a bad time, as the meal tonight was terrible. Furthermore, Hancock forgot to bring my liquor ration, so he has to drink some Belgian cognac of dubious vintage. So, both my ration and my health were saved a severe malling. I had enough to be a good host, and we sat up chewing the rag far into the night...

Although I managed to save my liquor, Elliot went through my pecans like a squirrel. He is quite close to me now, but is moving again in a day or so, and I don't know when we will get together again. I sent him off with a couple of Fields and a good dog talk under his belt, so he should have improved morale for a while. He can certainly stand it.

You were a little off in figuring my previous location, as I was about half-way between your guess and the folks. However, I am happy enough at being away from Verdun, which was one of the dreariest places I have hit in Europe and by far the least pleasant I encountered in France. Besides that I was in a Headquarters, all of which are undesirable, and that one was particularly so. Here I can sit out and survey my city of ruins, far from big brass and all the fool ideas which afflict it. I am more comfortable, and I am certainly doing a lot more good. As far as being dangerous is concerned, the most dangerous weapon the enemy has is our jeep, and if one of those doesn't kill me, I should reach a ripe old age.

I haven't been out of the house at night since I've been here - there's a sentry on the corner out here who thinks he is in No Man's Land, and I am scared to stick my head out the door without whistling Yankee Doodle, waving the flag, and calling the password at every step.

Visited by Lt. Co. Braennecke, CIC 15th Army - is staying all night. Two Jayhawk Lts. arrived announcing they were here for the take-over. Phoned Major Jensen who knows of no change. Phoned Major Ault who stated no take-over in the mill as of yet.

Mamma's letter made a very good guess at my location, which I suppose was not too difficult to figure out this time, I guess all of you are getting to be trained super-snoops.

As usual, there isn't much news in the way of exciting adventures on my part. I sit here all day, talking to various assorted characters who come in to put the bite on their personal enemies, business rivals, etc. or perhaps to get even with some of the nastys who deviled them during the past few years. Most of my associates are very repulsive and should all be in jail, but they are fine people as long as they make with the conversation. It is surprising how many upstanding citizens there are in this neck of the woods who will commit treason for a package of cigarettes. Don't I meet the nicest people? When I am not talking with these charming individuals, I am very busy taking all the papers out of my files, spreading them out on my desk, and putting them back again, thereby bringing the end of the war appreciably closer. Sometimes I even write notes on cards and carry them back to the file room, and when that is done, it is the same as another mile on the road to Berlin. The most fun I have, though, is saying, "Throw him in the clink!" every time somebody catches a questionable character. It certainly is fun not to have to worry about lawyers or constitutional rights or such matters in dealing with my nasty customers.

You see that I am getting to be a very mean and hard-boiled character...

Major Ault phoned and stated that no change was known at CONQUER Headquarters re Aachen situation. He is to notify us of any change.
Jayhawk people left afternoon (they are taking over from Armor.)

Last night I was up far into the night getting out one of these periodic reports, which of course I had put off until the last minute.

The past two days have been very busy ones, though I don't seem to have won the war. However, I have hopes that one fine day I will wake up and find that somebody else has done it for me.

Things go along about as they have for the past several days, my days being somewhat tumultuous. Things here are not quite as well organized as I would like, and I will be glad when I get in on the ground floor of the next place we work. I certainly spend a lot of time here talking to an assortment of strange characters.

This morning I managed to make the proper connections with the chapel services and heard a good sermon for a change. The text was: "As thy days are, so will thy strength be," or words of that effect, the gist of it being that when the time comes we will have strength enough to meet whatever trials there are, providing we don't make more trouble by worrying about things that haven't happened. It was a good thought, and worth bearing in mind these days.

I don't know whether Paul Mohr is doing as well as you thought. Being reassigned may mean that they simply ran out of a job for him, but ordinarily it carries a bad implication. I am inclined to wonder if he tried to drink all the whiskey in India. Of course, I don't imagine he would be particularly concerned, as long as he managed to avoid a court martial, but they usually have ways of doing something unpleasant to fellows under these circumstances. I know one who wound up in Iceland.

Did I write you the other day that I had a long letter from McGreevy? He is now at Sherman, Texas, at an air field there, and apparently is still successfully evading the draft, though he is probably more gray-headed than ever from worrying about it. He seemed to think he had a chance of missing the rap altogether. I envy him, though some day I will probably look back on it all and be glad to have been through all of this - I keep telling myself...

Visited by Major Ault of CONQUER CIC and Capt. Hallett of LUCKY CIC. ETO ribbons issued to all members of detachment.

...we haven't any lights. Our electric system moved out several days ago, and now our gas lamps are on the frits, so I am using an old-fashioned kerosene lamp, which is just about the same as being in the dark. We are having our own portable generator built out of a German electric motor and a German automobile engine, by a German mechanic. If the darned thing works and we don't either burn the house down or die of surprise, we will be all fixed up.

I have had a hectic day today, with people coming in in swarms, most of them just to take up a lot of time to no purpose. I hate days like that, because when it is all over I am worn out and jittery and can't look back at any one thing accomplished. I certainly meet some strange characters in my chosen profession.

Capt. Hancock and Walker go to Maastricht in P.M. Mendoza driving Lt. Col. Miner of 1st Army CIC dropped in. Cache of cognac confiscated by MG last week, was apportioned to units in town. Our share 1/2 liter per man, cost 3 M per man.

This won't be much of a letter, as I am tired and have a lousy headache, which I have enjoyed all day. No aspersions - I didn't have but one small drink last night! Besides, we have no lights, and trying to out-stare one of these gas lights will give you a headache if you don't already have one.

I thought I ought to write and send you some money just in case you are running low. The enclosed, at current rates of exchange, is worth a mere $2,000,000, which ought to be enough to keep you in pin money for a while. Of course, it is a little out of date, but you aren't supposed to keep up with European history, so I would suggest that you go down and buy you a nice fur coat and offer this for payment.

Today I ran across the first man from Helena I have seen over here, and he was just a part-time resident... Just in case you have been thinking that being in CIC and getting a commission over here is pretty hot stuff, he is and he did. I had an idea I was the only one in that part of the country who ever heard of the organization. He seems to be a very nice fellow, and we reminisced for a while. I think he left Helena to study law at Illinois or some such place and was there until the warring interrupted.

Capt. Hancock, Conahan and Kinch go to look over perspective area.

It was a pretty day today , so all the CICs for miles around were out visiting. They wander around and trade gossip like old ladies at a sewing circle. Harold was off, and I had to stay here and entertain dozens of visiting firemen who apparently had nothing to do while we were busy as hell. They finally filled my office up so that I had to move out and hide to get some work done.

Kinch and Walker to MASTER to pick up Capt. Hancock. Grainger says he is going out on the "usual investigation." Capt. Hancock, Kinch and Walker went to Alsdorf and returned at noon.

Agent Mendoza and John Marle 1st Army screen personnel at the Josephein. Lt. Higgens and an agent named Andy came in Saturday evening for information. All personnel read the new censorship directive. Agent for 2nd Armored came in for information concerning Technic Hoschcule. Major Hugh Jones of MG in for dinner as was Major Ault and Gregg. Major Gagan from Corp was in to see Capt. Hancock during afternoon.

Today your air mail of Jan 15 came, along with one of your Christmas packages, in which there were some candy, mints, a pair of socks, some soap, and razor blades. Yesterday your package with anchovies, cheese, biscuits, and candy came, and I am planning a feed for tonight. I am having my Christmas feasting now, a little late, but everything is in excellent shape.

As far as getting fancy beer mugs, I think that south Germany, down in Bavaria, is probably the place where they are found. At least I haven't seen any in these parts, but when I catch up with some you shall have them. Don't worry about the price; paying for things involves fraternizing, and you know that we can't have any fraternizing. There is an old saying that the Lord will provide, and another that the Lord helps him who helps himself. Between the two we manage to pick up a few souvenirs. As you know, I am not much of a hand at gathering souvenirs, so you have to let me know what you want if you think of anything. Some of the boys have sent home enough Nazi flags, helmets, and assorted junk to fill a warehouse, but I don't even want to look at such trash after the war, and doubt that anybody else will.

Meanwhile I have lots of moving around ahead of me.

This morning I went to chapel, and the old colonel who holds forth when he can't pass the buck off to someone else came up with a very good sermon. It was on the subject of Abraham Lincoln, and the old boy managed to get his thoughts together better than he usually does. I came back afterward and spent the balance of the morning straightening up my stuff and trying to get some small part of it in my foot locker instead of all over the room. Then this afternoon I came down and got a little work done. Sunday is usually a quiet day without too many visitors and gives a little chance to get things arranged.

Yesterday I took a little trip up into some of the more or less forward areas, and I observed that what has been done to this town is no exceptional case. Every place I saw was battered until it didn't seem possible that people could ever live there again, but some still do. It is certainly a lesson on the horrors of war, and I hope the krauts will absorb it.

One of the boys saw Elliott today in Headquarters on his way to join the 9th Air Force. He got his commission yesterday or the day before and got out of the division at the same time, so I imagine that he is happy for once.

When I was visiting the relatives in Dundee, cousin Jack Low (a fine old Scots gentlemen!) presented me a bottle of Haig's Pinch Bottle of pre-war vintage. It was so good that I have kept a gill of it against the day of victory. I have nursed it in five countries and into the sixth now, so I am ready to hit it.

A Belgian friend has invited me to come down to Liege and visit him and meet his family, but I don't see much chance of doing it. Would like to go, as he says he has some fine old Burgundy wine in his cellar which belonged to his father, and do I like Burgundy!

Tonight was a wild night outside of town. Germans staged an air raid. Some of us watched it out our 3rd floor window.

We stop at ARMOR FORWARD. Capt. Hancock goes to war room. When back in Aachen Capt. Hancock and Conohan looked over the Hotel Fuedellenhoff. Zan and Marks go to Leige on motorcycle.

Lt. May from 2nd Division Corps in at office, has two flat tires when it is time to leave.

Mendoza drives Capt. Hancock to Maastricht for Gikas's jeep. Capt. tells Conohan about monthly credential checks and also badge check.

T force men notified that they are to leave Friday. Kinch and Capt. Hancock to Maastricht. Capt. returns and states we will move soon.

Thoumsin and Capt. Hancock go to Alstof to Corp. Additional report on Aachen filed.

Today was Washington's birthday, but it passed more or less without event. For some reason our household made a very pretty cake and a sort of party with cake and coffee this afternoon - maybe that was what brought it on.

Last night I saw a spectacular sight - an RAF air raid on a German city. It must have been nearly fifty miles away - there aren't any closer - but you could hear the bombs exploding dully and see the glow in the sky. The most spectacular part, though, was that you could actually see the flash of the bombs - a great bright flash like someone blinking a flashlight in the dark, and then a beam shooting straight up to the clouds. It must have been terrific, and it lasted for nearly half an hour. I don't see how there is anything left or what keeps them fighting.

We have big news in these parts of late, and all of us have hopes that it will mean the end of the war before too long. We have been watching this and getting ready for a time with great interest and cussing the weather that held it up.

Dick Beebe was in today for a few minutes. He worked in Headquarters in Omaha, a 2nd Lt. then, and was an awfully nice fellow. He got married some time in the summer of 1943 and very shortly afterwards set out for overseas about the same time that Parker did, and both have been in armored divisions over here. He says that Parker has recently been shifted to take charge of a detachment in one of the newer divisions, which will probably mean a captaincy for him.

We are running sort of a crossroads hotel here, and everybody drops in. Sooner or later I would probably see half the people I know in CIC if I stayed here. We never know how many we are going to have for a meal, but can usually count on from two to six guests. It's very chummy, but sometimes makes it a bit difficult to figure enough to go around.

News is very good, and we have hopes that big things are in the offing. I have been most impressed with watching preparations for the big push, which were certainly awe-inspiring. The artillery bombardment the morning of the jump-off woke me up, and it was truly something to remember. I am glad I was listening to it from this side.

I am enclosing one of the trophies of war. I don't know what it stands for, but no doubt some kraut was very proud of it. It looks like a nice thing to wear on your hat, but maybe a better use would be to give it to Johnnie.

We are keeping a close watch on the war news, which certainly is good at the moment. We have high hopes that this will shortly bring us to that last lap, when we will only have to round up all the nastys and get on the boat home, though that may not be as simple a process as it sounds.

I haven't done anything of interest. Today I took off in the afternoon with Harold and made a little trip to the outfit in front of us to look at the situation map and see how the war is going.

On the way we saw truck loads of krauts coming home from the wars, and they certainly didn't look like superman. Then we went down to Headquarters, got the mail, and came back for supper. Lately the weather has been like spring, and it was very pleasant to be out. The trees are even beginning to bud.

As you say, I have my ups and downs, and the mail situation has a lot to do with it. Since I have been here I have stayed busy, and that is usually good for morale. As long as I feel like I am getting something done, I feel pretty good, but when I am idle I soon get down in the dumps.

It looks as if we may be seeing more of Germany soon. At the rate the lines are moving, we should have quite a lot of it under control before long and I won't mind moving, as the situation here has been quite unsatisfactory lately. Everybody and his brother has been moving in on us, wanting meals, overnight lodging, and all manner of foolish and unnecessary requests. I hope that we will be able to work off the beaten path and have a little time to ourselves.

It's time to stop and go to work, so 'bye now.

Capt. Hancock, Kinch, Mendoza, Young, Lindemann, Moses and Conohan leave Aachen for Rheydt. Capt. gets two billets for whole group. Maid at German home was mad as hell when we tell her to get out. The town was taken by 29th Inf. Div. last night and this morning and they were taken out for a rest.

...just one more day of plugging away. I did have the satisfaction of seeing a case which I started show some good results, maybe even more than that. I can't say that my contribution to the cause was exactly sensational, but at least I had something to do with it, and it may prove really worth while. The few live spies whom I have seen have been such ordinary looking individuals that they are awfully disappointing. They put on their pants one leg at a time like everybody else.

Munchen-Gladbach

This is a picture of a residential area in the near downtown district of this town. This town has been subjected to heavy air attack as the damaged buildings indicate. In this area as far as the eye could see there was not a single undamaged building.

This is Munchen-Gladbach famous water tower. It was located near the Military Government building, which was where the shopping district of one of the residential areas of the city. On the upper floors of this tower living quarters for homeless persons were maintained.

Kinch and Lindemann return to Aachen to bring the rest of Detachment to Muchen-Gladbach where Capt. Hancock and rest of the 1st group are moving today. Found good billet for all personnel in Muchen-Gladbach. Town is not too well set up. Capt. Hancock has conference with Major Gagan and the G-5 in the afternoon and with Major Gagan again in the evening - trouble with jail, among other things.

Rest of the detachment and attached men got to Muchen-Gladbach by noon. Capt. Hancock and Major Gagan try to get a jail. New dutch interpreter is billeting with us, came in today.

Thoumsin and Grainger arrive from Aachen. Begin screening of physician and nurses because of typhus. Capt. Slaughter, Major Ault and Reese up from CONQUER. Target teams are made up and sent out.

Meeting of all personnel this morning. The lady who lives near our parking lot gave us 6 cases of wine. Major Ault, Reese and two other men come in as advance party for CONQUER CIC. Screening for PWs big job and Young calls for men.

Arrangements for screening of all persons in city. Office is now in CONQUER FORWARD HQTRS. area and are completely surrounded by concentration wire. City registration by M.G. starts for Munchen-Gladbach. Major Ault inquired regarding the Kuppers, Arnold (Aachen case) picture. Gikas goes on a search for weapons as a result of complaint of Russian imprisoned worker. Mendoza is CQ. Major Baker comes in to see Capt. Hancock.

Major Hancock makes arrangements for new motors for Stewart's and Thoumsin's jeep. Gikas continues to work on the case involving the girl clerk from local Gestapo office. CONQUER CIC brings in Marie Mueller for questioning.

Today we moved up in pursuit of the war and reached another town which was German a remarkably short time ago but is now not even close to the front lines. It is a good sized place, and though it has by no means escaped the war without severe damage. We have again been fortunate - perhaps skillful is a better word - in getting a good house. We haven't yet got the heating and dining facilities fixed up as well, but with a little time should be better fixed up than ever.

We had a rather interesting trip and saw Julich, among other spots which have made headline recently. It is incredibly beaten up - simply nothing left - and makes even Aachen look well off. I have never seen a town so terribly blasted; I don't believe there is a building which is inhabitable, and habitable over here is a lot different from what you would think an impossible place in the States. Other places along the advance were evidently bypassed very quickly, because a lot of them seem to be in fair shape, but the larger towns have the characteristic marks of a German city.

It is interesting to see that there are lots of signs painted on the buildings in all the towns in three-foot letters, evidently in an effort to bolster civilian morale and war effort. There are things like "Everything for the armed forces," "We love our Fuhrer," "The SA is always there - Are you?," and lots of others, down to "Heil Hitler." Some of them are funny and must be a bitter pill for the people to swallow, particularly those about victory. I think the best one though, is one that some GI had put up: "Adolf Hitler said, "Give me five years and you will not recognize Germany." That is one of the few true statements he made.

The war news is excellent, and everybody is all pepped up. I hope that we will be able to make an end of this mess soon. It is difficult to understand how the Germans keep fighting, and they are certainly paying a terrible price for their madness. The GIs have certainly been having a picnic in these towns. They take an awful beating and have lived miserably all winter, and if they have a little fun, nobody ought to begrudge it to them.

I have had hopes of picking up a good German camera, but unfortunately a few million other Americans have the same idea. I guess I will have to wait until I get home and buy one. How awful!

The natives have kindly furnished us some fine Rhine wines.

You would not believe it, but I have right here in my office a real live cuckoo clock, and every hour the bird comes out and cuckoos. I think it is wonderful, and I would loot it immediately if I could just figure out some way to get it home and set it up again with all the weights and chains and things. We are fairly well set up in our new home, but have nearly frozen. Today we got the furnace going, and already the situation is much improved. We have been eating in an Army mess, which has been a pretty good one, but tomorrow we hope to get our own going again. We expect that soon we will be living in our accustomed style.

There is a lot of work to be done here. In some respects this will be a new thing to us, as we are in earlier than usual. There is a tremendous lot of confusion, as the town has been taken less than a week, and the drive went so fast through here that units are just now catching up. However, it is quite peaceable, and nobody seems disposed to start any trouble. On the other hand, people here seem more unfriendly than at our last location, probably because they are almost all Germans, with fewer Belgian and Dutch mixed in. They certainly don't care for us, and I can't say that I admire them any more.

Right at the moment I am doing all right with some very choice wines, but I am afraid they won't last until I get home. It was certainly nice of the Germans to accumulate all of them here for us from all over Europe.

We are getting very well established in our house now. We have heat and have our own mess going; found a French woman to cook for us, and even though we haven't been getting the very best rations lately, the improvement in the cooking was noticeable. There is no beating French cooking when it comes to taking ordinary stuff and making it taste like something different. We are pretty well fixed up except for bathing facilities. The hot water system operated from gas, which is definitely kaput, and it looks as if the baths will be of the hospital variety for a while, otherwise, though, we are doing all right.

We have a lot to do, but it isn't really as interesting as things were a while back. Everything is terribly confused at present, and it will be several days before we can gather enough information to really get started on the kind of work I like. I prefer to do investigating where we work on cases and accumulate information to the point of having a good case, but in this stage of the game it is mostly a matter of dashing around raiding people's houses and looking for somebody else if they are not there.

I have a nice Nazi Party button I wanted to send David Bridgewell, who is just the type for that sort of thing.

Ralph Harden has joined me, and we will be working together, or at least in the same town, for a while. He seems his usual cheerful self, and says news from Omaha is about as usual.

War news is really good these days, and everybody is in good spirits. I hope that it won't be long until we are on the home stretch. I don't mean on the way home by any means, but at least in that last period when we will know that we can go home after we finish that job.

I have accumulated a few trinkets which I will get off to you at first opportunity. Also, have a pair of matched beer mugs which are not just what I was looking for but may do, and a couple of others that are more or less mediocre.

I am quite busy and expect to be more so for some days to come, we are getting a little better organized now and can see a little better what we are doing. In a little while things will be fairly well systematized, but we will have plenty to attend to for a long time.

Seeing that it's Sunday, I guess I'd better get a note off to you. I am sitting here listening to Guy Lombardo on the radio and sipping a glass of good Rhine wine, so I feel in the mood for writing.

Last night I sat here with these same three fellows and polished off a nice bottle of wine to their radio. They are my pick of the team - Bill Miller, a serious, hard-working fellow; Bob Conohan, a Kappa Sig, who works in the office most of the time with me, a good-natured Irishman; and Paul Gross, a German immigrant with a terrific accent, but a nice fellow and one of the most capable investigators I have met in the Corps.

They are playing "Stardust" now. There aren't many prettier modern pieces. Now it's the news - very good news too. I hope we are getting near the end of this mess.

I stay busy all the time, and these days I don't see many visitors to pick up gossip. There is a terrible lot of work here, a lot of interesting things, but we are constantly interrupted with routine things that take time and interfere. Coming into a town early has many advantages. From now on it will probably be like this continually until the war is over, when I hope we will get a place and stay there, and we can make plans with the certainty that we will be there to carry them out. It rather takes the pep out of things to know that when you have figured something out and made all the plans somebody else will come along to finish the job and take all the credit.

I got a letter today from Elliott and one from Henry Gregory. The letter was quite a masterpiece, some nine pages, which is, I believe, the most letter I have received from anyone since I have been at the wars. Either he hasn't much to do or he is pretty lonesome. Elliott is in Belgium and is working with Hopper, who seems to have a commission. He seems in good spirits (Elliott I mean).

Today has been a beautiful day with a real feel of spring in the air. I celebrated by walking up to the shower point and getting the first decent bath I have had in ten days. Though it is in a tent, the weather was not too bad for comfort and the water was nice and hot. You don't know what a blessing a good bath can be.

I didn't get to write last night, as the generator pooped out just as I was getting my stationery out. So I retired back to Harold's room and polished off a couple of bottles of Rhine wine by lamp light. Rhine wine is a white wine, very light, and is an excellent table wine with very little authority. Still, one has to use what the country affords.

We have a French woman cooking for us, and she certainly puts the Germans to shame, though we had pretty good cooks in Aachen. It is remarkable what she can do with very little in the way of supplies. She served canned tomatoes with onions sliced in them, and it was the first time I ever thought they were good, except for cooking spaghetti or something of the sort. They put onions in everything, which is very good as long as one has no social obligations, which we definitely do not.

Everyone is getting very hopeful that we will soon see the end of the shooting over here, and I hope they are right. It can't come too soon.

Orders came through for Eric the Dutch boy to report PM office for duty. City electricity is moved into the billet.

Meyersberg picked up Heintges Frantz and NSDAP member involved in the sabotage case. Word comes through that we are supposed to get some Dutch interpreters.

Meyersberg and Grainger still working on the sabotage investigation they started on March 14th. Capt. Hancock sees Major Ault regarding new arrangement for operations.

Gross and Meyersberg interrogate two German stay

behind saboteurs and return to billet at 630 this morning.

The new Dutch interpreters are assigned to the team. Grainger and Meyersberg continue to work on the party member sabotage case.

Mendoza takes a CONQUER prisoner to Heerlen. City registration was suppose to begin again today, but if it doesn't, the job remains unfinished. Mendoza goes to Heerlen with three other prisoners.

Lt. Fritz from TAC comes in to see Capt. Hancock about sabotage etc. Held a drawing to see who wins the trip to Paris. Miller wins but turns it down, so then it is between Meyersberg and Mendoza, so they flip a coin and Meyersberg wins. Meyersberg gives it to Mendoza, so Mendoza goes to Paris.

Meyersberg and Grainger still looking for foresters who have information relative to bunkers to be used by saboteurs.

Meyersberg and Grainger still working on NSDAP sabotage case and today finally locate a forester who has some information regarding the markings of the hidden bunkers. Lt. Harden, came in from CONQUER.

Conohan and Gross hit targets during the afternoon. A character named Walter Kutschke was brought in wearing a German R.R. uniform. Miller and Gikas leave for St. Round.

Thoumsin, Gross and Conohan leave for Tonges. Report comes from CONQUER relative to the killing of the burgomeister in Aachen; nobody knows whether it is a rumor or the truth; stop in Aachen on the way back to get some information on it.

Stopped in the old billet in Aachen to get the dope on the killing of the burgomeister. The old kitchen help told them it was true and that everybody in Aachen is very nervous about it. The rumor is now going around that the Army is going to put a guard on all the burgomeisters.

Stopped in the old billet in Aachen to get the dope on the killing of the burgomeister. The old kitchen help told them it was true and that everybody in Aachen is very nervous about it. The rumor is now going around that the Army is going to put a guard on all the burgomeisters.

Today was sort of a busy day; work was more or less routine. Capt. Hancock says that he thinks that we will be moving out in a few days, or so, so things should be gotten in order. The 29th Division team, still in town, also expect to be leaving in a few days. All remaining records are taken over to Major Aults office. Capt. Hancock calls a meeting for evening and tells us of movement order.

Outfit moves out of Munchen-Gladbach at 915. Corp has moved to the vicinity of Haltern. Outfit crosses the Rhine River on G. Bridge at 1200 noon Easter Saturday. After going to Corp which is outside of Haltern, Lt. Walker was told that we are to stay in Haltern until further orders. Capt. Hancock gets us a billet on the outskirts of town, on a road overlooking the Lippen River and the canal. Fighting is going on, on the other bank and machine gun and small arms fire can be heard clearly. Can see their bombs hit. During the evening a patrol of the 17 AB division passes the billet. The village on the other side of the river is all in flames and looks like a giant red ball.

Munchen-Gladbach
March 31, 1945

This picture was taken as we were getting ready to pull out of town. Paul Gross, Bill Miller, Charles Meyersburg and Bob Conohan can be seen in the picture.

This building was the CIC Office and also our billet. The first floor was used for the office and the quarters of Capt. Hancock and Lt. Walker. The second floor was used for the dining room and the additional rooms were used for sleeping quarters for the remainder of the team as were the rooms on the third and fourth floor.

This town will be remembered for many things a few among them are as follows. The M.I. man from a document team that was checking the post office, on his first day in town he came to the office after working hours with a gunny sack (100lbs. potato size) crammed full of German money, he asked Lt. Walker and Capt. Hancock if he could leave it at the office and get a receipt for it. They looked at each other and then at him and asked how much was in the sack. He replied that he didn't know. Capt. Hancock then said who is going to count it. His answer again was he didn't know. They then said he could leave it if he would accept a receipt for "one gunny sack full of German marks" he said that was agreeable to him, it was a lot easier than counting the stuff.

The distillery that nobody knew about for three days and that Frank Mendoza just "happened to find" just as the G.I.'s were "requisitioning" their supply result 8 bottles of good wine per man.

The German lady that gave Charles Meyersburg a box of table wine for the fellows (the box was almost as big as a piano case, this added an additional seven bottles per man.)

The search of all party buildings for guns, we had the list of new Walther pistols that had been issued, but all them that received them got rid of them in a hurry.

On March 31, 1945 (Easter Saturday morning) at 1200 we crossed the Rhine river. We drove on for about another three hours after stopping along the road for lunch. The problem on this particular day was trying to find Corp Headquarters, everyone was moving so fast that everything seemed to be confused. We finally ended up in Haltern with orders to stay there until further orders.

We found a billet in the area that was going to be set aside for Corp. This was found not to have enough room so the Capt, Lt. Walker and Bob Kinch went out and found one on the outskirts of town. It had formerly been the billet of a German signal outfit.

On Easter Sunday the fellows went to their church services, Gross, Gikas, Miller, Grainger, Mendoza and Conohan went in the afternoon, on the way to Church we passed buildings that were still burning after being set afire during the previous days fighting.

During the late afternoon the wind started to blow extremely hard, we heard an explosion out in our parking lot, we looked outside but nothing was damaged. A little exploration revealed that the Germans had left a booby trap in one of the hedges that bordered the parking lot – nice guys.

I meant to write last night and even got out the stationery but couldn't think of a thing to fill a letter. I wound up by going to bed early and studying German in bed until I got sleepy – a hell of a way to spend one's time in bed.

I have made up my mind that I'm going to learn the damned language, since I have to live here and listen to it for some time to come. It is annoying as the devil not to be able to tell what a conversation is all about or to read a simple document. In France, I was never too good on conversation, but could at least follow the drift; and I could always read anything that was necessary. Studying a language at my age and with as much as I have to do is like taking medicine, but I am going to do it. We have lights now, and I can read in bed, so it isn't too bad. I have lived to be nearly thirty-five years old without reading in bed, but frequently I am not sleepy, so I might as well use the time. There is nothing like German to put you to sleep.

In honor of it being St. Patrick's Day and Saturday night and all that sort of thing I have just dragged out my last month's bottle of Scotch, which is hauled half-way across Germany more or less intact. Maybe it will make the fount of inspiration flow more freely. I admire Mr. Dewar's White Label product very much indeed – in Scotland I was told that it was among the better of the popular brands.

Mc is worrying about going to another school somewhere, but seems to be less concerned about the possibility of overseas service. I don't know – I surely didn't want to come over here and have been miserable enough while here, but when I think of those fellows and what everyone here thinks of them, I believe it is probably just as well that I am here. I have given up a lot, but not my self-respect. I may not have done much to win the war, but at least I am where it is.

I drove up and visited Dick Beebe for a few minutes and was supposed to get the address of another fellow whom the boy with me wanted to see. However, we learned that he was at the moment engaged at shooting at people across the Rhine, which seemed to me a rough and vulgar pastime in which I did not care to join, as some of them are so inconsiderate as to shoot back.

I am enclosing a picture which I found in the course of

prowling about one of the Nazi Party Headquarters in search of more important evidence. This citizen is no doubt one of the Nazi dignitaries, and he seems to be discharging an important function of his office.

Though he no doubt appears a bit silly, I feel sure that he felt much better at the time than he did when his wife saw the picture. That sort of thing must have been more or less routine, as none of the neighbors seemed to be paying much attention to him. Again I say – nice people!

I haven't got a letter off since Sunday night. I had to get out a report last night and didn't get to write. Started a letter this morning but was interrupted so much that I gave it up in disgust. Every time I put it down I had nothing to do, but before I could write a line people would pour in, so I threw it away.

Night before last I made a brave attempt to go to the movie for the umpteenth time since I have been in Germany, but couldn't get in, so tonight I tried again. This time I made it, and it served me right. I don't think I ever saw such a lousy picture. Unfortunately I got there after it had started, so I don't know the name and can't warn you against it. However I don't think it is necessary, as any theater in the States that showed such a thing would be closed for obtaining money under false pretenses; even free it was a gyp. It was about a dolly who blew her top on a count of she was scared of birds, so if you ever hear of such a performance, beware!

I have a fine German typewriter which is one of the spoils of war, and it is a good one. The main keyboard is like ours, only the y is where the z ought to be and vice versa; also a number of the smaller gadgets are moved around somewhat. It has lots of funny things, like: ß, Ö, Ä. Ü, ', ¦ §, and =, but what I am most proud of is ⚡, which is the symbol of the SS. It seems to resemble in general the Underwood and is quite sturdy.

Today I obtained a beer mug which is just the kind I have been looking for. It is a real novelty, a lawyer's mug with the outside designed like law books and a top that raises up and has a legal crest on it with a Latin motto. I admire it no end. I have several others for your collection, but though some of them are fairly nice, none of them are just what I want. However, I will get the collection off to you soon. I am glad I waited for this one, and think I will wait a little longer in hopes of getting one of the big ones with a peaked top to put on the mantelpiece. I have a little matched pair for us, but unfortunately they do not have the top.

Monday night when I tried to go to the movie, the evening wasn't quite a total loss, as they were selling Coca-Colas at the same place, and I got one. I don't know when I last had one – imagine me in a land of good wine enjoying a coke!

It looks as if I will have to stay over here. I read in the paper about the Mississippi flooding and breaking the levees and all the meat ration being cut off, so it looks as if I will have to stay at war to enjoy the comforts of home. Here I can even buy cocktail peanuts in cans at the PX, and I'll bet you can't do that – I can't either most of the time. The only trouble with this life is that it just isn't any fun. To date the Germans have been tame enough, but it has been almost too easy, and I don't know how it will be when we catch up with the big shots who are now so busy running away while they tell everyone else to fight to the last. They are an utterly perverted, unprincipled, and unscrupulous lot.

Today was another beautiful day, turning my mind to thoughts of spring and the air corps to thoughts of dropping much bombs on the dirty krauts. That was probably much more fun to your ex boy friends than to the recipients. They have certainly been working overtime these pretty days, and I hope that they will get things built up to finish this job in a hurry. I for one am getting good and tired of being over here, and it will be a relief to know that there remains only the occupation, which can't last forever.

News of the past few days has been wonderful, and it looks as if things are building up to a real crisis. I don't know – I have thought before that it wouldn't be long, and it was a long time and still isn't over. Still, it never hurts to hope, and I do feel really optimistic. I have hopes that we will soon follow along and see the other side of the Rhine, which will suit me fine, as I am not too pleased with the situation here. We are comfortable enough, but we are not our own bosses as we have been accustomed to being, and we get lots of annoying jobs that don't seem to accomplish much. I am pretty spoiled and like to have a town all of our own.

Tonight Harold and I went to the movie. It was Gloria Jean in "Destiny," a rather corny affair which could be figured out well in advance, but not too bad. She has developed in to a pretty chick, or maybe it is just the solitude.

Today I went to the church services for Palm Sunday. The chaplain was an old Army chaplain and did pretty well, but I much prefer the variety who haven't had too much GI life. It definitely stamps anybody who is around it too long – you will probably think I am a dirty old soldier when I get home. Next Sunday is Easter, and I am wondering what I am going to do about the services. There is an Episcopal chaplain with one of the Corps near here, and if they are still around I may go there. There will also be some Holy Week services here during the week. Today the services were in the local theatre, which was once a very fancy place, and they had succeeded in finding a couple of potted palms for the day.

This afternoon I continued with the theme that this is a special day by going over and getting a shower. It is quite a bit of trouble, but I manage to get around two or three times a week. So you see that maybe you aren't missing so much after all by not being with me. You probably wouldn't love me any more, and I could sell my sad story to one of the Lifebuoy ads.

The beautiful weather we have been enjoying has continued, but today it is clouding up some. I hope it will hold for a few days more, but it has been remarkable that we have had so much already. I never expected anything like it in this part of the world at this season. It has done wonders for our operations and has undoubtedly shortened the war by many weeks.

News has been wonderful the past few days. Although we are almost close enough to hear everything that takes place, we really know very little about it, and you probably get the news as quickly as we do, except for gossip, which is usually 100% wrong. However, there is no doubt that things are going very well indeed, and I am hopeful that before long we will be embarked on the last phase of our job here. It is my hope that we will be assigned to some place where we will stay for the duration of our time in Germany, and that by some chance it will be a decent place. I have visions of a Bavarian mountain resort, but am afraid there will be no such luck.

Putting Nazis in jail serves somewhat to vent my bad temper.

I took off yesterday with Hancock and went back to a little town back in Holland where he was located for a while last fall. Things had quieted down a bit here, and we thought we would get a little relaxation while we could, as we will probably soon be very busy indeed. It was a very nice place and had a good modern hotel which the team had occupied while there, and where we were welcomed like we owned the place. It was the cleanest, most modern place – I mean the town as a whole – that I have seen in Europe; it was a new town, built around a large coal mine, and I was impressed with how well-built and up-to-date all the houses are. There wasn't much to do, but I didn't want to do anything anyhow. We got in just before lunch, had a good meal, and enjoyed the luxury of an afternoon nap. We got up and walked around town, had a couple of beers, which were the strongest drink to be had, then had supper and went to the show. It was an American picture with Dutch sub-titles, Dick Powell in "Christmas in July." It wasn't new by any means, but was pretty good, and at least wasn't about the war. We returned to the hotel and visited with the people for a while, then went to bed after a hot bath (in a tub) and slept until ten-thirty this morning. Had breakfast at our leisure and went for a little drive into the surrounding country; then had lunch and returned to the wars. It was a good rest, and it was nice to be back where people smile, and you can talk to them. It was especially nice to be around kids, and I enjoyed giving them some of my surplus chocolate. It is remarkable how they have picked up English in the time since we arrived. Most of the people look fairly well-fed, but it is noticeable that the younger children have small, rickety legs, and none of them are fat.

News is almost too good to believe, and we are in hope that the end is in sight. That won't mean much to us except a chance to take a few drinks before going back to work, but at least that will be something.

No mail from home came today, but I got a letter from one of the boys on my old detachment enclosing the two pictures which I am forwarding. This will show you the horrors of trench warfare when the old Conqueror was liberating Verdun; it is no wonder that a million men were killed there in the last war. It will also show you the old Conqueror in his athletic days; that form will have Sammy Baugh worrying about his post-war future.

The war is progressing rapidly, and I shall probably do likewise one of these days. It will be nice to find a new place far removed from this Headquarters, a new town with bigger and better beer mugs, and, I trust, many fine wines and cognacs. Peace, it's wonderful!

Every day the news seems more promising, and we are in hopes that we will soon have the best news of all – next to that order home. I have long since got my fill of touring Europe, and I will be a happy soldier when I know we have made the last move. I take root very easily, and hate to leave every place I get settled, most just because I hate so much to pack.

Chapter 14

Germany – Ahlen, Braunschweig & more
1 April – 30 April 1945

Capt. Hancock, Lt. Walker and Kinch go to Corp., return about noon with the information that we are not
moving. Everything is quiet on the other side of the
river. The fellows get a chance to go to Church in the
afternoon at 4 o'clock. On the way to church we see
some large buildings burning to the ground. Small
explosions in parking lot during afternoon.

Another day finished, fifty miles or so covered, and still
so far behind as ever! This trip across Germany is assuming the
proportions of a wild dash. I don't know when we will catch up
well enough to do some work.

Today we passed through beautiful farming country which
looks very much like I own except that it is flatter. Spring has
everything blooming; the fields are green, and around the houses there are pansies and violets and other flowers. There has
been little fighting here, and the towns are too small to attract
aerial bombing, so there is not much sign of war except streams
of American vehicles moving up, truckloads of prisoners coming back, and hundreds of liberated French, Belgians, Dutch, and
Russians walking back – the most miserable-looking people you
ever saw, but smiling and making the V-sign. Men and women
were trudging along today in a pouring rain, carrying their pitiful
little bundles or shoving carts, striking out afoot for homes that
are hundreds of miles away and probably destroyed when they get
there.

We reached a pretty little town this afternoon, dispossessed
a typical bloated old kraut, and set ourselves up in a very comfortable house. The water isn't running, but we had to set up our own
generator for light and radio.

Capt. Hancock Lt. Walker and Kinch go to Corp, return around noon and tell us we are moving immediately to the town of Ahlen. The day is miserable. It
is spilling rain at the time we leave. When we arrive
Capt. Hancock picks out a nice house, and we moved
the people out. It is an architects home.

This picture is included because it was so typical of the thing that we saw time and time again namely evacuates return to their homes carrying all of their worldly possessions on their back or on a small cart or anything they could get to serve this purpose. For about two days people were constantly going by our billet. Most of them were returning to the East Bank of the Rhine or one of the Allied nations.

This picture was taken in the downtown area of Ahlen as the picture indicates not too much damage was done to this town the reason for this was that Ahlen was declared an open city because the Germans had many hospitals in this town and as a result they did not put up a fight for it nor did our troops attack the city.

Capt. Hancock, Lt. Walker and Kinch go to Corp, return with the news that we are not to move. Outfit will stay in town but will remain non-operational. We are eating with an Ordinance outfit stationed at one of the towns fire houses. Mendoza and Grainger find a place that sells cognac made out of rye; the fellows are a little skeptical about drinking it. Refugees, especially Russians and Poles are running all over town.

This is a picture of the CIC office and of our billet in Ahlen. Paul Gross is standing in front of the fence. The home was the home of another architect. We seemed to have a weakness for the homes of architects, they seemed to meet our requirements as for space. This was a nice place only the neighbors wouldn't speak to us.

As for the town of Ahlen itself, it will be remembered for a number of things. First of all it was a pretty little town and not badly damaged. A beautiful stream ran through the center of the town and large white birds that looked like swans were constantly swimming in this stream. The town was peaceful and quiet but just so we didn't forget we could hear day and night the big guns shelling Hamm. It was easy to tell that there still was a war going on.

I think that this was the town that made many of us realize what it was to be an American and to thank God for being one and for having spared our people from the fate that had befallen the Europeans. What made us realize this more than anything else was the scene that took place at meal time. We were eating in an ordnance utfits chow line and the DP's in the area would swarm around our eating area and especially around the large GI cans that we emptied our mess kits in, and as the fellows emptied their mess kits the DP's would ask up for the pieces of bread, meat, etc. that were left in our mess kits, and when there wasn't any in our kits they would reach in the GI cans and take out whatever looked edible. It made us realize that we had no room to complain and so much to be thankful for.

Capt. Hancock, Lt. Walker, Kinch and Mandoza go to Corp, come back with the news that the team is going to be split up into two groups. During the evening Lt. Walker tells us how we are to be divided up.

There isn't much news, but since mail will probably be slow getting through I will take every opportunity to write. I haven't had any mail for five days, but Harold has gone back to Army Headquarters tonight and I hope he will bring back a big haul tomorrow. We are way out in front of them, and they don't know where we are, so we can only get our mail by going for it. It's about like your driving to Little Rock for your morning mail delivery, and in a jeep that's no pleasure spin.

Our progress across Germany has been held up when we stopped to do a little work for a change. However, we will soon put all the local nastys in durance vile and look for new fields to conquer. A little of this, and you get a sort of wanderlust and want to keep pushing on. I am still looking for my Bavarian mountain resort to spend the occupation there, but this looks like a pleasant enough country. We are in a nice-looking old town, not too large, and not greatly damaged. The surrounding country is pleasant farming land, with a solid, prosperous look and a gentle roll that looks very much like Iowa.

This has been a very interesting experience. For the first

time we have seen a part of Germany which is not beaten all to pieces and has most of the people left. The advance was too rapid for all the big shot Nazis to run away as they did before. As a special reward they will get put in jail here instead of somewhere else. They are apparently the only ones interested in carrying on the war, and that's only to save their own dirty hides a while longer.

The fount of inspiration is being replenished with a little German "korn" liquor, which seems to be a very desirable fluid. Some of the boys have drunk it already and survived, so I am hopeful. It lacks the power of the Arkansas variety of "korn," but is alas less nasty. Incidentally, "korn" in German means rye or almost any grain except corn.

We have moved our time up an hour, and the evening passes quickly. It is late now, and I have killed the whole evening writing this between interruptions.

The team has been operational since yesterday. During search it was found that the record at the Kriesletung were almost complete. Mendoza and Stewart bring back a good German trailer.

Lt. Walker calls a meeting at 430 Capt. Hancock, Lt. Bauer, Miller and Young, Gikas, Mendoza and Kinch as well as Eddie and Paul the two dutch boys move out for Lipstadt.

Three fellows from the 29th came in to get some information about the surrounding towns. Veech and Brown from the 95th also came in, requested us to screen a German movie actress.

Stewart leaves to join Capt. Hancock at Lipstadt. Lt. Walker decides that we will move to Beckum in the morning. At 630 a Captain from a field artillery outfit brings a truck load of Germans to the billet. He claims that the Russians told him that they were German deserters that had changed to civilian clothes. Lt. Walker told him to take them to the PWE at Beckum and we would screen them in the morning.

Outfit of Lt. Walker leaves for Beckum when we move in with the two fellows, Lt. Simon and Charlie Meyersberg, "My Friend" Claus who stayed behind when MG moved out. Lt. Walker and Conohan go to Lipstadt in the afternoon. On the way out of town, they are stopped by some DP's and break up a fight between some Russians and Germans. Gross screened the truck load of Germans that the field artillery Capt. brought in last night. Interrogations revealed that the Captain had arrested most of the Beckum police who had been sent out by MG to round up the Russians.

Thoumsin and Meyersberg are working Ahlen from Beckum. Lt. Walker is running the office. Young, Stewart, Kinch, Gross and Conohan get typhus shots. Lt. Walker and Gross go to Hamm during the afternoon.

29th Division comes into the area to take over the control of the DP's who are a terrific problem. MG men move out of the billet and French Lt. who is to take their place moves in.

Grainger, Joe, Gross and Conohan take a load of prisoners to the PWE, and because of poor marching on the road cannot find it. 29th Division regimental PW cage finally takes them off our hands, on our way back find CONQUER PWE where we were headed for. Miller brings in a report on how Bauer and he broke up a potential HJ sabotage ring in Lipstadt.

Today was mail day, and what a day! I got nineteen letters, plus four letters of clippings, two copies of the Field, and a couple of Law Reporters.

We have been settled for three days now and feel like old residents. All of you were pretty far off on your guesses as to my whereabouts – the Ninth Army didn't go towards Cologne. This is a pretty country, and, as one of the boys remarked today, it's a shame the people couldn't mind their own business. I think they are beginning to have the same idea about the matter.

We have a terrific amount of work to do, so much that it is hard to find a place to start. There is terrific confusion in newly occupied territory, and it is really remarkable that order can be produced as quickly as it is. It just seems one day that a lot of things have suddenly adjusted themselves, and the country seems quite normal. But until that day comes, everybody seems to go in circles, hollering at somebody else to do something.

I am in a rather interesting neighborhood, and lots of things are going on within a few miles of me. They might as well be in China for all I know of them. I have to listen to the radio to find out how the war is going ten miles away.

On the way up here I passed and visited briefly an old castle or palace of some German princes, now somewhat in disrepair but housing three real live princes and the princess. I didn't meet any of the royalty, but have no doubt that all were bloated and sloppy krauts. However, the place is like a picture, set in a wood, with landscaped grounds covered all over with statues in the most horrid Victorian style. The palace is surrounded by a moat with drawbridges and all that sort of thing, and is an enormous place built in a quadrangle around inner courtyards. It must have been quite a show place in its day, though definitely ornate rather than beautiful. The castles on the Rhine which are so famous are further up, and the lower part is nothing to get excited about.

We are fortunate in having a good house with furnace heat and electric lights. It has a fine bathroom too, but unfortunately the water system is not functioning. We have a pump in the basement, which is a help, but also a nuisance. I hope we will be here a few days longer before we again hit the sawdust trail, but one never knows.

Yesterday was a beautiful day, though a little cool for this time of the year. The Air force heavies were out on a big raid, and in just a few minutes watching I counted more than a hundred and fifty of them passing this one point. They were beautiful big silver ships, up so high they looked like toys and seemed to just float along. The fighter escorts were so high that they looked like little silver specks flashing in the sun. Today dawned foggy and

242

raw, but about noon it turned off into a beautiful day, just right to go somewhere. But all I did was stay here. Tomorrow I think we will move up to the next town, only a few miles from here and in even better shape. We already have our eyes on a house with a genuine bathtub, and hot water!

We are practically out of communication with our Headquarters, and the lack of mail is about the only disadvantage to that. It is funny how everybody dislikes Headquarters, and yet there are so many of them. We are very fortunate in that we usually operate in the field detached from any of them, and we are always griped when we get caught by one moving into town on us.

We keep pretty busy these days, and in spite of that have to leave a lot to be done by the outfits that come along after us. The war is just moving too fast to keep up with it. It is amazing to see the numbers of prisoners being brought in – great trailer trucks loaded with all that can be packed in standing and coming in long convoys. They are a miserable looking lot – I guess all prisoners are, but it must still be a relief to them to know that it is all over for them. I don't see how this can last much longer, or why, but apparently the Nazis are determined to drag everything in Germany down with them.

I was surprised to find that people in this vicinity seem the least hostile of any I have met in Germany; in fact, a lot of them seem glad to see us, and the kids have already started begging for chocolate and gum just like those in England, France, and everywhere else. The non-fraternization policy forbids giving it to them, but they must have had some luck somewhere, as they are all beginning to ask. I suppose it is because they were more or less bypassed by the war and got off with very little damage in these parts and hence have less reason to feel sore.

In spite of the work being interesting and plentiful, this life gets awfully monotonous, but then I think that the time will come one of these days that it will have been worth all the waiting and the long unhappy nights.

There has been no mail for several days now, and I don't

even know where my Headquarters is so I can't send and get it. I have settled down in a town and started to run it for our purposes, and the war has gone off and left me. I don't think anybody knows where I am, and I am sure nobody knows where we are supposed to be, especially ourselves.

We are living in the finest house I have been in Europe for the purposes of good living. It is very modern, with indirect lighting in some rooms, a tiled bath as big as an ordinary bedroom, overstuffed leather – upholstered furniture, and wonderful china, linen and other fittings. We are sleeping in feather beds made of some sort of down which is very comfortable and warm and must cost plenty of money. The people are evidently very well heeled and have a lot of snapshots of traveling in Switzerland or some other beautiful mountain country. They moved next door when they were dispossessed, and the woman is supervising the kitchen, waiting on the table, and cleaning up for us. This is probably heresy and a scandal, but she seems like a very nice person, not at all what Germans are supposed to be. I have no doubt that she is very proud of her home and is trying to look after it as best she can, and you would think that we were her guests instead of the enemy who kicked her out. She seems very cheerful and pleasant about the whole affair, and I guess we are at least doing her the favor of keeping the Russians from looting the place, in which event it would look more like a stable.

This town is untouched by the war, and a very nice comfortable-looking farming community. Today I drove over to a neighboring city, which is one of the big targets for bombing and has been repeatedly worked over since the heavy bombing started, besides being fought for street by street. It was in about the same shape as Aachen.

The most terrible sight you see over here is the thousands of forced workers who have recently been liberated – displaced persons as we call them. They are terribly undernourished, ragged, and dirty, and they have no homes, no money, nothing. The Army has moved too fast to bring up facilities to take care of them, and about all that can be done is to get them a little food, and not too much of that. They are a pitiful and yet a repulsive sight, filthy and broken in spirit. Their hatred of the Germans is a terrible thing, and I suppose that one has to see what was done to them to appreciate it. Here we see all nationalities, though Russians seem to be in the majority, and the Germans are really terrified of them. Their chickens are really coming home to roost, and they certainly have every reason to fear what may come to them. In spite of our best intentions, the American Army is more of a protection than a conqueror in the German eyes.

War news is better than could be anticipated – the only thing better would be to hear that it is all over. We are listening to our radios at every opportunity in the hope that the news will come any time, but they seem determined to finish themselves off. Maybe I will be writing you soon from Unter der Liinten. However, I really have little desire to go to Berlin; I would much rather get established in a quiet country town in nice country like we are now occupying. There is no chance that we will remain here, but I have hopes that we will get some such nice section of the country.

We have been enjoying beautiful spring weather, but I am afraid it is getting ready to rain again. The warm days have brought out lots of flowers, and there is a particularly pretty tree right across the street covered with blossoms. I don't know what it is. There are a lot of flowers around the house which I have seen at home, but I don't know the names.

There are days when this seems a long, discouraging pull, and this is one of them. My morale varies more or less directly with the mail service, and that is very poor too. Everything always seems to be confused, and there is always something else to do. On every hand over here you see nothing but misery and terrible-looking people. In this part of the country the Germans are in very good shape, but that will soon be different. It is hard to see what will be the end of it all. The foreign workers and prisoners are so miserable that you feel terribly sorry for them, and at the same time they are such a dirty, shiftless, broken, and lousy lot that they are completely repulsive, and one hates to be around them. Their home countries, the Russians particularly, don't seem to be worrying too much about them, and the Americans are too busy fighting the war.

I have obtained a very pretty little pistol that one of the Gestapo decided he didn't need any longer. It is a very nice job and practically new, but I still like the one at home better. I hope that after the war I will have no occasion to touch one again. Before I leave, I may pick up a good shotgun – the Belgian firms make some excellent ones – but there too I doubt that I will find anything I like better than those I have at home.

Capt. Hancock and Kinch stop at Beckum. They have lunch with Lt. Walker and the fellows and tell us that we are to leave our two towns this afternoon as soon as we can, stop over night and rendezvous at Oschersleben the following day. Lt. Walker's team leaves Beckum at 1500, stops off at Army and then proceeds to the town of Lemgo where we stay for the night.

Lt. Walkers team leaves at 0900 and arrive at Oschersleben at 1700. We all have chow at 2nd armored mess. The team is all together again and we get a billet and some rich manufactures home. We are told that we will leave the next morning for Braunschweig.

17 April

The town abounds with work and as usual we get reports from stolen bicycle to strong arm stuff. The biggest catch to date was brought in a S.A. Standartenfuhrur and a ortsgruppenleiter.

Twenty four PW's and internees are taken to TORNADO CP by Gikas and Mendoza. Thoumsin and Mendoza gets two SS obersturmbaunfuhrers, one was the highest official in the county. Miller and Gikas find a stock of gym suits and sweat suits of the SA and also a supply of daggers.

Business the same as usual, namely the office packed most of the time. Americans who came over here in 1938 and 1939 on the promise of jobs etc., and to visit continue to come in to see how they can return to the States. Numerous soldiers both British and American come in to see if they can get guns, daggers and souvenirs.

Miller and Gross still working on the Gestapo, building up material and getting information. CONQUER is starting to move in and the advance party is in and already set up. Lt. Harden and one of the fellows came in for information about a billet for the CONQUER team. Two of the fellows from 8ᵗʰ Armored Division also came in and picked up a few arrest forms.

Capt. Hancock helps Lt. Harden get the billet for CONQUER CIC. Miller and Gross are still working on the Gestapo. Office still full most of the day and we have more business than we can handle. Capt. Hancock goes down to Wolfenbuttle to see Capt. Gross of 2nd Armored who is in charge of this area and division for which we are working Braunschweig for.

Yesterday and today we were on the move, a tremendous jump of more than 150 miles. It was very interesting, more like a scenic trip than a military operation. First we had a prosperous, rolling farm country, then very pretty wooded hills, then great open farming plains like the west. The smaller towns are not usually damaged, but the larger industrial places are beaten absolutely to a pulp.

I am enclosing a post card of the hotel which we commandeered last night. If you will look closely at the lettering on the front, you can read that it was built in 1631. In spite of that it had been modernized and was quite comfortable. It was a picturesque old town with lots of old places like that. We also saw where the Pied Piper did his stuff. Now I am practically ready for a little drive to Berlin – it's no trip at all – but I understand that they aren't quite ready to receive me.

We are in a new town – actually had to move back to take this one, as we had got a little ahead of ourselves and couldn't go as far as we had expected. It is one of the better known air targets, and is really beaten to a pulp. I can't make up my mind whether or not it is worse than Aachen, but it is one of our better jobs. Nevertheless, we are living in a very good house with lights and water. We are quite comfortable, and the nice Germans have left lots of good wine and cognac for us. They drink some pretty vile stuff, though – the only good liquor they had came from France.

Here we have found the usual multitudes of foreign forced labor, and the first bunch of liberated American and British prisoners that I have encountered. Some of them have been prisoners for four or five years, and they are in pitiful shape. They have been fed just enough to keep them alive, and have had some horrible experiences. It is partly the result of German savagery and partly the result of not having it. It is very touching to see how glad they are to see us, and the real pleasure they get out of ordinary Army food, though I might say that the "ordinary" food we get up here is really something to marvel at. The other day I had breakfast with one of our most famous combat divisions, and had three fresh eggs for breakfast! That is not by any means normal, but it shows what a wonderful supply job is being done.

Harold Hancock is still my CO and does a very good job; he is still the same old Harold of the Health Haven, but he knows his business. I saw Ralph Harden a couple of days ago on my way up here and had a good time, as usual, giving him the berry about being "rear echelon," and inviting him up to see how the war is going. He usually follows right behind us, but neither of us is exactly up with Mauldin. However, I have actually shot at a German; didn't hit him but scared the hell out of him, which was about all I wanted to do and certainly all my pistol marksmanship is calculated to do at 100 yards – result 1 surrender.

There's no mail again today, but I guess I have been pretty lucky to get what I have, in view of our communications. We are scattered so far that it's a wonder they get it up at all.

We are awfully busy and will continue so for some time – in fact, as far ahead as I can see. We have got far enough along that all the Nazi big shots can no longer run away, and we are beginning to round up some. They are just as lousy and contemptible as small fry, and I don't see how they told them apart. They are yellow as gold for the most part and come slinking around like whipped dogs.

I wrote you the other day that I had a nice Gestapo pistol, but the funniest thing happened. It has turned into the nicest camera you ever saw and should neatly solve our post-war camera problems. It is a swell job, and I hope I will be able to get it home OK. It is a Rolleicord and uses a standard size film size "120," taking a picture approximately 2 ¼" x 2 ¼" without enlarging. It has a gadget to look in the top and focus it exactly and is remarkably accurate. All this came about because I had a pistol and a GI had a camera, and each wanted the other.

Another nice thing that has turned up is a little table radio about a foot long by six inches by eight inches. Unfortunately it is a Nazi radio and prefers to get the Wehrwolf or some station playing the Horst Wesel Lied.

That clipping about the jump boots is one of the best Mauldin has done, and I was very pleased with it. Unfortunately, jump boots are scarce as hen's teeth. I wear combat boots, which are similar in style, but not in beauty, being a rough finish. I am afraid that I am so used to GI shoes that I will never be able to wear anything else, but they are really comfortable.

Tonight I found how to get the water heater in our house percolating, and got a good hot bath. What a luxury a bath can be. German homes – at least the type we appropriate – have pretty good plumbing, better by far than the French or English, but not equal to ours.

This has been a long, hard day, and I am plenty tired. This is the largest town we have worked, and we got here early, so there was a lot to do. A lot of the big shots didn't get away, and we are busy night and day rounding them up. It is by far the most interesting place we have worked, and there is a terrible lot to do. However, Harden caught up with us today, and that is usually our signal to hit the road, so I guess we will have to find us another town.

The past few days have been beautiful, and spring seems to be with us, though it is pretty cool at night. There is nothing pretty about a bombed out city, but around the edges and out in the country the fruit trees are blooming, and things are turning green.

All of us were shocked to hear of Ernie Pyle's death. Very few men have made themselves so universally liked. I was also shocked to hear that Roosevelt had died. Even those of us who disagree with him felt that it was a tragedy, particularly in view of his successor.

Just got another picture of our last home. Note the sign on the tree and the old soldier leaning against the fence.

The character walking down the street is a typical refugee. This was one of the nicest houses I have been in Europe, not the largest or most elaborate, but thoroughly modern and livable.

We continue to be awfully busy but feel that we are accomplishing something. This work can be very interesting when things are going right, but sometimes we almost go crazy with stupid interruptions. Everyone takes us for a general information service, and I'll bet I answer a thousand fool questions every day about things that are no concern of mine.

This is a lonesome Saturday night – no place to go, nothing to do, nobody to love me. I am awfully tired of this kind of life, but there isn't much I can do about it except long for the day there will be no more lonesome days or nights.

CONQUER team begins operations here. Lt. Harden and Connelly comes in to see about the Division of work between the two teams. Major Ault and Reese also comes in. Capt. Hancock goes out to see Major Ault about the division of work and it is decided that they would handle all of CONQUER'S security problems, and have nothing to do with the Gestapo. Miller and Gross would handle all that. Gikas and Kinch picked up a character named Bahr who was an employee of the Gestapo.

Lt. Hardin leaves the office and this team takes over the whole town and will handle the work that CONQUER CIC would handle. Quite a few people came in denouncing being Wehrwolfs.

Office is jammed all day. One of the frequent occurrences now is for women to come in and ask where her husband is. Lt. Fritz from TAC comes in to see Lt. Walker and Capt. Hancock. Young is assigned to handle the Wehrwolf cases, and it looks like he will have plenty to do.

CONQUER moves to their new town. Miller and Gross still developing lead on the Gestapo set up. Capt. Hancock and Lt. Walker decide that we need a stenographer in the office to help get caught up on our records.

Meyersberg and Thoumsin are at work getting the Sachs Bunker straightened out. Capt. Hancock, Lt. Bauer and the Chief of Police have a conference to come to an understanding regarding the arrest made by the city police.

Meyersburg and Thoumsin get the evidence to prove a Voighlander official is an Abwehr agent. Miller and Gross have a field day and get three Gestapo agents. Capt. Hancock hires a girl, Elizabeth Wachtelborn who is an American citizen and comes from St. Louis to work in the office. She will start Monday morning.

Air Corp outfit brings in Standartenfuhrer. Meyersburg and Thoumsin working on the abwehr case.

Miller and Gross leave town to pick up what they think will be one of the prize catches in their Gestapo case. They return in the evening with the news that the Braunschweig police have completely bundled up this angle of the case and as a consequence they lost their man.

Elizabeth Wachtelborn, an American citizen, starts to work in the office.

This is a picture of our billet in Braunschweig Germany it was formerly the home and garage of the owner of an automotive electric shop it was an ideal billet if there ever was one.

He had a 8 stall garage in the rear of the house so we had room enough to park all of our jeeps and trailers inside. The living quarters were large enough to accommodate all of the team personnel and we had a large dining room and also a day room. Most of the other buildings in the area were pretty badly damaged but this one was practically untouched.

We all remember this old church. We went by it every day on our way to the office, as the picture indicates this was about the only skeleton of a building that was left standing in this vicinity.

This is a postcard and a picture of the Court House square showing the extensive damage done in this area.

We have piddled around until Headquarters caught up with us, and that had the good result of bringing mail, though that was about the only advantage of being near a Headquarters.

It looks as if we might stay here a while, so I have un-packed some stuff and settled down a bit. That will probably be a signal for us to leave at once. We are not set up as luxuriously here as we have been in some places, but have a very comfortable house which is well suited to our needs and quite modern. I am rather pleased at the chance to stay here, as this is one of the most interesting places we have worked, and we are off to a good start. There is a terrific amount of work to be done in Germany.

This is a picture of Charlie Grainger, Bob Conohan and one of the British Field Security Police standing in the square in which our office was located. The picture is of interest only because we were standing in the exact spot where Hitler had made a speech just three years before. It sort of shows in what a short time the course of history can radically change.

Young and Paul pick up a new motorcycle from an SS man.

It looks as if this just isn't the night to write. I just had another interruption. I'm getting so I throw people in jail as casually as I say "good morning."

Tonight I opened my last package of your Ward Bryant fudge. It came just before we took off from Munchen-Gladbach, and we have been moving so much since that I haven't unpacked enough to get at it. It is remarkable how well it keeps, and it is excellent. Everybody enjoys it, and if you have time to fix up some more, it will be most welcome. The big pecans on top made it very pretty, besides being good.

We are now enjoying our own mess, which is a great convenience and allows me an extra hour of most welcome sleep in the morning. In spite of the horrors of front-line soldiering, I have consistently slept later since I have been in Europe than I ever did at home. Even in the GI outfits that is true, in comparison with Army life at home.

Just to show that virtue is rewarded, one of our German department, the Gestapo, found that he no longer needs his pistol where he is going, so like the nice fellow he is, he contributed it to me. So now I have my nice pistol back and my camera too.

War news is looking up again, and now they have got around to talking opening about how unconditional is unconditional surrender, so maybe we are actually reaching the stage where we can safely say it won't be long.

We are awfully busy, and have been having pretty good hunting, all things considered. We have met better luck here than at any place we have been, and we are somewhat encouraged about the prospects for future operations. There is a tremendous amount of work to be done, and I can see why it is going to take a long time. Still, there seems to be more reason than might be expected to believe that the job will not be as hard as we anticipated.

Chapter 15

Germany – V-E DAY
May 1945

Thoumsin and Meyersberg finishing the Ruhland and Abwehr case.

Capt. Foster, one of his Lt's. and three civilians came in this afternoon. They made arrangements with us to hold one of their prisoners until he can be turned over to the 8th Armoured Division. Big news of the day was the unconditional surrender of the German Armies in Italy and western Austria.

Miller and Gross pick up another Gestapo agent in the afternoon, during the evening one of our informants brings another Gestapo man in and turns him over to us at our billet. Young's motorcycle has a flat tire and when Paul goes to have it fixed he finds more holes in the tires.

A group of about a dozen American PW's who were liberated by the Russians turn up at the office looking for some help to get to the proper authorities in order to be evacuated. Two of them had been prisoners for fifteen months.

Gross and Miller are still working on the Gestapo angle of this business. Miller has some leads for today. Thoumsin and Meyersburg have completed the Ruhland case and are now making up the memorandum. Young still working on the Wehrwolf case.

Sunday, half of the fellows off in the morning and half in the afternoon. Lt. Beebe said that the 2nd Armoured had picked up a Gestapo man by the name of Walter Hildebrandt. Miller and Gross had furnished them with the information relative to subjects location. The office is plenty busy today, as it usually is. Grainger went back today to pick up a suspect whom he had seen yesterday but did not pick up because subject had a broken leg. Today Grainger found out that last night subject stole a bicycle and beat it. Radio Luxemburg announced the end of the war at 1800 hours. Later in the evening the radio stated that tomorrow will be VE Day and tomorrow Wednesday will be a holiday.

I got your package mailed March 21, and it is choice. It had cheese, nuts, and sea food, along with beaten biscuits, candy, and chewing gum, and I never got a package in better shape. Last night I got into the cheese and tonight the smoked oysters; Chaplain McDonald back at Verdun used to talk about how good they are, and he wasn't kidding. Tonight, quite by accident, I picked up the best bottle of wine I've had in Germany, which went nicely with the oysters.

We just heard over the radio that Hitler is dead. It is great news if true, but the scum is probably trying to cover up while he runs away like the rest of the Nazi heroes.

This has been another day of turmoil, trying to do three or four things at once and talk to somebody while I am trying to think of something else. At the end of the day I am usually thoroughly confused and worn out, and often cannot see that I have accomplished much. Last night I had to go out after supper to chase an SS man who, when I caught him, turned out not to be one after all, a not unusual result, particularly when people rush up with something that can't wait for a minute. I hate to turn people down when they are trying to be helpful, but as a general thing amateur spy-catchers are about as useful, pleasant, and helpful as a carbuncle.

Last night the British Military Government detachment had the whole team over to dinner, and it was really quite a party. They have taken over a hotel with the complete staff, and the service was something fine. Furthermore, they have in one way and another acquired all the fine wine in this part of the country, and they were not a bit stingy with it. They are an unusually nice bunch of fellows and a lot of fun after you get to know them and they unbend a little. It was a large evening, and I didn't get home until about one o'clock, being then and there somewhat the worse for wear. This morning I was off duty, and I celebrated by sleeping until eleven o'clock, at which time the results of the celebration had worn off somewhat.

This afternoon I went out to Headquarters. While there I visited with Harden, who was in fine spirits. He is wondering whether he will stay here or go to the Orient, and I don't think he cares much, as a trip to the Orient would probably give him some time at home. However, I don't think I could stand to leave again.

I understand that today censorship was called off except for some minor particulars, and the Army is going back into dress uniform, so I guess peace is settling down upon us. I am now getting anxious to get to the place where we will operate permanently and get started on the last job – at least I hope we will have only one more place to clean up. It will be nice to get to a place where we can unpack and know that whatever work we do will be building for our own future operations and not someone else's.

We continue to be very busy, and I think we could work for six months on what we have on hand now if nothing new came in, as it does every day. It is a very interesting operation, but there appears to be no end to it. Tomorrow is Sunday, and I hope to be able to find a church service in the morning, and if it is a pretty day will try to get some more pictures, as I have captured quite a nice supply of film.

We are settling down to a lot of work for a while, as there is a lot to be straightened out here. It seems that everywhere we go we are the first to try to do things with some method and to keep records, so everything is always a mess when we start out.

I see that Congressman Gore from Tennessee has introduced a bill to send wives over here, so you can tell Took that it is no use; Gore has beaten him to my vote for President. The only way he can salvage my support is to pass a law to draft the FBI to take my place.

Walker & Hardin

V-E Day the office is not very busy. The air forces, 9th, part of which is stationed outside of town, put on a demonstration over the town, flying in formation, they made the letters V and E and the U.S.A.. Lt. Hardin and Reese from CONQUER came up and stayed for supper. Lt. Hardin paid us last month wages. After supper Thoumsin took a group of pictures of the gang.

Picture of team members taken at Braunschweig, Germany
Rear row: Harold Hancock, Christos Gikas, Wesley Young, William Miller. Middle row: Frank Mendoza, Serrvious Thoumsin, Charles Stewart, Paul Gross, Paul (Dutch Army), Joe Nartier (Dutch Army), George Walker

One of the boys just gave me this sheet of stationery, saying he had been saving it especially for V-E Day. We have been looking forward to this day so long that it has come as a sort of anti-climax. For one thing, the prolonged negotiations and the delay between the event and the formal announcement took the pep out of the day.

Last night, by way of celebration, I opened a small bottle of pre-war Haig & Haig that I had carried all the way from Glasgow across four countries and half of Germany awaiting this occasion. It was excellent, but not nearly enough.

Tonight in honor of the occasion we all got out and got a group picture, then took a bunch of individual shots. I took up a roll of 12. You never saw so much photographic equipment in your life. I'll bet there was $3000 worth of cameras in the yard at one time.

I am enclosing a snapshot which one of the boys took of our camera club. V-E Day doesn't promise any immediate change for us.

Gikes goes to MG Court to act as a Greek interpreter. Miller and Gross get some more good leads relative to their Gestapo work and if they come through, tomorrow promises to be a big day.

Conohan and Bauer have to go to MG Court on the Eckart concealed weapon case. Defendant found guilty and gets three years in prison. Gikas goes to MG Court on the hidden dynamite case which is a poor case to start with and it is also poorly presented, with the result that the dynamite charge cannot be proven, but defendant also had ammunition in his home, on this charge he was found guilty and fined 800 RM. Miller and Gross find that their leads of yesterday paid off. They picked up a number of Gestapo men and S.D. men.

Gregg and Callegora of the CONQUER team move into the billet with us. Gross and Miller go out on a Gestapo call in the evening that proves to be a false alarm. Gikas, Meyersburg, Joe, Kinch, Kinch's friend Lou and Conohan also go out in the evening for four SS men and they all prove to be false alarms.

Young got a policeman on a false fragenbogen and found him with a concealed weapon, it promises to be a good case.

Today is Mother's Day and a really beautiful day. Not much business at the office is as to be expected because today is Sunday. In the afternoon, Chris, Bauer, Walker and Conohan go out in the country and get some eggs. A telephone is now installed in the office, so they can get us at night if necessary.

Today is the same as all of the other Mondays, namely we are busier than "all get out." There is a big line waiting for us when we get here in the morning. Miller and Gross go out and move Mrs. Kuhl and Stalinsky and their children. Meyersburg and Thoumsin are getting ready to close the Kuhl case. The weather still continues to be the tops, it is hard to stay inside.

Col. Clemens calls this morning at 815 looking for the

Captain. Meyersburg and Thoumsin still working on the Abwehr case. Miller and Gross go out to a small town near Braunschweig after a Gestapo man, only to find that he had turned himself in this morning as only an SS man, and was subsequently released. As a result, Miller, Gross and part of regiment from the 83rd have to comb the country side to try and find him, with no results. Miller and Gross make arrangements with the 83rd to search subject's home at 11 tonight and seven in the morning and pick up subject if he is there. They then came back to the billet at 9 P.M.

Gross and Miller are notified that the fellow they went out to pick up yesterday has been apprehended. This evening is the pay off; Gross was taking a cot down to the office for Bill Miller and on the way down he recognized a Gestapo man walking with three other men. He stopped to pick him up and found out that all four were Gestapo men on their way to the office to turn themselves in. Dr. Kuhl, the head of the local office and Stalinsky were among the four. Gikas is out returning Mrs. Kuhl and the others to their homes. Miller and Gross are at the jail interrogating last nights haul.

Gross and Miller are still working at the jail on the four Gestapo men that turned in the night before last. Book one and the book of lists are finally brought up to date.

Today isn't busy being Saturday, and nothing big comes into the office today. All of us have to have a profile physical exam by next Thursday. The British 103rd MG detachment gives us a big party in the evening, wonderful food and plenty to drink. The fellows did not get in until after midnight and all of them are pretty well tanked up.

Today is Sunday and all of the fellows feel like resting today after last night's little party.

Miller and Gross are working on the Gestapo report.

Hold a drawing at noon to see who wins the trip to Paris. Gikas wins, but gives the trip to Thoumsin who will leave tomorrow noon. Lt. Walker gets his orders confirming his promotion to 1st Lt. Miller and Gross finish their Gestapo report; it contains 15 pages when finished. Then in the evening Miller and Gross go out and pick up 4000 more marks that belonged to a stay behind agent. At supper time we notice that our motorcycle is gone.

Luxembourg

Dear Dave,

The afternoon's mail brought a letter April 19th. ETO mail has always been slow, but I think that the present instance sets some kind of record.

Enjoyed the snaps of the puppies very much---they are certainly a fine looking bunch of hopefuls with what I think are extra nice heads. Having obtained permission of the copyright owner mine shall bear the name of Beau Essigs Becky. I sent full shipping instructions to Mr. Walker. If my last letter takes the usual ETO course, he should have it by the fourth of July! Here we go again:

> Hugh F. Elliott
> c/o Dr. S.W. Haigler's Dog and Cat Hospital
> Delmar Blvd and North and South Road
> University City, (5), Missouri.

The Doc is a good bird hunter and can check her to see if she made the trip in good shape or whether she needs a Bromo-Seltzer. I assure you that he will also return the crate by the same truck that brings the pup! I am quite enthusiastic about the young lady and will try to arrange things so I can return home and supervise her education.

Everything here is running along fine. I have always enjoyed Luxembourg and don't know how I could be better off in the ETO. Don't think anyone who was in the armored force should ever after be called a rear echelon so and so though and am prepared to take up that crack the first time I see the Lord of the Walker manor! Have lots of room here, plenty of rations, and a small amount of spirits on hand usually-so if you can stop your self proclaimed spearheading I can offer a few days rest and recuperation here!

Moved here about the first of last month and was told of leaving Namur and coming here and related how the AF did not wish to jeopardize the non-fraternization policy by taking Hopper to Germany and how I had to drive him to Paris—a heck of a chore!

Had a little trouble last Saturday night when my jeep was stolen, but being an expert investigator I organized a search party Sunday and recovered it some forty miles south of here and caught the culprit red handed! Quite a character, threw the top away, busted my handcuffs getting them off the steering wheel, tore a lot of the wiring out-just plain damned meaness. Gave him a free ride back to the scene of his crime and tossed him in the pokey.

This point system leaves me cold—about 15 degrees or points too cold. Hopper is gloating over his 89 points but I think it will be several months before they get around to him. How do you stand?

That about concludes the broadcast from this department for this evening. Thanks again for the lovely little lady and lets hear from you again soon.

Fourth Platoon reports the arrival of the Fields and two letters from "The Reich" dated 27 April and 5 May 1945. Thank you again for the Fields, these were an interesting assortment. (Note in one of them that Mr. Hawse recovered ZERO some thirty miles from where he was lost-sounds like a fox-hound, doesn't it!)

No late dope on the Frierson rumor-will send on any further dope received on this point. Have written for complete details, but no answer to date. Apparently it will turn out to be as unfounded as the Major Hopper—Hero story.

The thought that with the coming of peace in Europe, redeployment, etc. that you might be able to spend a few days rest and recuperation here in Luxembourg. Have the same old stand that the flying snoopers have always had in this town and if you are unfamiliar with its location, inquiry at the town CIC or almost any pretty girl you encounter on the street will reveal its location. (The latter condition grew out of Hopper's occupancy of the home for a short period.) Am presently moderately supplied with spirits- and not of the vile Heinie champagne variety either. What can you do about this?

Contrasted with your heavy schedule, I have been kept only moderately busy here but everyone seems happy so I am not going around trying to stir up trouble. Not many spies have fallen to my trusty six shooter in recent weeks but neither have any been positively identified in our various CPs. In a recent report to our Hqs I stated among other things "no new cases of espionage have been brought to the attention of these agents during the period of this report." Was interested in a squib which appeared in Readers Digest the other day. It seems that a group of Heinies were denying that the majority of Germans were in favor of Der Fuhrer and all reports to the contrary were "dirty Jewish, communistic lies."

That about concludes the broadcast from this department for this evening. Thanks again for the lovely little lady and lets hear from you again soon.

Lots of luck, Hugh

Chapter 16

The Braunschweig Gestapo Report
18 May & 28 May 1945

Dearest Son,

Two years ago today was the high light of my life. It was Frances' Baccalaureate Day, and in the morning Daddy and I had all of you with us at the morning church service. I was fairly bursting with pride and I am deeply grateful to have been given that hour. That memory is one of my most cherished possessions.

Yesterday was a good day – three letters from you, two to me written on the fifth and V-E Day respectfully. The latter was a most splendid letter and one I shall reread and then read again. The newspaper is most interesting – though of course I can only manage the English version. I am watching to see if D will attempt the French side. One is English, one French, one German, is the fourth Dutch? We do not recognize that at all.

Daddy finally made an extra effort and sent Elliot's pup. He kept the prospective Blue Beltons. Freckles and the pup make such a pretty picture - laid stretched out on the grass in the shade of the pecan tree and both asleep. Freckles is tied so she can't take the daughter off hunting.

Please excuse this worse than usual scrawl – yesterday afternoon Rochie stayed to help me and we pulled grass and weeds all afternoon. I could scarce move this morning when I first woke up. But today is special cleaning day and Priscilla came to help us do the dining room.

Now – 2 PM- it is all clean except the oak china cabinet – all the rest of the room has been scrubbed, the china and silver all washed and polished, and the wall cupboards too – and I'm TIRED.

D is working on some Home Improvement stuff

for Daddy.

The madonna lilies are at their peak today. I want to cut them late this afternoon and take them to the cemetery for Francis.

Bye now – always I love you,
Mamma

A picture of our office and the British Military Government Building next door. The two fellows standing by the Jeep are Bill Miller and Paul Gross. They were just getting ready to leave for their days work. They were working on their Gestapo investigation.

This is a picture of the building in which the SS troops had offices, the front of the building leaves a false impression it appears to be in fairly good shape when in reality it was so badly damaged that it was almost impossible to move around inside.

A picture of the entrance to our office. The window at the right is the window of the record section of our office. Elizabeth Wabhtelborn (An American citizen who was a resident of Braunschweig) who worked as a typist for us and Bruce Harbottel of the British Field Security Police can be seen looking out of the window. Chris and the little girl that used to call every day to get her stick of gum or piece of chocolate candy can be seen sitting on the bunker out in front of the window.

Questioning about the motorcycle seems to get us no-where.

Miller and Gross go down to the Hartz Mts. and pick up two more Gestapo agents and the mistress of one of them. They are pretty tough cookies, and when Miller and Gross takes them to the jail here in Braun-schweig Dr. Kuhl looked at them, then at Miller and Gross, then asked Miller and Gross if they picked those two characters up. Then they answered in the affirmative, Dr. Kuhl said, "good, the City of Braun-schweig owes you two a vote of thanks."

Today is evacuation day and we ship out thirty-five men and some of them are really tough cookies. Young goes to Court on the fragenbogen cases; one of the defendants gets eighteen months for falsifying the fragenbogen.

Miller, Gross and Gikas have to go back down to the Hartz to pick up the money of Heyser and Meyer. In the afternoon they go over to the jail and both Heyser and Meyer decide to talk.

HEADQUARTERS NINTH US Army
309th CIC Detachment
Tactical Reserve Team No. 4
APO 339   US Army

Braunschweig, Germany
18 May 1945

MEMORANDUM FOR THE OFFICER IN CHARGE

SUBJECT: GESTAPO of Braunschweig.
RE: Report of Investigation.

On 20 April 1945 these Agents initiated investigation of Braunschweig GESTAPO personnel and submit the following report reflecting the result of said investigation to date.

There were two main GESTAPO offices in the city of Braunschweig. These were located at Leopoldstrasse 23/25 and at Friedrich Wilhelm Löperstrasse 20. Across from the latter location at NO.52 Friedrich Wilhelm Löperstrasse there existed a sub-office for the use of informants (V-men) and to the rear of this was located a GESTAPO air-raid shelter equipped with telephone exchange and other operational facilities.

A search of these premises revealed that all records had apparently been removed or destroyed. However, in examining the office at Friedrich Wilhelm Löperstrasse 20 these Agents discovered a few personnel card records of GESTAPO Agents with names beginning with the letters D, E and F, the same having obviously been overlooked when the balance of the personnel files were removed by the GESTAPO. These names plus two or three others obtained during the search of all sites constituted the original leads for investigation. These were supplemented on 22 April 1945 by a list of some GESTAPO personalities obtained by CONQUER CIC from one Herman Gustav RAUTMANN, former doorman at GESTAPO Headquarters at Leopoldstrasse 23/25, who had been picked up by local police and turned over to CIC. Investigation of the original leads in Braunschweig proved negative and clearly disclosed that prior to the arrival of the American in the city a mass evacuation of GESTAPO personnel had occurred. This was soon confirmed by subsequent investigation, the earliest definite information being elicited through interrogation of one Rudi (Rolf) LEICHTWEISS, a KRIPO Kriminal Kommissar of Braunschweig. LEICHTWEISS, who had been arrested by reason of his status as SS Hauptsturmfuhrer but subsequently released because he held only nominal rank, was interrogated by these agents on 21 and 22 April 1945 and voluntarily revealed details of the evacuation. This information, supplemented by further data obtained from him and through detailed interrogation of apprehended GESTAPO officials, including Dr. Gunther KUHL, Chief of the Braunschweig GESTAPO, and from other sources, resulted in the revelation of the following details.

EVENTS PRECEDING EVACUATION. The events immediately leading up to evacuation begin with happenings transpiring from about 1 April 1945 at which time and thereafter messages and orders were received at GESTAPO Headquarters over the teletype from the Reichssicherheitsamt in Berlin. These embodied information concerning the location of the advancing American spearheads and divers orders of a general nature indicating the course to be taken by GESTAPO personnel in the event of a continued American advance eastward. The messages reflected that the lives of all GESTAPO personnel and their families were threatened; that everyone must aid in the defense of Germany; that food and weapons were to be gathered and stored in hiding places for future use; that the GESTAPO was to let the enemy overrun Braunschweig and adjoining territory and then were to use all means to hinder and harass the Americans through sabotage and other methods. Prior to the teletype messages evacuation plans of a general nature had been forwarded to the GESTAPO from the Reichssicherheitsamt. Reference to these plans was included in the teletype messages which indicated that time had come to perfect the same and be prepared for evacuation.

The details of the evacuation plan were discussed at a number of meetings held between Dr. Joseph KREUTZER, SS

Standartenfuhrer and Inspector of the Sicherheitspolizei in Braun-schweig, and Dr. KUHL at the former's office in Breizemeratrasse 42, Braunschweig. At the first of these discussions was present a representative of the Reichssicherheitsamt. These conferences, at which general plans were discussed, were followed by meetings in GESTAPO Headquarters attended by both GESTAPO and KRIPO personnel. At this time it may be noted that about 4 April 1945 Dr. Kuhl assumed a new position created by the Reichssicherheit-samt, viz., Chief of the Sicherheitspolizei in Braunschweig. This position was created in view of the emergency and gave him ju-risdiction over both GESTAPO and KRIPO although he remained subject to orders from his superior, Inspector KREUTZER.

The meetings in GESTAPO Headquarters were attended by Dr. KUHL, his chief assistant Carl DIRKS, Heinz Gunther EN-GELMANN, Kriminalrat and chief of the KRIPO and the follow-ing GESTAPO members: Hermann SCHARFE, Kriminal Ober-sekretär; Fritz FLINT, Kriminal Kommissar; Polizeirat (FNU) STRROHMEYER. At one of these meetings the heads of the GE-STAPO sub-office in Bad Harzburg, Watenstedt and Salzgitter also were present. They were: Leo KOWITZKE, Kriminal Inspector, Bad Harzburg; Albert MEYER, Kriminal Inspector, Watenstedt; Fritz RAABE, Kriminal Obersekretär, Salzgitter. According the Dr. KUHL, he assigned the details connected with the evacuation to his assistant, DIRKS, and to SCHARFE who became his right hand man. The evacuation plan involved the issuance of false cre-dentials and this was handled by KRIPO Chief ENGELMANN. All details in connection with the distribution of money was taken care of by STROHMEYER and the latter's assistant Franz BAU-ER, Kriminal Inspector. According to plan, each evacuee was to be given 1500 marks while others, left behind on missions, were to receive 2000 marks each. Dr. KUHL was not certain as to the exact total amount involved but guessed that the amount received from the Braunschweig Police Cashier for all evacuation and mis-sion purposes was 80,000 or 90,000 marks.

On 9 April 1945, the situation having become tense, Dr. KUHL called a meeting of all GESTAPO personnel at which he stated that their lives and those of their immediate families were at stake; he informed them that a secret order of General Eisenhower had been captured which indicated that all personnel connected with the Sicherheitedienst and GESTAPO, together with their families, would be shot; that there was no alternative for them except to follow orders; that evacuation plans had been completed and that the evacuated personnel would be divided into groups and assigned to certain territory to carry out certain missions. In general terms, Dr. KUHL explained that orders had been received from Berlin directing the GESTAPO to operate behind the American lines and to harass and hinder the enemy wherever possible. This proposed activity for the GESTAPO was given the official name of "Buntschuh" (same meaning as Wehrwolf).

During his interrogation Dr. KUHL disclosed to these Agents that the alleged captured secret order of General Eisenhower was never seen by him but that he was advised of the same by Dr. Kreutzer, Inspector the Sicherheitspelizei.

Following the general meeting of the GESTAPO personnel, there was a meeting of department heads, including KRIPO Chief ENGELMANN, and group leaders were appointed. Actual evacuation commenced on 10 April 1945. This evacuation, hereinafter referred to in detail, did not involve any women personnel; they and certain older GESTAPO and KRIPO employees along with others who held minor positions and some who were deemed unsuitable for evacuation or missions were discharged prior to evacuation and advised to leave Braunschweig.

ISSUANCE OF FALSE CREDENTIALS. As previously noted, the evacuation plan and the execution of the proposed GESTAPO missions involved the issuance of false credentials. This detail was given to KRIPO Chief ENGELMANN. It called for the issuance of new civilian credentials (Kennkarten) in place of official credentials. These Kennkarten, bearing the signature of one GRUNKORN and signed by him for the Police President. Braunschweig, contained a false name of the individual's own choosing and reflected an occupation other than GESTAPO or KRIPO. Specimens of these Kennkarten were submitted on 23

April 1945 for transmission to CIB for inspection and dissemination of information concerning the same.

On 25 April 1945 these Agents arrested Ernest GRŰNKORN, signer of the new Kennkarten. Interrogation of Subject revealed that he was discharged from the Wehrmacht on 17 January 1945, his discharge having been effected by request of Branuschweig Police President FUCHS. Subject explained that prior to his entry into the Wehrmacht on 3 May 1941 he was Oberregierungarat and assistant to the then Braunschweig Police President; that when he was discharged from the Wehrmacht FUCHS, whom he knew previously from the Braunschweig SCHUPO and who only became Police President in the latter part of 1944, advised him that he needed his services as legal assistant and for this reason had effected his discharge from the Wehrmacht.

GRŰNKORN stated that he resumed his police duties on 22 January 1945; that on about 5 or 6 April 1945 he was given a batch of new blank Kennkarten to sign, possibly 100 or 120 as he recalled, with the explanation that they were to be issued in place of official police credentials. He declared that he regarded this procedure as unusual and advised Police President FUCHS that he should obtain approval of higher police authority. According to Subject, FUCHS contacted the HSS-PF in Braunschweig and received the answer that the execution of those Kennkarten was a military order and to proceed therewith; GRŰNKORN thereupon proceeded to sign the Kennkarten which were completely blank. He expressed complete ignorance of the later use, distribution and ultimate possession of the new credentials. He himself possessed a previously executed proper Kennkarten in his own true name. Interrogation of Subject and further investigation indicated the probable veracity of his story and he was released.

These Agents had been informed that in some cases Wehrpasses had been exchanged for red-colored AUSMUSTRUNGSSCHEINE or INVALID cards donating exemption from military service by reason of physical or mental disability. However, investigation and interrogation has failed to establish proof of that fact. In one instance, an arrested suspect admitted having possessed a falsified FUHRERSCHEIN (Driver's License) issued to correspond with the false name on his new Kennkartens.

It appears that the distribution of the new Kennkarten was effected unmethodically. They were made available to GESTA-PO and KRIPO personnel at their convenience and were filled in by the individual. At this point it may be noted that some of these Kennkarten and Fuhrerschein were apparently obtained by individuals from other localities; further details in connection therewith are presently unknown.

STAY-BEHIND MISSIONS. In accordance with Reichssicherheitsamt orders, prevision had been made to leave behind in Braunschweig certain personnel to accomplish assigned missions. It appears that these assignments were made by Assistant GESTA-PO Chief DIRKS. Investigation has revealed the existence of 4 independent groups of KRIPO and GESTAPO personnel to whom such missions had been assigned.

Group 1. This group consisted of GESTAPO Agent Karl MACKE, in charge; (FNU) WISEE, GESTAPO messenger; Wilhelm OTTO, KRIPO beamter; and Kurt WENZEL, KRIPO Angestellter. The first information concerning this group was elicited by these Agents during interrogation of OTTO who had been denounced as a GESTAPO Agent. Preliminary questioning revealed OTTO'S KRIPO status and his admission that he had not been evacuated along with other eligible KRIPO personnel created a suspicion that he had been left behind on a mission. Further interrogation drew his admission that he, MACKE, WENZEL and a fourth man from the GESTAPO whom he did not know (later identified as WIESE) were assigned to the duty of supervising the activities of the Volkasturm. He stated that he and WENZEL had been given 16 Panzerfausts for use of the group; that, after the GESTAPO had evacuated, he and WENZEL buried the Panzerfausts, after removing the fuses, and abandoned their mission.

On 22 April 1945 these Agents arrested WENZEL at his home in Braunschweig a few hours after his return from hiding out in another part of the city. He admitted his mission but asserted his intention not to execute the same. Subject corroborated

OTTO'S statement as to the disposition of the Panzerfausts and pointed out the place on the grounds of the Giliesmarode Hospital in Braunschweig where they had hidden their pistols and KRIPO credentials, which were recovered.

Both OTTO and WENZEL were carrying new Kennkarten when arrested. OTTO'S was issued in the name of Wilhelm OTTMER while WENZEL'S were the name of Kurt WEGENER.

The third member of this group, Karl MACKE, was found to have committed suicide. Investigation, including examination of the death certificate, interrogation of a doctor who signed same, also subject's parents and relatives, revealed that MACKE hung himself in the attic of his home on 12 April 1945.

During the investigation of MACKE'S death, the name of the fourth and last member of this group was established as (FNU) WIESE, GESTAPO messenger. WIESE'S whereabouts is presently unknown.

Group 2. This group consisted of the following three KRIPO members: Heinrich AUSCHRA, Kriminal Obersekretär: Walter ZEHME, Kriminal Sekretär; Hermann LANGERWICH, Kriminal Sekretär. It appears that on 6 April 1945 Assistant GESTAPO Chief DIRKS ordered this trio to engage in the following proposed mission; They were each given the sum of 2000 marks with instructions to immediately disappear in the vicinity of Wolfenbuttel and then to return to Braunschweig in the event the Americans overran the city and there to engage in acts of sabotage; they were also advised to hire others to effect their mission; AUSCHRA was made leader of the group.

Investigation revealed that AUSCHRA advised the others to meet him in his apartment in BRAUNSCHWEIG on 18 April 1945 and not to do anything in the meantime. It appears that AUSCHRA returned to Braunschweig on 16 April 1945 and contacted ZEHME. It was decided to wait until the return of LANGERWICH on the 18th and then to report to the KRIPO in Braunschweig. It further appears that on the 18th LANGERWICH did not appear and that on said date AUSCHRA and ZEHME reported to the Braunschweig Police and advised of their mission and the money received therefor.

These Agents questioned AUSCHRA and ZEHME on 5 May 1945. At this time both had resumed their employment with KRIPO. Both said that they never had any intention of carrying out DIRKS orders. These Agents checked their story, including their reporting to the Police on the 18th and investigation indicated their probable lack of intent to execute their proposed mission in addition to verifying the fact that they had reported to the Police on the 18th. Each turned over to these Agents the sum of 2000 marks received from DIRKS and under the circumstances no action was taken against them. Thereafter both AUSCHRA and ZEHME were arrested by Agent Young of this Detachment for making false statements in their fragebogens and are presently awaiting trial by Military Government on that account.

The whereabouts of LANGERWICH, the third member of the group, is presently unknown. A check at his home in Braunschweig and the home of friends in Neindorf was negative. However, his wife was contacted in Braunschweig and stated that he disappeared before the arrival of the Americans and was not heard from since. He had given her 500 marks from the money received for his mission and this was turned over to these Agents.

Group 3. This group was also composed of three KRIPO members who similarly received 2000 marks each for the accomplishment of their mission. They are: Karl VOGT, Kriminal Sekretär, leader; Karl KASTEN, Kriminal Sekretär; Reinhard ROHRMAN, Kriminal Angestellter.

KASTEN and ROHRMAN have been arrested by these Agents. On questioning, KASTEN admitted that the trio had been given a mission by assistant GESTAPO chief DIRKS on 6 April 1945 but denied knowledge of the purpose of details thereof, stating that VOGT, the group leader, never revealed the same to him. ROHRMAN declared that his understanding of their mission was that they were to return to Braunschweig after the Americans overran the city and were to observe the actions of German civilians so that they might be properly dealt with later on.

Information for other sources indicates that the missions of

Groups 2 and 3 were similar. At the present time these Agents are following up leads on VOGT who, if apprehended, should clarify the exact nature of the Group's mission. Of the 2000 marks given to ROHRMAN, 1500 marks were recovered 2000 marks were recovered from KASTEN.

Group 4. This three-man group consisted of the following GESTAPO personnel; Hermann KADEN, Kriminal Angestellter, Salzgitter office; Hubert (?) BREMEN, Bad Harzburg office; Wolfgang WIEZKE, Police Inspector apprentice, Braunschweig office.

According to WIEZKE, who has been arrested by these Agents, he, Fritz RAABE, head of the Salzgitter office, and BREMEN were called into assistant GESTAPO Chief DIRK'S office on 6 April 1945 and advised that they would be given a special mission and funds provided for that purpose. The details were only given to RAABE and arrangements made to meet again on the 7th. On that date KADEN appeared in place of RAABE and distributed the funds received from DIRKS,viz., 2000 marks to WEIZKE, BREMEN and himself. Arrangements were made then for the trio to meet again in WIEZKE'S apartment in Braunschweig on the 9th. WIEZKE stated that neither KADEN or BREMEN ever appeared and that finally on 24 April 1945 he moved to Helmstedt. The sum of 1800 marks was recovered by these Agents from WIEZKE.

By memorandum dated 25 April 1945, these Agents advised POWERHOUSE CIC of the probable whereabouts of KADEN. He was arrested by that Detachment on or about 2 May 1945. At that time nothing was known of his involved in any mission. When this was recently made known these Agents contacted his fiancée in Engerede and recovered from her the 2000 marks he had received and which he left with her.

At the moment nothing definite is known concerning the purpose of the mission of this group. However, it has been indicated that this group was to act as liaison between stay-behind and evacuated personnel.

EVACUATION. The actual mass evacuation of GESTA-

PO and KRIPO personnel other than those assigned specific missions or discharged or otherwise left behind, as already noted, apparently commenced on 10 April 1945 at 1100 hours. At that time the main body, under the leadership of Fritz, FLINT, GESTAPO Kriminal Kommissar, proceeded to Walohausen, near Eitzum. GESTAPO chief Dr. KUHL and others remained behind in Braunschweig. After arriving at Waldehausen and remaining there a few hours, a messenger from Dr. KUHL contacted FLINT with orders to form a small group under the leadership of GESTAPO Polizei Obersekretar Eduard KNOOP which group was to proceed to Tetzelstein, in the Elm Mountains, to await further instructions. This was done and the larger group remained at Waldchausen until the early afternoon of 11 April 1945 when Dr. KUHL and the rest of the personnel who had remained in Braunschweig arrived. The entire body then proceeded to Clara Bad, near Helmstedt where they were joined by KNOOP'S group which had likewise been instructed to go to that place.

It appears that while the entire body was thus assembled at Clara Bad, Wilhelm (?) DYROFF, SD Chief in Braunschweig entered the town on foot with the story that the Americans had stopped his car, questioned and released him. When this was made known there was considerable confusion in the group and a few KRIPO members, including Kriminal Kommissar LEICHTWEISS, previously mentioned, seized upon the opportunity to take off and depart for home. It appears that shortly thereafter the remaining personnel proceeded to some woods outside Helmstedt where they were divided into groups. At this time it may be mentioned that by reason of the confused situations and the element of pressure caused by the rapid advance of the Americans, the groupings differed from that originally planned. In addition, some of the personnel failed to appear. At any rate, it is known that the following group leaders were appointed at that time; the names of the known members of each group are also indicated.

Group I.   GESTAPO Kriminal Inspector Hermann SCHARFE, leader, and the following GESTAPO personnel: GESTAPO Chief Dr. Gunther KUHL; Kriminal Sekretar Wilhelm

SCJLEICHER; Kriminal Angestellter Oskar STALINSKI; Kriminal Angestellter Helmuth WIPPER (Dr. KUHL'S chauffeur). Also including the group were five French informants who were also evacuated with the GESTAPO at the suggestion of STALINSKI for whom they had worked. They were Jan AMIOT, Rene SCJWARTZ, Jean SAVOIA; Michel BERGES; (FNU) PARVILLIER.

Group II. GESTAPO Kriminal Kommissar Fritz FLINT, leader, and the following GESTAPO personnel: Kriminal Angestellter Hans RODIGER; Kriminal Sekretar Hermann WEILMAN; Polizei Sekretar Walter VOGEL; Kriminal Angestellter Bruno BIEGEL; Kriminal Angestellter Heinrich JAHNS; Kriminal Angestellter Hermann MARTIN; 9FNU) STANDER; (FUNU) HOFFMAN. The last two named were newcomers, arriving in Braunschweig a short time before evacuation.

Group III. GESTAPO Polizei Oberseckretar Deuard KNOOP, leader, and the following GESTAPO personnel: Kriminal Angestellter Wilhelm BAUMGARTEN; Kriminal Angestellter Peter WINDOLPH; Kriminal Sekretar Hermann FRISCHE; Oplizeirat (FNU) STROHMEYER; Polizei Inspector Franz BAUER.

Group IV. GESTAPO Kriminal Obersekretar Herbert STEINBORN, leader. At the present time the names of the members of this group are not definitely known.

Group V. KRIPO Chief and Kriminalrat Heinz Gunther ENGELMANN, leader, The names of the members of this group, all KRIPO personnel, have not as yet been established.

As previously pointed out, pressure, confusion and failure of personnel to appear resulted in a change of original grouping plans. For example, KNOOP replaced Kriminal Obersekretar Albert MEIER, head of the GESTAPO office in Watenstedt, as leader of Group III, when MEIER failed to appear; also STEINBORN replaced GESTAPO Kriminal Kommissar (FNU) HEINZ who also failed to appear. Another group was scheduled to be under the leadership of one of Karl SCHEUERMANN, KRIPO apprentice. However, it seems that when SCHEUREMANN reached Clara Bad by motorcar with the main body, his group of KRIPO members who were supposed to follow by bicycle failed to appear. Investigation established that apparently as soon as they were divorced from GESTAPO leadership after leaving Waldchausen these KRIPO personnel depart from their homes.

After the groups were formed, rations and money were distributed. Each individual present was supposed to have received 1500 marks; this also included the five French informants; the balance of the money, amounting to 11,000 marks was turned over to Kr. KUHL by Franz BAUER who had distributed the money. It appears that formation of the groups and distribution of rations and money was done very hurriedly and that the group members disappeared as soon as possible.

ARRESTS TO DATE

The following are the arrests effected by these Agents to date. They are listed according to groups rather than in chronological order.

Group I

KUHL, Dr. Gunther; GESTAPO Chief in Braunschweig since November 1942; SS Obersturmbannfuhrer; member of GE-STAPO since July 1938; NSDAP since 1 May 1933. KUHL, together with SCHARFE, SCHLEICHER and STALINSKY were arrested in Braunschweig on 16 May 1945 while in the process of surrendering themselves. The surrender of these Subjects was the result of action taken by these Agents relative to their wives and families. On 11 May 1945 Helmuth WIPPER, Dr. KUHL'S chauffeur, was brought to these Agents by Fraulein Ilse NIEPER, Dr. KUHL'S secretary, who had been previously interrogated and instructed to report the presence of any GESTAPO personnel in Braunschweig. Interrogation of WIPPER, who was also in Group I, revealed that he had returned from the Harz region about 10 days previously. He said that he had left the other members of the group there, except the French informants who had been dismissed, and then returned for the obvious reason of sizing up the situation in Braunschweig and supposedly retuning to Ilseburg to advise the others. He declared that he had no intention of ever doing so.

He confirmed the fact, known to these Agents, that on 5 April 1945 the wives and children of Dr. KUHL, SCHARFE and STALINSKI had been removed from their respective homes outside of Braunschweig and brought to a small farming community in a different locality. This removal was accomplished without knowledge of anyone else except the principals involved and WIPPER. He identified the location as Alvesse, a town about 20 miles outside Braunschweig. WIPPER also gave minute details concerning the appearance of Dr. KUL, SCHARFE, SHLEICHER and STALINSKI.

On learning of the possible whereabouts of Dr. KUHL, these Agents proceeded to Ilseburg accompanied by Kriminal Kommissar LEICHTWEISS, previously used as an informant. LEICHTWEISS was established in the town for about 36 hours in an attempt to spot Dr. KUHL and the others. However, no results followed and additional checking indicated Subjects were not in the vicinity.

The only other apparent way to attempt to apprehend Subjects was determined to be to remove the wives and children of Dr. KUHL, SCHARFE and STALINSKI from Alvesse to Braunschweig having in mind that Subjects might attempt to contact them in the very near future. On 14 May 1945, these Agents brought the wives and children of Dr. KUHL and SCHARFE to Braunschweig and placed them under house arrest in the home of Mrs. SCHARGE'S sister in law. Mrs. STALINSKI and her children were left in Alvesse for contact purposes.

The following day 15 May 1945 Subjects, who had come up from the Harz area, tried to contact their wives in Alvesse. On learning the facts they decided to surrender, which they did on the following night.

Dr. KUHL possessed a new Kennkarten issued in the name of Gerhard Welter. This was the only identity document in his possession and he stated that he had used it since evacuation without difficulty. He and the others had also obtained food stamps in Ilsenburg under their assumed names. A total amount of 11,800 marks were recovered from the four Subjects.

Relative to WIPPER, no action was taken in view of his merely being a chauffeur and not regarded as a security threat. However, these Agents obtained from him the 1500 marks he received.

2. <u>SCHARFE</u>, Hermann, alias Hermann STEINBERG; Kriminal Inspector; member of GESTAPO since 1 March 1936; in charge of informants department of Braunschweig GESTAPO since September 1945; SS Untersturmfuhrer; SS anwarter since 1941: NSDAP from 1 May 1938.

The Informants Department headed by Subject was located in a separate building at Friedrich Wilhelm Loperstrasse 52. A sign indicated the premises to be that occupied by a private firm known as Kaufmann was displayed in front. It was revealed that Subject's department employed more than 100 informants, mostly foreigners. Informants, many of whom were inmates on concentration camps, received no direct pay. They were usually given easy jobs in the establishments in which they were placed. On occasion, when good reports were turned in, they were sometimes given a bonus of cigarettes or liquor.

SCHARFE stated that the Reichssicherheitsant in Berlin was particularly concerned with the maintenance of an extensive informants system and that submitted reports directly to that office.

3. <u>STALINSKI</u>, Oskar, alias Franz BEHREND; Kriminal Angesstelter, employed in GESTAPO since June 1940; since December 1942 in Informants Department under SCHARFE and considered his right hand man; has been denounced for having administered beatings to subjects and is primarily responsible for odious reputation of Informants Department.

4. SCHLEICHER, Wilhelm, alias Willi ROBER; Kriminal Sekretar; SS Oberscharfuhrer; member of GESTAPO since April 1939; brother-in-law of SCHARFE; last in Department IV-1-A handling cases involving remarks against Reich and listening to

foreign broadcasts.

All four Subjects are now in Braunschweig Prison for further interrogation before evacuation for internment.

Group II

5.   FLINT, Fritz, alias Ernst Thie; Kriminal Kommissar; member of GESTAPO since October 1935; in charge of Departments IV-1-A & B and IV-2-3-5 and 6-B; ranking Kommissar in Braunschweig GESTAPO; SS Obersturmfuhrer; awaiting evacuation for internment.

Subject was apprehended by these Agents in Suepplingen, Germany, on 30 April 1945. Shortly before Subject's arrest, two other members of this group, Hans Rodiger and Hermann Weliman, had been arrested and interrogated. Information obtained from them indicated that, after leaving the woods near Helmstedt, where they had received money and rations, the entire group went to Suepplingen where they stayed overnight in a hayloft. On the next morning, the town having been overrun by the Americans, the group broke up and apparently left the town individually and in groups. It was learned that the members of the group had hidden their weapons in the hayloft and had also disposed of their official GESTAPO credentials.

On 30 April 1945 these Agents searched the hayloft in Suepplingen. One machine pistol and six automatic pistols were recovered in addition to some small arms ammunition; also, FLINT'S GESTAPO credentials were found hidden in the rafters. Since FLINT was later known to have visited the towns of Rottdorf and Helmstedt, it was assured that he also and left Suepplingen as to whether he had seen anyone who had exhibited a new Braunschweig Kennkarten and were informed that a man named THIE possessed one. These Agents located "THIE" in a furnished room in the town and identified him as FLINT. At first FLINT attempted to represent himself as THIE by exhibiting his new Kennkarten and only admitted his identity when shown his GESTAPO credentials. These agents recovered 1500 marks from Subject.

6. <u>RODIGER</u>, Hans, alias Heinz ROEMER; Kriminal Angestellter; member of GESTAPO since 1939; employed in Department IV-3; SS Unterschargfuhrer; served in SD (Untersccharfuhrer) in Jugoslavin from May 1944 to February 1945. Arrested in Braunschweig on 26 April 1945; evacuated for internment on 28 April 1945; 1500 marks recovered.

7. <u>WELIMAN</u>, Hermann, alias Fritz BAER; Kriminal Sekretar; member of GESTPO since March 1939, SS Hauptscharfuhrer; SD Hauptscharfuhrer; employed in Department IV-1-C; surrendered himself in Braunschweig on 28 April 1945; evacuated for internment on 16 May 1945; 1500 marks recovered.

8. <u>VOGEL</u>, Walter, alias Willy DOSCHNER, Polizei Sekretar; member of GESTAPO since September 1938; SD Staffelsturmscharfuhrer; employed in administrative branch of GESTAPO; arrested in Braunschweig 16 April 1945; evacuated for internment on 16 May 1945; 1500 marks recovered.

9. <u>JAHNS</u>, Heinrich, alias Henrich PINKENELLA; Kriminal Angestellter; member of GESTAPO since October 1939; employed in Department IV-3; SS Staffelscharfuhrer. Subject was arrested by these Agents in Sophienthal, Germany, on 2 May 1945; evacuated for internment on 16 May 1945; 1500 marks recovered.

10. <u>MARTIN</u>, Herman, alias Herman MARX; Kriminal Angestellier; member of GESTAPO since September 1942; worked in Department IV-1-C; SS Unterscharfuhrer. Subject was arrested by these AGENTS on 3 May 1945 in the home of friends in Wehnsen, Germany. Evacuated for internment on 16 may 1945; 1500 marks recovered.

Group III

11. <u>KNOOP</u>, Eduard, alias Peter WEDNT; Plizei Obersekretar; member of GESTAPO since January 1939; employed in Administrative Department; SS Untersturmfuhrer; SD Untersturmfuhrer in which capacity served in Russia from July 1941 to May 1942. Arrested by these Agents at the home of relatives in Helmstedt, Germany, on 11 May 1945; evacuated for internment

on 16 May 1945; 1500 marks recovered.

12. <u>WINDOLPH</u>, Peter, alias Heinrich KLINGEN-HOFER; Polizei Assistant; member of GESTAPO since July 1941; Allgemeine SS since October 1932; also served in Waffen SS 1934-1938 and 1939-1941- highest rank Unterscharfuhrer; SS rank in GESTAPO-Oberscharfuhrer. Subject, employed in Administrative Department, arrested by these Agents in Helmstedt, Germany on 11 May 1945. Subject was working in that town as a bricklayer under his alias when apprehended. Evacuated for internment on 16 May 1945; 1500 marks recovered.

Another member of this group, Wilhelm <u>BAUMGAR-TEN</u>. Kriminal Angestellter, SS Oberscharfuhrer and Allgemeine SS member since 1932, was arrested by BLACKBIRD CIC on 15 May 1945 near Bahrdorf, Germany. Subject had surrendered that same morning to a local unit handling Military Government affairs in Bahrdorf. He was sent to the unit's CP in Vorsfelde and shortly afterwards released. Agents of BLACKBIRD CIC visited the CP shortly after Subjects release, were informed about him, and picked him up on the road to Bahrdorf.

It may be stated that Subject's surrender was the result of these Agents having contacted his wife in Bahrdorf in the early part of May and by coincidence these Agents contacted his wife again in Bahrdorf on the day he surrendered. Since disappearing with the rest of the group on 11 April 1945, Subject worked on the farm of relatives in Mackendorf, Germany. After learning of Subject's surrender that morning, these Agents went to Mackendorf and recovered 1500 marks. After Subjects arrest, he was interrogated by these Agents in the jail at Helmstedt after these Agents had first contacted BLACKBIRD CIC in Schoenningen.

STAY-BEHIND MISSIONS

Group 1

13. <u>OTTO</u>, Wilhelm alias Wilhelm OTTMER; KRIPO beamter; member of Braunschweig KRIPO since 1940; SD Unterscharfuhrer, serving in Hungary from March to November 1944;

arrested in Braunschweig w1 April 1945; evacuated for internment 25 April 1945. No money recovered since this group apparently not given funds.

14. <u>WENZEL</u>, Kurt alias Kurt WEGENER; KRIPO Kriminal Angestellter; Allgemeine SS since 1933—Oberscharfuhrer; SD Oberscharfuhrer, serving in Russia in April and May 1943; arrested in Braunschweig 22 April 1945; evacuated for internment on 25 April 1945.

Group 2

No arrests made. See original reference on Page 5.

Group 3

15. <u>KASTEN</u>, Karl alias Karl KUHNERT; KRIPO Kriminal Sekretar; member of KRIPO since 1934; not SS or SD member; had evacuated to Helmstedt and then returned to Braunschweig where arrested by these Agents on 10 May 1945; 2000 marks recovered; evacuated for internment 16 May 1945.

16. <u>ROHRMANN</u>, Reinhard alias Rudolf RIEMERS; KRIPO Kriminal Angestellter; member of KRIPO since February 1938; for HJ member; SA member since February 1932 with rank of Unterscharfuhrer; also member of Allgemeine SS since December 1935 with rank of Oberscharfuhrer. Subject had evacuated to Helmstedt and returned to Braunschweig on 10 May 1945 and learned that these Agents had contacted his home. Subject reported to this Detachment on 11 May 1945 and was arrested by these Agents. A total of 1500 marks out of 2000 marks originally received by him were recovered by these Agents from Subject's wife in Schoenningen. Evacuated for internment on 16 May 1945.

Group 4

17. <u>WIEZKE</u>, Wolfgang alias Woldemar WUNDELICH; Polizei Inspector (Anwarter) working for GESTAPO since 1 May 1943; Allgemein SS (applicant) since 1942; nominal rank of SS

Hauptscharfuhrer; worked in Administrative Department of GE-STAPO. Subject was arrested by these Agents in Helmstedt on 11 May 1945; 1800 marks out of the 2000 originally received by Subject recovered. Evacuated for internment on 16 May 1945.

As previously noted (Page 6), another member of this group, Hermann KADEN, was arrested by POWERHOUSE CIC on or about 2 May 1945. These Agents had on 25 April 1945 submitted a memorandum to POWERHOUSE giving Subject's whereabouts at which location on 18 May 1945 these Agents recovered the sum of 2000 marks from Subject's fiancée.

Miscellaneous

18. DURING, Paul; Interpreter for GESTAPO since July 1944; arrested on 22 April 1945 after detention by local police; served as Sonderfuhrer in PW camps from August 1940 to January 1944; evacuated for internment on 28 April 1945.

These Agents had submitted to POWERHOUSE information concerning HILDEBRANDT and the whereabouts of his wife by memorandum of 25 April 1945 which also included information concerning GESTAPO personalities. At the request of these Agents HILDEBRANDT was transferred by POWERHOUSE to Braunschweig where he was interrogated and evacuated for internment on 16 May 1945.

COMMENTS: During the course of the current investigation, these Agents have interrogated, besides apprehended Subjects, numerous suspects, GESTAPO informants, GESTAPO personnel who held minor positions and who were not regarded as security threats or within the automatic arrest category, and informants. Special emphasis has been placed on eliciting information concerning the possible whereabouts of Subjects' wives, families, relatives and close friends as a means of locating Subjects. Such information has proven invaluable in a number of instances, the outstanding example being that culminating in the arrests of Dr. KUHL, SCHARFE, STALINSKI and SCHLEICHER. A number of other of such leads have been followed up to the point where wives and families have been located and contacted but who profess to have no knowledge of Subjects whereabouts and not to have seen or heard from them since their disappearance. In these cases, wives and relatives have been told of the advisability of the surrender of Subjects on their return and Military Government units in the locality advised of the facts. Eventually these locations will be contacted again and re-checked and it is felt that in some cases, at least, the apprehension of Subjects should be effected. It may be noted that there is a possibility of the non-return of some of Subjects who may have been picked up as PWs, involuntarily or otherwise.

These Agents have also endeavored to secure as detailed descriptions of Subjects as possible; also photographs, whenever available. In addition, a course was adopted whereby certain apprehended Subjects or suspects have been retained in custody in Braunschweig Prison and evacuation to CONQUER Internment Center deferred until the individual had been fully exploited as a source of information.

To date, these Agents have recovered the total of 38,600 marks of GESTAPO funds used for contemplated missions and future activities. Additional recoveries are expected and further arrests anticipated. While it has been estimated that 80,000 or 90,000 marks were involved in the proceedings, the exact amount apparently can only be confirmed though apprehension of the STROHMEYER or BAUER, who handed the finances, since the records of the Braunschweig Police Cashier which would reflect the amount drawn, apparently were destroyed. Some of these funds are probably beyond recovery as, for example, that paid to the five French informants who accompanied the GESTAPO on evacuation. They formed part of Group I but were subsequently dismissed and indicated that they would make their way back to France. An attempt is being made to obtain information concerning their backgrounds and location of their homes in France with the idea of turning the same over to French liaison authorities with CONQUER.

19. WOHLTMANN, August alias Adolph WOHLMUT; Kriminal Sekretar; member of GESTASPO since 1939; last worked

in Fahndungs Department and prior to that in Department IV-2-A. Subject was one of GESTAPO personnel relieved from duty prior to evacuation and not included in any evacuation or mission plans. He left Braunschweig on 10 April 1945 and returned on 27 April 1945. Subject was arrested by these Agents on the following date at his home. Evacuated on 4 May 1945 for internment.

20. HICKMAN, Max; Kriminal Sekretar; member of GE-STAPO since 1938; employed in Watenstedt office, Department IV-6; Subject relieved from duty prior to evacuation on account of age; not SS member. Arrested in Braunschweig on 3 May 1945; evacuated for internment on 10 May 1945. POWERHOUSE CIC advised.

21. SCHEUERMANN, Karl alias KURT SCHAFERS. Subject, former lieutenant in Wehrmacht who was discharged for wounds on 13 April 1944, was arrested by these Agents in Helmstedt on 11 May 1945. Subject had been reported as a leader of one of the evacuated groups; also that he was an SS Obersturmfuhrer in the SD. Subject, who became associated with KRIPO only in March, 1945, admitted having been originally appointed a group leader and that he evacuated with the rest of the GESTAPO and KRIPO personnel. He claims that the members of his group failed to appear at Clara Bad and that Dr. KUHL, GESTAPO Cheif, then relieved him of all further participation in the proceedings; he claims that he was also released because of his physical disability; also that he had received no money. He denies being in the SS or SD but admits having worn an SS Oberstrumfuhrer's uniform merely for the purpose of impressing others. Subject will be retained in Braunschweig Prison pending further investigation.

22. FRICKE, Ernst; Kriminal Obersekretar; member of GESTAPO since 1937; SS Untersturmfuhrer; member of Allgemeine SS since 1934; also SD since 1935—SD Untersturmfuhrer. Subject, residing in Oelpher, surrendered on this date, 18 May 1945, after these Agents had contacted his wife on two occasions and left instructions for Subject to report on his return to Oelpher. Subject in Braunschweig Prison, to be interrogated.

23. STAHLMAN, Alfred alias Carl NAMUTH; Kriminal

Angestellter; member of GESTAPO since June 1935; most recently employed in Department IV-1-A. Subject had been relieved of duty and was not included in evacuation or mission plans; he left Braunschweig on 8 or 9 April 1945 for Clausthal-Zellerfeld in the Harz area; returned with family on 16 May 1945. Arrested in Braunschweig home on this date, 18 May 1945. Subject member of Allgemeine SS since April 1932—was SS Hauptscharfuhrer; states he left SS and became SD when he entered employ of GE-STAPO; held rank of SD Sturmhauptscharfuhrer. In Braunschweig Prison pending evacuation for internment.

In addition to the foregoing arrests, these Agents were advised by POWERHOUSE CIC on 6 May 1945 of the arrest by that detachment of Braunschweig GESTAPO Agent Walter <u>HILDEBRANDT</u> alias Wilhelm HOLSTEIN.

The employment of former KRIPO Kriminal Kommissar Rudi (Rolf) LEICHTWEISS and his wife as confidential informants, and in an undercover capacity, provided excellent results. On the date of 25 April 1945, these Agents submitted a memorandum relative to LEICHTWEISS, shows he offered his services as informant, recommending the use of his services. Thereafter he and his wife, using the assumed names of Mr. and Mrs. Rudi BECK, were established in Braunschweig in the home of former Minister KLAGGE at Loewenwall 3; authorization for quarters and ration stamps in their assumed names were secured for them through Military Government. Informants remained at this location for about a week during which time they compiled a report containing much information concerning GESTAPO and KRIPO personalities. Since these Agents had previously sealed former Minister KLABBES office, contact with informants was made under the guise of checking the premises and occupants.

Investigation had revealed that some Braunschweig GE-STAPO personnel had evacuated to Helmstedt and possible were still in town. In an attempt to ferret out these individuals, these Agents suggested to the LEICHTWEISS'S that they transfer to Helmstedt for a few days to try and spot any suspects. Informants agreed and these Agents transported them from Braunschweig to

Helmstedt on 6 May 1945 where, with the cooperation of Military Government, they were established in a local hotel. There was no other CIC Detachment in Helmstedt at the time, ARMOR CIC having vacated shortly before. These Agents contacted informants again on 10 May 1945 and learned that they had spotted four Subjects in the meantime. On the following day these Agents arrested the four, viz., KNOOP, WINDOLPH, WIEZKE and SCHEUERMANN.

As already indicated, LEICHTWEISS was also used in Ilsenburg in an effort to locate Dr. KUHL and other.

Wherever possible these Agents have contacted other CIC Detachments when operating outside Braunschweig. Investigation of Braunschweig GESTAPO is continuing and a further report will be submitted in due course.

Today is our last day of operation here and there is plenty of work to get done. Miller and Gross are putting the finishing touches on their Gestapo operations. Lt. Walker makes up our evacuation list and gets it up to date.

Lt. Walker takes Millers and Gross's report out to CONQUER as well as our evacuation list. While out there we find that Lts. Walker, Bauer, and Gikas, Grainger, Joe, Gross, Miller and Conohan are to go to Frankenberg as per order of Captain Hancock. Capt. Hancock also stated that Meyersberg is to stay behind and wait for Thoumsin to get back from Paris.

28 May
Lt. Walker and the English Captain work on the American citizen that has been a big shot in the Hermann Goering Works, it looks as if maybe a treason case. Major Ault and the Captain and their fellows from the 9th Armored drop in the billet and stay overnight.

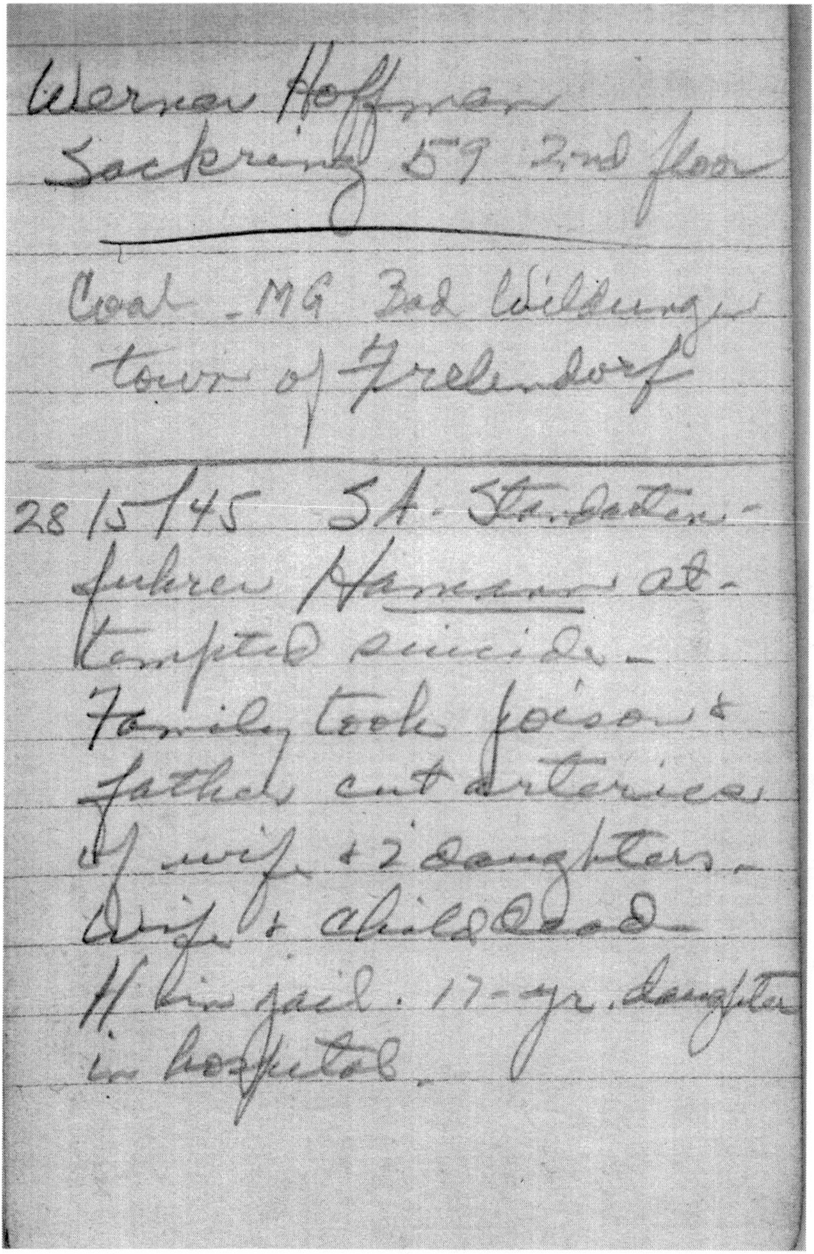

Werner Hoffman
Sackring 59 2nd floor

Coal - MG Bad Wildungen
town of Frelendorf

28/5/45 S.A. Standarten-
fuhrer Hansen at-
tempted suicide -
Family took poison &
father cut arteries
of wife + 2 daughters -
Wife + children dead
H in jail. 17-yr. daughter
in hospital.

Braunschweig, Germany
28 May 1945

MEMORANDUM FOR THE OFFICER IN CHARGE
SUBJECT: GESTAPO of Braunschweig.
RE: Second and final Report of Investigation.

The following final report of investigation of Braunschweig GESTAPO personnel supplements the initial report submitted by these Agents under date of 18 May 1945. The instant report
is submitted in connection with the current "take-over" of operation in Braunschweig by a British FSS Detachment.

Since the submission of the previous initial report, additional information has been obtained concerning matters and personalities noted therein and the same will be referred to in this
report with a corresponding reference to the first report.

ISSUANCE OF FALSE CREDENTIALS
(Page 3, Initial Report)

The possession of re-colored AUSMUSTRUNGSSCHEINE cards
denoting exemption from military service by reason of physical
or mental disability has been verified in two cases, both KRIPO
personnel who had evacuated from Braunschweig with the GE-
STAPO. It appears that these cards were available to GESTAPO
and KRIPO personnel, if desired, but were not issued as a matter
of form, the same situation existing in the case of false FUHRER-
SCHEIN (Drivers' Licenses). It seems that these two type credentials were made available in the office of the KRIPO and this, plus

the fact that GESTAPO personnel secured their false credentials more or less at the last minute, may account for the failure of GESTAPO personnel thus far apprehended to possess either a fast AUSMUSTRUNGSSCHEINE or FUHRERSCHEIN. However, the possession of both in addition to a false Kennkarten is possible.

EVACUATION.
(Page 6, Initial Report)
The personnel of Group V has been definitely established as follows: Heinz Gunther ENGELMANN, KRIPO Chief and Kriminalrat, leader, and the following, KRIPO members: Wilhelm BARTSCHAT, Brune MANTHEY, Rudof ELLBRIGHT, and Friedrich CORNELIUS.

The following new groups have also been identified:

Group VI
GESTAPO Kriminal Sekretar Kurt HEYER, leader; GESTAPO Kriminal Angestellter Whilhelm GRIMM; and Rene MAILLE de GIRVES, French Interpreter for the GESTAPO.

Group VII
GESTAPO Kriminal Sekretar Herman MEYER, leader; GESTAPO Kriminal Angestellter Werner BASSO; GESTAPO Kriminal Sekretar Wilhelm LAMPE; GESTAPO Kriminal Angestellter (FNU) REICHERT; and two unidentified Russians who worked for the GESTAPO.

ADDITIONAL ARRESTS
The following additional arrests have been effected since the initial report:

Group III
24. FRISCHE, Hermann; GESTAPO Polizei Sekretar. Subject was apprehended on 20 May 1945 in Wenschet, Germany,

by members of a local Bolld M. G. unit acting on instructions of these Agents. Several days previously these Agents contacted Subject's wife in Wenschet where she was living with Subject's parents; she stated she was unaware of Subject's whereabouts. These Agents, who had knowledge that Subject was in the vicinity of Wenschet, advised the local Military Government unit of the facts and requested a spot check be made on the home of Subject's parents. FRISHCE returned to Wenschet on the evening of 19 May 1945 and was apprehended next day. He was evacuated through PW channels after questioning by BLACKBIRD CIC. These Agents recovered 1500 marks from Subject's wife.

Group V

25. HEYER, Kurt alias Kurt HINZ, GESTAPO Kriminal Sekretar; SS applicant since 1937—SS Staffelsturmscharfuhrer; member of GESTAPO since 1935; worked in Department IV-A-1.

Subject, together with GESTAPO Kriminal Sekretar Hermann MEYER, alias Thee MAYER, was apprehended by these Agents on 24 May 1945 in a hide-out in the Harz Mountains near Neuwerk. These Agents had received information that MEYER, a woman posing as his wife, and another unidentified man, were hiding out in the Harz area near Neuwerk. Enlisting the assistance of two members of the acting military government unit in nearby Rubeland and with the aid of a Neuwerk resident, acing as guide, these Agents located the hide-out in the mountains and found Subject, MEYER, and two women there. Subject and MEYER presented their false Kennkarten and refused to admit their identity. One of the women, later established as Hella (Heda) KOLLE, GURSCH, presented a false Kennkarten purpertrating to identify her as MEYER'S wife. The other woman, Eran RIEHN, Kehlrauschstr 25, Blankenburg, a friend of Frau KOLLE, was released and Subject, MEYER and Frau KOLLE brought back to Braunschweig.

On questioning Braunschweig, Subject admitted his identity and that he had evacuated with GESTAPO Kriminal Angestellter Whilhelm GRIMM and a Frenchman, Rene MAILLE de GIRVES, Interpreter for the GESTAPO, on 7 April 1945; that he separated from the other two in GESLAR and went to Blankenburg where he met MEYER who already arranged for the hide-out; he explained that his meeting with MEYER was accidental.

MEYER stated that he had also evacuated on 7 April 1945 with the other members of his group (See Group VII) and went to Blankenburg; that after several days the others left, most of them to go to their wives and families, and he remained behind, that the German military authorities in Blankenburg, then still in German hands, advised him of where he could hide-out.

Frau KOLLE finally admitted that she was a Kreisleiterin of the NSF in Hanover and had met MEYER in Blandenburg and that he had secured false Kennkarten for her at that place.

HEYER and MEYER are awaiting evacuation to CONQUER Internment Center while Frau KOLLE is being detained in Braunschweig Prison pending further investigation.

Group VII

26. MEYER, Hermann alias Thee MAYER; GESTAPO Kriminal Sekretar; member of GESTAPO since 15 May 1934; Allgemeine SS since 1930; SS Hauptsturmfuhrer; alleged to be fanatical Nazi and admitted NSDAP member since 1927; worked in Department II-H (Schutzdienst) and since 1936 in charge of protecting eminent personalities visiting Braunschweig area. Apprehended with Kurt HEYE on 24 May 1945 in hide-out in Harz Mountains where 4000 marks also recovered. Awaiting evacuation for internment.

Miscellaneous

27. BEUSSE, Wilhelm; GESTAPO Kriminal Sekretar; member of GESTAPO since 1939 working in Department III-D; also Ortsgruppenleiter of Ortsgruppe Ruehme, Braunschweig, since 1939/1940. Subject, apparently assigned to no group, evacuated from Braunschweig on 7 April 1944. He was arrested by these Agents on 21 May 1945 in Supplingenburg, Germany. SD

Sturmscharfuhrer since 1941. Evacuated for internment on 25 May 1945.

28. <u>WOLTER</u>, Ludwig alias Albert WARNECKE; GE-STAPO Kriminal Sekretar, Bad Harzburg Office; SS Untersturmfuhrer—member of Allgemeine SS since 1933; member of GE-STAPO since 1934. Subject had lived in US from 1922-1926 and 1927-1932.

Subject surrendered to local police in Braunschweig on 23 May 1945; had evacuated from Bad Harzburg without GESTAPO personnel from that office; group had gone to Blankenburg, then to Halle, and then dispersed; false Kennkarten obtained in Blankenburg destroyed by Subject. WOLTER awaiting evacuation for internment.

29. <u>DUSDIEKER</u>, Wilhelm; GESTAPO Kriminal Sekretar; SS applicant since 1937, claims no rank; member of GESTAPO since 1937; last worked in GESTAPO office in Fallingbostel, Germany, since 1943 and prior thereto in Braunschweig. Arrested in Braunschweig by local police. Awaiting evacuation for internment.

Group VI

30. <u>MAILLE de GIRVES</u>, Rene; French National employed as Interpreter by Braunschweig GESTAPO since February 1945; member and Organizer of French pro-Facist organization known as F.P.T. (Doriet movement). Subject surrendered to French authorities in Braunschweig; remanded to Braunschweig Prison on 23 May 1945 for interrogation and evacuation by CIC. As a member of this Group VI Subject received 1500 marks of GESTAPO funds out of which these Agents recovered 500 marks.

<u>SPECIAL NOTES RE GROUP V</u>. This group consisting of five KRIPO members including KRIPO Chief and Kriminalrat Heinz Gunther ENGELMANN, was definitely identified by these Agents on questioning of Friedrich CORNELIUS, a member of the group, CORNELIUS, a Kriminal Sekretar, had returned to Braunschweig about 20 April 1945 and reported back to the KRI-

PO. He continued his employment there until about the middle of this month when arrested for allegedly falsifying his Military Government Fragebogen by failing to state his SS rank and connection. On m22 May 1945 while interrogating GESTAPO agent SCHARFE (see Initial Report, Page 9), these Agents learned that CORNELIUS had been a member of Group V and that his group had received GESTAPO funds when the same were distributed in the forest near Helmstedt. CORNELIUS, who was in Braunschweig Prison awaiting trail on the falsified Fragebogen charge, was questioned and revealed the following information.

Subject identified the rest of the group, besides ENGELMANN and himself, as Wilhelm BARSCHAT, Brune MANTHEY and Rudolph ELLBRIGHT. He said that following the receipt of funds in the forest on 11 April the group hid out in a nearby town; that on 13 April 1945 they decided to break up and go to their wives or families and, except MANTHEY who remained behind intending to go to Eitzum by bicycle, they proceeded in the direction of Halberstedt, ENGELMANN on a motorcycle and the other three in a motorcar. While enroute the motorcar was struck by a shell and BARSCHAT injured. CORNELIUS stated that the others continued on their ways while he remained with BARSCHAT and brought him to his wife who was in Lochtum.

According to CORNELIUS, neither he nor the other members of the group had received any specific mission from the GESTAPO or from ENGELMANN. He said that he had received 6000 marks for distribution but that he only distributed 2000 marks which he gave to BARSCHAT, and still retained the balance. He admitted that he had not mentioned the receipt or possession of said money to anyone since returning to Braunschweig. These Agents recovered the 4000 marks from CORNELIUS'S wife.

Under all the circumstances, including the absence of any proof that CORNELIUS had been assigned any specific mission, these gents took no action against him. He will, however, be prosecuted on the falsified Fragebogen charge and Military Government notified of his failure to report receipt of GESTAPO funds. CORNELIUS had destroyed a new Kennkarten issued to him in the name of Fred CAMEN.

Group VI

On 26 May 1945 these Agents located group member BARSCHAT in St. Josephs Hospital, Wiedelah, where he is a patient under the name of Wilhelm Bartels, the name of his new Kennkarten. BARSCHAT also stated that no orders had been given the group to perform any specific mission. He stated that he had received orders from the KRIPO in Braunschweig to report for work and intended to do so when released from the hospital. BARSCHAT had given the 2000 marks received by him from CORNELIUS to his wife and the same was recovered from her in Braunschweig.

A third member of the group, Bruno MANTHEY, reported to the KRIPO on 25 May 1945; he was detained in Braunschweig Prison and there interrogated by these Agents on 27 May 1945. He stated that he had obtained no new Kennkarte and verified the statements of CORNELIUS and BARSCHAT as to the absence of any specific mission. He said that he had received 1600 marks from ENGELMAN at the time of general distribution in the forest but that after the accident to BARSCHAT, ENGELMANN had contacted him and declared that all his money and personal belongings had been in the car and were destroyed and requested 800 marks from MANTHEY which he gave him. MANTHEY stated that he had spent the remaining 800 marks paying debts and purchasing necessities and said that he believed he was justified in doing so since he had not received any salary from the KRIPO since January 1945. He explained that he had been working in the KRIPO in Bromberg, East Prussia, until January 1945; that, due to the Russian advance, he had to leave and did not arrive in Braunschweig until about 1 April 1945. MANTHEY was not found to be in the automatic arrest category, was not deemed a security threat, and was released on 27 May 1945.

COMMENTS: With the submission of this report the investigation of Braunschweig GESTAPO by these Agents is concluded. A total amount of 50,600 marks of GESTAPO funds recovered during the course of the investigation has been turned into CONQUER Finance Office. All information and leads on unapprehended personalities are being given to the succeeding FSS Detachment. In these cases where information disclosed the probable location of suspects in specific places outside Braunschweig, the same will be submitted to CIB for dissemination to appropriate CIC Detachments.

WILLIAM F. MILLER

PAUL GROSS

Special Agents

Chapter 17

Germany - Braunschweig, Frankenberg & Marburg
29 May – 21 July

Dear Dave:

Congratulations upon your promotion to First—one more bump and you will be an officer instead of a lieutenant!

Thank you for the pictures. Had I been in a position to have voiced a choice of the litter, the white one is the very one I would have picked!

Sorry to hear of the abortion of the bitch and to Little Smokey. You do have your troubles with pregnant bitches – first the Beau Essig litter is killed and now this one.

Where in the hell is Marburg? Can't find it on my map and in spite of a few weeks at Ritchie you didn't send any coordinates. Can you possibly make it here for a visit. Call me on Glider 526 (there Gangway) if you can and I will pay my last bottle of Scotch!

Life in the AF CIC continues to be one of beer and skittles and thoroughly enjoyable. It is certainly a good thing that I didn't know about this last winter when I was in a slip trench ducking Army bullets and mortars or I would have really been pissed off!

Note with interest your great round-up of the ortsgruppenleiters. My attention has been largely confined to attempting to protect my own truck, ¼ ton, 4x4, 20516523. To date it has been stolen once and recovered by my own Philo Vance technique; shoved a block and a half before the prospective thief gave up on the deal; and last night it was sabotaged! The dirty son of a bitch cut the oil line and pulled off all the wiring. Life in the rear echelons has its own perils!

That is about all there is to report from here. If you are still with Hancock tell him Hello-Moyen we

say here-and to you

                                        All luck,
                                        Hugh

Dear Bud:

Your letter of 27 May and one to Mother came in this morning. I was much interested in your wonderful hunt, which sounds like you might have been hunting in Phillips County so far as results were concerned. I will be much interested in seeing your new gun. I have never shot an over and under. Now, if German officers have good saddles, and I have no doubt they had fine ones, I feel sure they have no use for them and if you can run across a good one I would be much interested in having it especially if it should turn out to be a gift from the German people. Your SS General for instance should have some good ones he no longer needs.

I seem to be making a thorough mess of keeping your dogs for you. Anyway a few nights or weeks ago along comes a stray dog and a big fight develops in which both the white pups and a small cur he had were involved. He killed the visiting dog, and fastend up the other three and all three developed rabies and died.

MANLY WORKLESS PERFORM
Third in the Open All Age State

I will mark a picture in the copy of the Field I am sending you today. It will give you an idea of what the

305

Beau Essig pup will be like (in color), and I want you to suggest a few good names.

I hope you like your new location and the associations that go with it, and will find your work interesting and that you can stick with it long enough to accomplish something. By the way, did I write you that P.I. Judd, the kid who was back from the Pacific(and of whom Frances was so fond) recently, has been reported missing. He was on a carrier, and evidently was the victim of some of the Jap suicide planes. Recently (Mrs. Atkins told Mother) her boy, who is a C-B I think almost bumped into Billy Berry and at first neither recognized the other, and of course had no idea they were in the same location.

Yesterday John Ike got a telegram from the War Department declaring Jack officially dead. He wanted me to advise you. I have not seen the message but I understand it stated that Jack was on the Jap prison ship which was torpedoed last October about 200 miles off the China coast; that there were only five escaped, and from their statements the War Department felt certain that Jack was killed, and he was therefore declared officially dead, and as I understood it, his pay stopped as of June 16th.1945. John and Mary are continuing to take it with chin up as they have had before inasmuch as none of the survivors actually saw him killed. That of course is alright, but they cannot really hold any hope. I wish I could do or say something to comfort them but as usual I am totally dumb on such occasions.

. Bob Orr got a lucky break for himself and family. He has been stationed at some prison camp in Oklahoma I believe. Anyway he has been transferred and placed in command of the prison camp at Elaine.

Nothing more of interest, so will sign off till next time.

Lots of love.

Dad

The past three days have been beautiful, and today was

306

warm as summer. After supper I went for a little ride in the country – like "making a block." The country around here is very pretty, and it is certainly a relief to see it after the rubble of the city. The lilacs are in bloom, and around here they grow to true size and several shades. You can smell them as you drive past, and there are other flowers too. Everything is fresh and green. It is the farmers and people of the villages who have got off fairly light here; they have suffered and will suffer little compared to the city people.

As far as we are concerned. The war has been over for us for nearly a month, and we have still had plenty to do. We are busy enough now, but the warm weather and the natural reaction have produced a sort of super-spring fever.

Just heard the demobilization plan broadcast; it doesn't apply to me, and wouldn't do me any good if it did. I guess I have a beautiful military career ahead of me.

This morning I got to church for the first time since Palm Sunday. In honor of the occasion I dressed in class A uniform, with necktie and low-quarter shoes and overseas cap, for the first time since I left Paris. It was a very nice service, in an old German military chapel, which would have been very pretty except that all the windows got bombed out. The chaplain announced that there would be an Episcopalian bishop here tonight who would hold an evening Communion service, so I went charging back tonight. However, he failed to show up, and the service was by the same guy. Anyhow, I had lots of religion today.

This afternoon I went with some of the boys for a little ride down the Autobahn.

It is a wonderful road, and the country is pretty. I got some pictures, as well as some fresh eggs.

Braunschweig, Germany

The Ninth Army says I can tell you where I am, so now you are in on the latest military secrets. In case you had trouble following me, after I left Aachen I went to Munchen-Gladbach, then to Haltern, Ahlen, Beckum (where I had the fine house), then up to Oschersleben, my nearest approach to Berlin, and back here.

Tonight I was out at Hq. and saw a movie, Ann Miller in "Eadie Was a Lady." It was a corny story, but the dancing was good, the clothes tight-fitting and revealing, and the whole thing entertaining and a bit sexy.

As a result of this hilarious evening I got home late, and then got in a big bull session, talked with Harden for a while before the show.

The pictures of the pups came. Elliott would be greatly pleased with that white puppy.

It's late, and I have been trying to write this while talking post-war problems to a room full of people and drinking some very fine wine which the British looted and I bummed off them.

I am glad that you find that some of my friends still remember me. I have never capitalized on my acquaintance with Gen. Kose to the extent I might have, but he is an awfully nice fellow. I took him hunting and fishing several times.

I continue to be busy with double summer time, it doesn't

get dark until after ten o'clock.

Heard's letter affected me about the same way as Heard always did. I am no hero and certainly didn't come here voluntarily. In spite of all I have put up with, I am not sure I would change places with those fellows who stayed in the States, now that I know what everyone thinks of them. I will still be a much happier soldier if I meet them over here, as I may yet.

I am sipping an excellent French dessert wine which I scrounged off the British, whom I caught taking it from you know who. Also I have a bottle of Monet champagne set aside for my promotion party, which is still about as uncertain as V-E Day was.

Tonight Harold and I walked out to Headquarters to see the movie. It was a beautiful moonlit evening and a very nice stroll of about a mile and a half each way. The show was a "Crime Doesn't Pay" job with Joan Blondell and some guy whose name I can't remember who looks like Frederick March, the deal being about the dollie and the insurance salesman insuring the old gent and bumping him off. It is reorienting us for our return to civilian life.

Today my orders finally came through and confirmed that I have been a 1st Lt. since May 1, which is most gratifying to me. It will mean a respectable increase in my monthly check – thirty dollars or so – and an additional bonus in self-respect since I am no longer completely at the bottom, this is probably my last promotion, and I am well pleased to have gone this far. CIC has had a lot of drawbacks, mostly in the way of rank, but as I look back on it I am inclined to believe that I made as good a choice out of ignorance as I could have after these many years of being a warrior.

I can't tell you my exact point total, as there are some changes in the campaign stars, and I don't know exactly how many I have. Any way I can figure them, however, I don't have enough, and the system doesn't apply to officers anyhow until they are declared surplus. I don't anticipate any immediate surplus in any kind of CIC personnel.

Our work is settling down into more of a routine after the first mad rush, though we still have plenty to do. I wrote a report last night on our first month of operations here, and was greatly please at what we have accomplished. From now on it will be slower, with more work and less spectacular results, but I am unable to see why we should be required here for any tremendous time if we have equal success everywhere. I don't think that I or many other CICs earned our pay until we hit Germany, but since I believe we have repaid what was spent on our education and have given ourselves reason to be proud of the organization.

We are still busy, but it looks as if we might soon be seeking greener pastures. I hope that we will go to our final location on our next move, but am inclined to doubt it. We are all getting tired of being gypsies, and are looking forward to the time when we can really settle down for the duration, or the plus six months, or whatever time it is we have to go.

This month's liquor ration included a bottle of Benedictine – a lovely fluid. It is a particularly fine after dinner liqueur, and I am just enjoying a little sip.

I have acquired a very nice shotgun, and think I have a hunt lined up on the preserve of a big Nazi general whom we unfortunately had to throw in the clink. It is out of season, but I am not particularly concerned with the future of the German game supply, whereas I am quite fond of pheasants. I also understand that the old scoundrel had practically a corner on the German deer supply, and I am not above working one over with a carbine, or my pistol.

You will never guess what I did this afternoon – I went deer hunting! We obtained the services of a German forester and went out to the estate of an SS general who will not be hunting for a few days. There were undoubtedly deer there, as we saw lots of fresh tracks, as well as places where they had pawed up the ground and had been rubbing their horns against the brush, it being that season of the year when they go in for such things. However, we didn't go at the right time of day for best results, and the whole deal would have been helped considerably by a couple of Earl Wells' hounds.

German Forester, Eddie, Dutch Interpreter & Waffen

It was a beautiful wood, and I enjoyed the stroll anyhow. I really wanted a pheasant, but the old scoundrel said there weren't any of them there. I think he sabotaged me.

Tonight I am busy with one of the favorite things I would rather not do – preparing to move. There is nothing I hate more than packing,. However, I have hopes that this will prove our last move. According to reports we are going into an interesting and pretty region, and I think we are getting a good break in that it is a small town with little damage.

Last night I went down to the British MG for a farewell drink, which was quite a protracted one, so much so, in fact, that Bauer, our other Lt., has been in bed all day with a hangover. Being of a hardier or more temperate nature, I suffered no ill effects and put in rather a full day.

This picture was taken on the morning that we left Braunschweig.

We will all remember Braunschweig for many things and I think especially for the fact that it was while in this town we received word that the War in Europe was ended.

Captain Hancock noticing a whole German convoy going through town unescorted while the War was still going on. He flagged the lead car down and inquired as to where they were going and who was in charge and he was informed that they were on their way to surrender, he then asked the logical question as to why they were coming from the East and into this area if it was just to surrender and he was informed that the officer wanted to surrender to the Americans instead of the Russians. (I guess that officer knew which way the wind was blowing away ahead of time.)

The DP's threw the Police Presidium up for grabs when they found all of the food stored in there.

The morning we came to work and someone reported that all of the flags on the city hall were down except the Russian flag - Result one city official removed (I think it was the Chief of Police) from office and given more comfortable quarters – the city jail.

Our motorcycle being stolen and our inability to find

it. (I think that we all know who did it but he returned to Holland before we could prove it.)

The party given to us by the British Military Government Officers.

All members of the team except Meyersburg leave for Frankenberg. Meyersberg will proceed to Marburg and join Capt. Hancock.

Lt. Walker finds out that he is to leave us and take over the Marburg detachment. We move in our new billet in the evening.

The day is spent setting up the office and making the proper contacts in town, namely MG, the town Mayor and CC of the Artillery Brigade charge with the security guard of the area.

Arrangements have been made for a truck to go to Marburg tomorrow to get coal.

Not to much business at the office. Capt. Hancock drove over to pick up Lt. Walker and move him over to Marburg.

Lt. Bauer interviews a ministrialrat from Berlin who has a very interesting background on who personally knew many of the Nazi big-wigs. Grainger and Joe pick up an Ortsgenppenlieter from Cologne who lives at the same village the ministrialrat did.

We called the Marburg office and find out that Capt. Hancock has flown up to 9th Army Hdqrs, at Braunschweig. Lt. Walker tells us that six IPW men have joined the team today and that two will come to Frankenburg. Claus Pappenheimer and Lt. David Neuwirth of the IPW men joined the team at Frankenburg early in the evening. Capt. Hancock calls stating that he is back from Braunschweig and that he has seen to it that all appropriate entries will be made in our service records prior to their being shipped to CONQUER REAR then to Group.

Today was a good day as far as informants were concerned, some of the better type have come in. Today

313

has been a pretty fair day for arrests. Among them was one SS Oberschaufuher.

Lt. Bauer and Gross return about nine with the news from Group which briefly is:(1) We will go home when our time comes (2) We may get the four stars (3) Mendoza is leaving the team on Tuesday and report to Group (4) Group Hqtrs. is well pleased with the way things are going.

Today there was only one arrest an SS Oberschaufuher. No new news from Marburg.

Today has been a real busy and we had four arrests, two SS men and two ortsgruppenleiters. Mendoza transfer is to 12th Army Group effective as of this date.

This morning we evacuate our first load of prisoners. There were 17 in the load, which included Dr. Ernest Krause, ministrialrat from the Ministry of Economics in Berlin, who Gross arrested this morning. During the afternoon Conohan goes to Marburg to bring the CIB copies of the arrest reports. Mendoza is going to be transferred to Com. Z instead of 12th Army Group. Gikas and Neurwirth go to the POW hospital at Haino and screen the patients for ultimate release. Town Mayor comes to office to see if the patients at the Frankenberg POW hospital have been screened. The MD in charge of the Frankenberg hospital calls to say that patients are going to be transferred from Frankenberg hospital to the Haino hospital.

We evacuate all our prisoners this morning. Had only one arrest for the day when Grainger picked up an Ortsgruppenleiter.

Today was a pretty busy day with four arrests.

Capt. Hancock goes to Corp for a meeting of team leaders.

Today hasn't been such a bad day, made four arrests but none of them amounted to very much. Dr. Jung from Haino was one of them, he is pretty clever and it took most of the day yesterday for Neuwirth and Conohan to get enough evidence to pick him up today.

Miller and Gross uncover 20 arrestable SS men at the Frankenburg PW station No. 9. Quite a few of them have on the totenkaupfrebunde which is the special SS group from which the concentration camp guard was made up. Neuwirth and Conohan arrest the undergaufraunschalesterin. At 2115 Bauer and Miller go out with the raiding party from Group (artillery) to Rodda. At 220 they raided the town.

Miller and Gross are working with MG on fragenbogen and other business of that nature. Conohan and Lt. Neuwirth were working out in the surrounding town and picked up an SS man.

In the morning Neuwirth and Conohan pick up a former Kries official and during the day investigated those other cases that all turn out to be duds.

This picture was taken when we stopped for lunch while we were on our way from Braunschweig to Frankenburg. I think that we will all remember this trip because of the really beautiful heavily wooded country that we went through. This was the same trip that took us by the German underground factory and also around the city of Kassel.

Today was a slow day only one ortsgruppenleiter was arrested.

Today was a little better than yesterday, two arrests. Charlie Grainger says arresting ortsgruppenleiters is like cutting off the dragons head – cut off one and six more grow on in its place – and that seems to be the case.

As I write this I am looking out my fourth-floor window across red tile rooves to a pasture with Holstein cows grazing and a little river winding through it.

On the other side a wooded ridge rises sharply, and along the bottom there are several houses with peaked gables and red tile rooves, and in the middle of them is a story-book hotel with lots of gables and blue windows. Off in the distance to the right there is a long, slowly–rising hill with green fields and patches of some kind of yellow flowers. From here I can hear the water rushing over the rocks a couple of hundred yards away. How's that for a scene?

This is one of those post-card German villages which lacks only storks on the chimneys to be exactly what you think of as South Germany. It is rather a sleepy little place, stronger on scenery than sanitation, though our house is fairly modern. On account of having to fight our part of the wars in the British sector, we arrived on this scene rather late and had a little difficulty setting ourselves up in our customary style. This was accomplished only after ejecting three families of Germans to the accompaniment of much weeping; these krauts certainly turn on the tears when the going gets rough.

In case you have difficulty locating this spot, it is between Kassel and Frankfurt, about 50 miles south of Kassel. I am not staying here but just helping the boys to get set up and then moving down to Marbug, the next town about 25 miles south, to join Harold and the rest of the team.

We came down yesterday, a hard drive of about 150 miles, but through very pretty and interesting country. We skirted the Harz Mountain region, which isn't much as mountains go but is strong on scenery. Most of the country is wooded, and the woods are beautiful. I couldn't tell whether underbrush doesn't grow in them or is cleared out, but anyhow there isn't any. The trees aren't very big, but are quite thick.

We aren't as far south as I thought we would go, but we may stay here. Somebody will work this area, and it may as well be us. This is something of a resort area, and when the troops move out there should be some hotels available.

Frankenburg

Today I went to church services conducted by an Army chaplain in an old German church. It was up on top of a hill overlooking the whole town, and I got some pictures before it started.

During the morning I went out on the pistol range and fired a few clips for target practice, the first time I have had any in nearly a year, and the results plainly showed it. Then I had to spend the rest of the morning cleaning my pistol, and I cleaned my other one and shined my shoes for good measure while I was at it.

Last night we saw "Rhapsody in Blue," the life of George Gershwin, at the local GI movie, and I certainly enjoyed it. Maybe it was from not seeing many movies lately, but I thought it one of the best I have seen in a long time, and the music was beautiful. There is a very nice theatre which the Army has taken over, and they show a new picture every other day.

This has been a beautiful day. There is a dam across the river here which makes a small swimming hole, but I have not tried it yet, as it is a bit cool and I am not too sure of the sanitary features. The Germans in this part of the country are very much like the French in that they have their barnyard animals right up in the middle of the town, and the result is more picturesque to sight than to smell. This is a very old place, and some of the old houses look as if they would fall down if you leaned against them.

Judging by the number of kids in this town, the krauts must not have much to do either, and they evidently go in for fraternizing in a big way.

Today I didn't have too much to do, so I spent the greater part of the day reading up on the operating instruction under which I have been working for a couple of months, and having mastered that subject, I read all the law reports I had on hand. That is very weighty matter, and I feel very erudite now.

We are very comfortably established here, and I hate the idea of moving down to Marburg. It is a bigger place than this and a more important assignment, I guess, but I like this quiet country life. I understand that the section of the team there is luxuriously established, so I won't lose anything in that respect, and it is supposed to be a resort town with very beautiful surrounding country too.

This was a sight that was familiar to all of us. The

318

German Army returning home through the courtesy of the United States Army.

We will all remember how the big trucks jam packed with prisoners went through the towns day after day taking the Germans to areas where they could be released to return home and how the German civilians gave them bread, etc., as the trucks went through the towns.

Here I am established in my new home, which I hope will be my residence for the occupation, or so much thereof as I have to worry with. This is the finest residence I have had yet; Harold and I have a big five-room apartment with two bedrooms, a dining room, a sitting room, a bath and a kitchen, all of them fine big rooms and well furnished, including a grand piano. We have a whole apartment building, with the rooms of the boys, the dining room, and the office occupying the other three floors. I have got further unpacked than at any time since I have been on the continent and am very comfortably set up.

I came down last night and am very much pleased at the beauty of the town and the surrounding country. This is a very old university town, having been a well-known place in 1200. Martin Luther lived here in the 16th century, and I took a picture this morning of the house where he lived. It was one of the centers of the Protestant Reformation, and there are many historical scenes and buildings here dating back to that period. I will be busy taking pictures; however, I have a folder written in German, Dutch, and English which I will enclose with this if I can find a large enough envelope, and it has some splendid pictures.

The country around is also very pretty, with wooded hills and beautiful rolling valleys. The little villages are very picturesque, just like they have been for centuries. It is just impossible to understand how a people from such a quiet, beautiful, peaceful country could go around all over Europe raising so much hell.

It will probably be just as well for you to start writing me for the time being at 12th Army Group; use the address: CIC 970/4, G-2 Section, Hq. 12th Army Group, APO 655, c/o PM, New York, N.Y. That may not be any better than the other one, but I think it will improve matters a little during the period while we are getting settled.

It will probably be just as well for you to start writing me for the time being at 12th Army Group; use the address: CIC 970/4, G-2 Section, Hq. 12th Army Group, APO 655, c/o PM, New York, N.Y. That may not be any better than the other one, but I think it will improve matters a little during the period while we are getting settled.

While describing the country, I forgot to mention that this is Hessen, the home of the Hessians, who are principally famous for getting drunk and letting George Washington paste them plenty at the Battle of Trenton in the Revolution. After getting whipped three times by the Americans, they should be about convinced.

Today, being the anniversary of D-Day, was proclaimed a holiday by Gen. Eisenhower, and we did not wait for official orders. I spent the morning taking it easy and bulling with visitors. This afternoon I went for a long walk through the town, taking pictures and looking at the interesting sights. We walked up to the park adjacent to the castle overlooking the town, and had a picnic there. Afterwards Harold and I went for a jeep ride out in the surrounding country, and I thoroughly enjoyed seeing it.

I got some film today for my 35mm camera, the newest one I have acquired, and used it. It is an Eastman Retina, said to be the best American-made camera, though this is the German model. I think I will like it very much, though it is not as simple to operate as my Rolleicord. The 35mm will take color film slides just like the Bantam. I believe these scenes would be wonderful in color. It may be difficult to get it developed, though I expect censorship regulations will be greatly relaxed as far as film is concerned.

Today was Sunday, and we have started operating more or less on a six-day week, though it is necessary to do a little work. This morning, having been warned that the GI chaplain is a stinker, I decided to go to the big German church in the hope that the music would make up for not being able to understand the sermon. They have a magnificent organ, but I was a little disappointed at the choir. The interior of the church is not as impressive as the exterior. It sounded strange to hear the old familiar hymns, many of which are original German tunes, and not to be able to understand the words. I am picking up a little German, but not enough to follow the service. To make it worse, the damned fellow preached for a solid hour; I think he did it on purpose and am seriously considering putting him in jail. That is a good plan for any preacher who holds forth for an hour, anyhow.

After supper we drove out in the country a way to some of the small villages. The women were all dressed up in peasant costumes, and I was sorry I didn't go earlier when I could take pictures.

Dispensing with justice:
Brunswick.
Across their desks passed
arrest reports for the nastiest
Nazis. 63

I have only two of these prints taken in the office and do not have the negatives, as they were taken by one of the boys when I was busy and didn't know it. You can see the conquering there just in the act of taking place and can almost hear the guns roaring.

I am particularly proud of the shot of the old church which I am sending, as I think it is really very clear and well done.

I wish you would tell Graham and John Ike of my new address. I don't want to have to go where the Ninth Army is going in order to get my mail.

I belong to the 7th Army now instead of 9th Army, and I don't even know where 7th Army is or who we are supposed to be working for there. As it is now, mail comes in either to Army or Group and is forwarded to Corps, and then we have to drive about forty miles to get it without any assurance that there is any.

Yesterday I rounded out eighteen months of overseas service and became entitled to wear three stripes on my sleeve. This is a respectable enough number to wear them, so I guess I will have to get some and have them sewed on. I also am entitled to four and maybe five campaign stars. If you just stay in the Army long enough and do little enough, you can become quite distinguished. However, I am distinguished enough in that respect, and am amply ready to call it a day.

Yesterday I got a hair cut and noticed that the barber had a fine fish head mounted on his wall. We got into an animated discussion in my very broken German and our mutually unsatisfactory French, and it may be that fishing trip will result. He had a very good American Shakespeare reel, but "malheureusement," as he said (unhappily), his rod was broken, and he could get no line. Also malheureusement, a munition plant has polluted the river and killed a lot of fish, but there are other streams.

This place has lots of possibilities.

This morning I got tied up in the office about church time and didn't get to go. It was a beautiful day, so after lunch Harold and I went for a ride. We got out of town a few miles and saw an old ruined tower on top of a high hill. We decided that we would have to go up and have a look at it, so we struck off on a little back road that headed in the right direction. After winding through the woods, driving over rocks, and cutting across people's fields, we finally got there – and found a good paved road leading up from the other side. It was worth the trouble, however, as it commanded the whole surrounding country, and there was a wonderful view for miles in every direction. I got some pictures, and while we were there about twenty kids came rushing up and adopted us. They all seem to know that the rule against playing with kids is suspended, and they are just like the British, French, and all the other kids in begging for gum and chocolate. A piece of gum seems to undo all the Nazi training, and everywhere you go the kids practically mob you. Maybe it is just being a long way from home and lonesome, but everywhere over here it seems that the kids are awfully cute. German kids seem more like Americans in that they run and play and make a lot of noise, and aren't so amazingly polite and well trained as the British and French, particularly the latter. Of course, manners is the great grace of the French; they aren't much good, but they are so darned nice about being worthless that you can't help liking them.

Last night I went out and visited the officers of the local security troops, who seemed to be a nice bunch of fellows and in addition had the rare virtue of having a great quantity of drinking whiskey. Unfortunately they aren't going to stay here, so I guess we will have to work up some more friendships.

This afternoon I tried to get a couple of pictures of my apartment, the first time I have tried anything inside. If it turns out, you can see exactly how we live. In today's Stars and Stripes I read where the Secretary of War has said to Congresswoman Somebody that he is well aware how badly the poor soldiers need their dollies (which I doubt) and that she is going to do something about it one of these days when she gets around to it. That is about as encouraging as anything I have seen so far. It was indicated that it would apply only to those cases where it appeared that the sucker was going to be over here a long time, and that will probably be the catch in it. They may require the signing of some sort of agreement to stay around a year or something like that in order to bring a wife over, but I am about in the notion to do anything. I signed up for a year to get a commission, and it is obvious now, as I thought then, that I didn't give anything away, since I would have been around just as long anyhow. At any rate, the prospects of going home any time soon don't look so good, so I may as well figure on making the best of it over here.

As for buying the lots on the hill, the main thing I had in mind was a sort of romantic notion I have had since I was a kid that I would like to own those hills, which were my favorite playground as a boy. I have never approved of the use to which they have been put since they were graded, and I would like to own them just to return them as nearly as possible to the way I knew them. It is a small investment and probably too late, but I am tired of them being the city dump. They run almost back to the Stephens' property, and it used to be a beautiful place to walk or run puppies or shoot an occasional partridge or one of Old Man Harry's pet squirrels.

The lots in the town which Dad was talking about buying are yet another project. At the risk of having a fine lawsuit, which I wouldn't mind, they are practically sure fire to make some money, and it is hardly possible to lose any on the deal. I have never approved of people not paying their taxes when given a reasonable opportunity to do so, especially when it means higher taxes on their neighbors, and there are some citizens of Helena whom I would like to leave holding that sack. I am getting so used to evicting people and listening to the wails of widows and orphans that I should be prepared to continue my career of crime, or perhaps it is proving that crime doesn't pay.

That should be enough of moralizing and talking business.

I haven't any news, but heard the father of all rumors today. I won't repeat it, as it might get you unduly excited, but it is a good one. Harden is the source.

Tonight I was going to the movie but was interrupted just as I started out the door to go harass some krauts. The raid proved a rather colorless affair, but on the way back we found a place where some GIs had some cold beer, so the evening was not a total loss. It was fairly good beer, too, as German beer goes. If anybody ever tells you that German beer, or English ale, or any other such stuff other than good American beer, is tops, tell him that he is lying like a rug. Maybe in peace time when they had the proper ingredients it was better, but I wouldn't trade a bottle of Budweiser for all the beer I have tasted in Europe.

This evening after supper I had to drive out in the country to see a character, and it turned out that he lived in one of the quaintest little villages you ever saw. It is right on top of a high hill which rises quite suddenly out of the plain and seems just big enough to hold the little town on its top. At the very top there is an old church, you can see the steeple for miles. There was a wonderful view, and the old place looked just as it must have in the days of Martin Luther. You can't imagine a less likely place to look for a Nazi, though you would readily conceive of some feudal baron sitting up there and pouring boiling water down on anybody he didn't want to come visit him.

Last night I went to a movie, Humphrey Bogart and Lauren Bacall in "To Have and Have Not." She is certainly a steaming number.

Nothing much goes on here, and I have settled down to a quiet rustic life. We have plenty of work to do, however, as the nastys seem to have been quite numerous here. They didn't get much of a patting as they did in the big cities so they are not as fully convinced of the error of their ways, though none of them seem too anxious to try again. Out in the country the people seem to have forgotten the war already; the kids are about as friendly as they were in France, and every time you stop the jeep they swarm all over you.

This morning I went to the GI chapel services which were conducted by a captain with a nasal mid-western whine who impressed me as probably being of the Holy Roller faith or some such. It was not a very uplifting service, but I guess it is good for me to go anyhow. After lunch I took a nap and then went for a drive; the country is pretty in every direction, and I never get tired of looking at it. After supper Harold and I drove down to Giesen for a visit with Bill Clark. He is an awfully nice fellow, and we talked over all the old times and all our friends who are still fighting the battle of Omaha and other tough campaigns. Needless to say, we have something less than cheers for them. His team is set up in a small hotel complete with bar, and has some very good beer, which we enjoyed.

One of the boys has been back to Brunswick (hence the mail), and he says that Harden has made 1st Lt. He is definitely on his way home. He will be sure to get a furlough. His stay in the States is not likely to be all that long, but he may be lucky and find a way to remain there. Of course, everybody who goes home has some such idea and not many of them will be able to swing it, but some will.

There has been some talk about danger, but it is negligible. In our own case, CIC being always different from everybody else, housing and messing facilities. I have no desire to remain here or anywhere else in the Army one minute longer than necessary, but, I could look forward to the prospect of another year without going completely into a decline. I try to convince myself that it won't be that long, but as a matter of fact it will take nearly that time to get home the 85-pointers and the troops on their way to the Pacific, without considering us who have a job to do. We should be able to have the greater part of our work done however, there will have to be some kind of CIC or similar personnel here as long as the occupation lasts.

News from you is still coming through by snail courier, or maybe the mailman couldn't get a pass to go through all the other zones to get here. Yesterday I got a letter from Elliott which made it all the way from Luxembourg in the brief interval since May 25. He could have walked up here and told me his news in less time than that. Apparently he didn't have much anyhow, though his letter was as entertaining as usual. His was the first letter I have received through 12th Army Group, and if it is a sample, I can see that I am not going to like the new arrangement.

In addition to my other troubles, my finance office has moved away, and I will have no end of trouble getting myself paid this month. I am due one month's difference in pay between the grade of 1st & 2nd Lt., as I didn't get it fixed up in time last month, so I should be quite rich.

I was down at Bad Nauheim to get paid, and it is a very fashionable resort or spa. The Army has taken over a lot of the better hotels and is holding forth in style and comfort. It is a very pretty place, and the drive down there is something to see. I am very much impressed with the beauty of this part of the country, just as much as with the worthlessness of the people.

> July 4th – day off by order of General Bradley.
> Miller and Gross go to a PW Stalag outside of Bad Kruezmach and pick up Heinrich Gruenwald the Landserat of Kries Frankenburg.
>
> Gross and Miller said Gruenwald was a sad looking sack, he had been in a PW cage since the end of March, had a months growth of beard, and was really sunburned.
>
> Miller and Gross arrest an SS man that had a blood mark taken off. During the interrogation Miller and Gross found out that woman doctor with Kries had removed it and she is now being investigated.
>
> Thoumsin and Conohan return from their pass. On the way back to Marburg Thoumsin is stopped and asked for a trip ticket by some joker from the air force group stationed here, who passes himself off as a CIC officer.

The Army gave me a holiday, and then took it away, all on account of some GI decided to go out and get himself fraternized and couldn't think of any better way to do it than to tell the dolly he was in CIC, and she had better, or else. That is very annoying to all of us boys who have character, discretion, integrity, and loyalty, on account of we don't get anything like that out of our work, so it became necessary for us to go out and find this character, which wasted a whole day. Now he no doubt wishes he would not have done it, or at least would have used some more simple and direct method like pulling his pistol, on account of we would then not have been interested in the matter, and he would not have got caught. Such a waste of time.

The Fourth of July passed very quietly hereabout, as most people didn't seem to realize the importance of the date and thought it was only a national holiday.

Capt. Hancock comes over from Marburg tells us of the picnic planned for next Sunday and also tells us that he is working on getting the battle stars settled for us.

Lt. Bauer gets a notice from Group concerning meeting of all S2 and CIC officers of this area next week on July 17th. Day is rather slow, we arrested just one ortsgruppenleiter and he turned himself in.

Sunday – team picnic in the woods outside of Marburg.

First customer is a character named Rumpf's wife. Comes in with the old song and dance "where is my man."

Grainger and Neuwirth go to the office of the Kreisletung and pick up the Kries records (about four jeep loads). In the afternoon Bauer and the Captain attend the meeting for the S2's and CIC officers for the Kreis Frankenberg and Marburg.

Neuwirth went to the local jail and interrogated our prisoners there. Mrs. Gruenwald, the landserat wife, came in and wanted to know if we could get her in the hospital to see "her man." Mrs. Krause came in and talked to Bauer, more "crap" about her man. In the evening Conohan goes to Marburg for mail and information. When he gets there he finds out that Lt. Walker had found out today that he is leaving tomorrow for Group to go back to the States to teach at Ritchie.

The two packages of bars came yesterday, too, and the cloth ones in your last letter. I have even got my four stars mounted on my ETO ribbon and am having three overseas stripes sewed on my sleeve, so I will soon be able to dress up with the best

329

of them. And since you wonder how I came by all these stars, I will enumerate them: Normandy, Northern France, Rhineland, and Central Germany; I will probably also be entitled to the Battle of the Bulge, but am rather ashamed to take that one. All of that adds up to eighty-one points, by virtue of which I am entitled to honorable mention on the going home. I was talking the other day to a CIC officer who had 120 and didn't expect to get home, but I told him that if I were in his place it would only be a question of whether they decided to send me in or out of the straight-jacket.

I'm sorry if I unduly aroused your curiosity about the rumor, which I had hopes would be a real surprise. Harden called me up one day and told me I was being ordered back to Ritchie to teach at a school. It sounded to good to be true, and I didn't believe him, as I didn't know anybody to get a thing like that accomplished. Sure enough, it turned out to be a mistake of some kind, and nothing ever came of it. I didn't want to get you all excited at the time, because I had an idea it would turn out this way.

It's been a hard day, and I am tired and have no news anyhow.

Stewart took Walker to Group this morning, when they got there Walker was told he was supposed to be there on the 12th and that now he was leaving almost immediately for Paris via air and would probably fly all the way to the States.

The secret operation started this morning at 0430 hours, the operation is a search of all building in the territory occupied by U.S. Troops. As a result of the operation the town is wild with rumors for example "the Russians have attacked the American forces, Kassal has been bombed." A BDM girl shot an American soldier and that is the reason for the searching. So far at noon the search has not yielded anything of any importance. In the evening Conohan goes over to Marburg for the mail. Thoumsin has taken over Lt. Walker's job.

Wiesbaden

It looks like this is it! If I'm lucky, I will at least talk to you before you get this, maybe even see you. It has all happened so suddenly that I can't yet be sure what's going on, but I seem to be on my way home!

Yesterday we made a routine call to this miserable Headquarters, and they demanded to know why I wasn't here. It developed that I was supposed to be here a week ago, but nobody bothered to tell me. There followed a wild packing with frantic efforts, then a trip here today. Tomorrow afternoon I fly down to Paris, where I am supposed to start the next lap of this adventure, which I hope will be an early plane to the States.

The deal is that I am supposed to become an instructor at Ritchie, why or in what I don't know. It will last several months, with a good leave either before or after. Then – nobody knows – either reassignment in the States, return here, or at best a discharge and at worst the Pacific. It is a gamble, and I could have turned it down. Then, I think that with 19 months overseas, 81 points, and 35 years, I should get some break.

I will wire you from Paris and call you from whatever place I hit first.

This last picture was of a small church in Frankenburg, Germany. It was chosen because I thought it
would be a good note up which to close this journal. I
think we all well remember the comfort and consolation that was ours when we had the opportunity to attend our respective churches. It was an opportunity
for which we were all thankful and this was a part of
our way of life which we cherished.

He Goes Quietly

While history goes on his will
He will go quietly.
Passed to another fair-haired boy.
Boy of inquisitiveness
Bounds on.
All the rubber-band airplanes,
All the Beagle and Setter pups,
All the shotguns, horses, and Model Ts,
All the slow delta Perch and Bass,
All the fly rods and popping bugs,
All the eagle, scholastic, and fraternal awards,
All the law, teaching, and writing,
All the esteemed honor and glory; bronze star,
campaign ribbons...
All the intelligence and intrigue,
All the lessons of history rest on his will
While history goes on, and man repeats it;
He will go quietly, the fair-haired boy,
The man we all knew, but did not know.

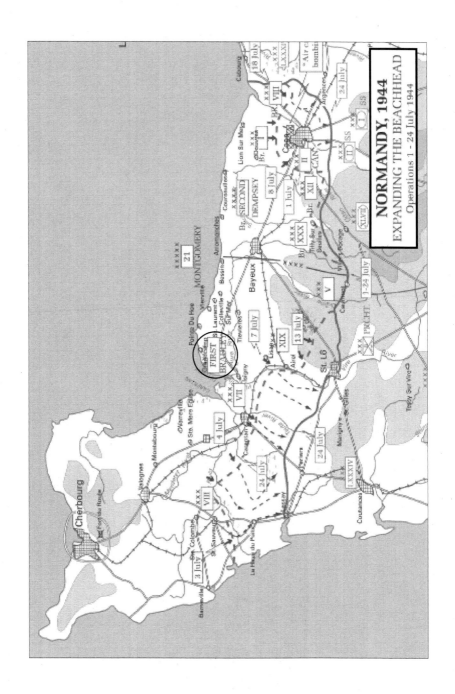

NORMANDY, 1944
EXPANDING THE BEACHHEAD
Operations 1 – 24 July 1944

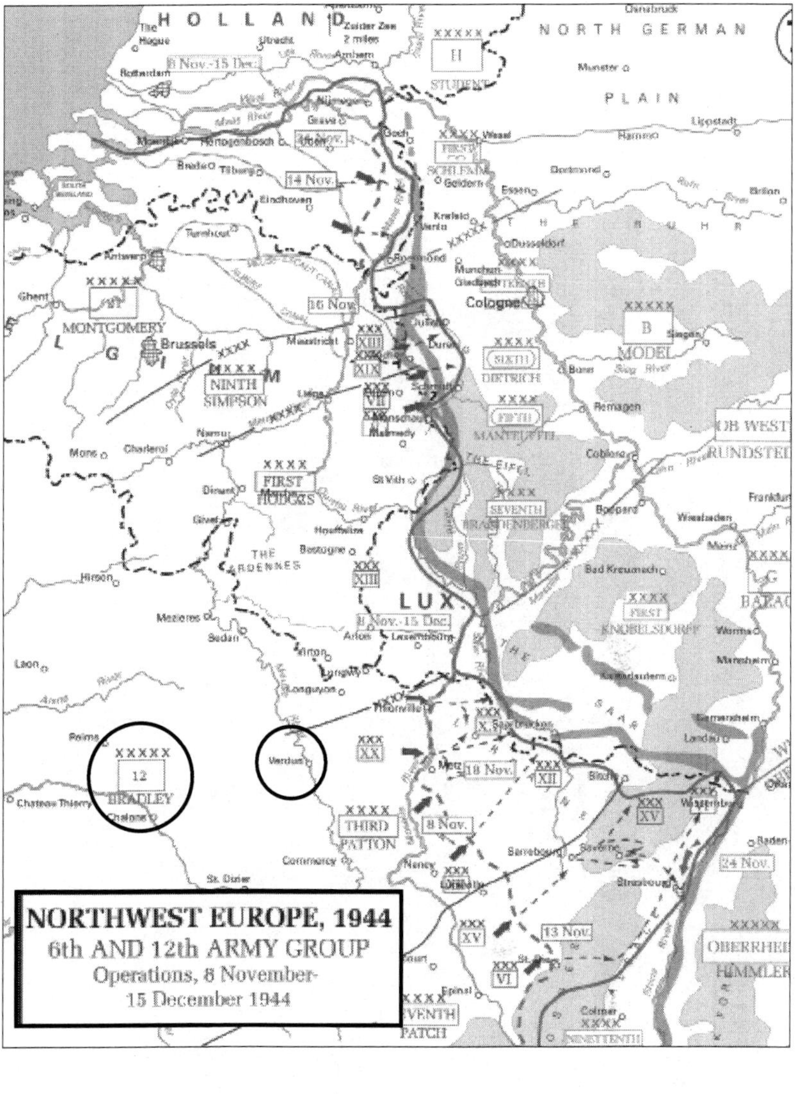
NORTHWEST EUROPE, 1944
6th AND 12th ARMY GROUP
Operations, 8 November-
15 December 1944
HOLLAND
NORTH GERMAN
PLAIN
MONTGOMERY
Brussels
NINTH
SIMPSON
FIRST
HODGES
THE ARDENNES
LUX.
THIRD
PATTON
BRADLEY
MODEL
DIETRICH
MANTEUFFEL
BRANDENBERGER
KNOBELSDORFF
OB WEST
RUNDSTEDT
HIMMLER
STUDENT
Cologne
Verdun
8 Nov.
13 Nov.
14 Nov.
16 Nov.
19 Nov.
24 Nov.
8 Nov.-15 Dec.

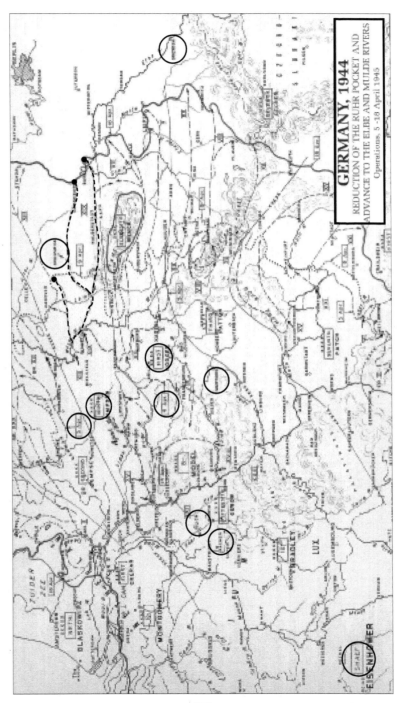

GERMANY, 1944
REDUCTION OF THE RUHR POCKET AND
ADVANCE TO THE ELBE AND MULDE RIVERS
Operations, 5 - 18 April 1945

Glossary

5th Column - A fifth column is a group of people who clandestinely undermine a larger group such as a nation from within. The term originated with a 1936 radio address by Emilio Mola, a Nationalist General during the 1936–39 Spanish Civil War.

Abwehr - German military intelligence (information gathering) organization from 1921 to 1944.

Alfred the Great - (848/849 – 26 October 899) was King of Wessex from 871 to 899. Alfred is noted for his defense of the Anglo-Saxon kingdoms of southern England against the Vikings, becoming the only English monarch still to be accorded the epithet "the Great."

Alien Registration Act - Also known as Smith Act of 1940, it is a United States federal statute that set criminal penalties for advocating the overthrow of the U.S. government and required all non-citizen adult residents to register with the government.

Allgemeine SS - The Allgemeine SS was the most numerous branch of the Schutzstaffel (SS) paramilitary forces of Nazi Germany. It was managed by the SS-Hauptamt (English: SS Main Offices). The Allgemeine SS was officially established in the autumn of 1934 to distinguish its members from the SS-Verfügungstruppe (which would later become the Waffen-SS) and the SS-Totenkopfverbände concentration camp guards.

American Field - is the oldest continuously published sporting dog journal in the United States.

Antwerp - A province of Flanders, Belgium, the capital city of the province of Antwerp.

A/P/O – Army Post Office

Armistice Day - Also known as Remembrance Day is on 11 November and commemorates the armistice signed between the Allies of World War I and Germany at Compiègne, France, for the cessation of hostilities on the Western Front, which took effect at eleven o'clock in the morning—the "eleventh hour of the eleventh day of the eleventh month" of 1918. While this official date to mark the end of the war reflects the cease fire on the Western Front, hostilities continued in other regions, especially across the former Russian Empire and in parts of the old Ottoman Empire.

A.T.U. - Alcohol & tobacco unit

AUS – (Army U.S.) The civilian branch of the War Department Ausmustrungsscheine - An Ausbesserungswerk is a railway facility, the primary function of which is the repair of railway vehicles or their components. Between the two world wars these facilities were called Reichsbahnausbesserungswerke (RAW) (Reichsbahn repair shops).

Auslanders Organization - Ausländer is a German word meaning foreigner.

Bangalore Torpedo - An explosive charge placed on the end of a long, extendible tube. It is used by combat engineers to clear obstacles that would otherwise require them to approach directly, possibly under fire. It is sometimes colloquially referred to as a Bangalore mine, bangers or simply Bangalore.

Battle of Bannockburn - Blàr Allt a' Bhonnaich in Scottish Gaelic (24 June 1314) was a significant Scottish victory in the Wars of Scottish Independence. It was the decisive battle in the First War of Scottish Independence.

Battle of Culloden - Blàr Chùil Lodair in Scottish Gaelic was the final confrontation of the 1745 Jacobite Rising. Taking place on 16 April 1746, the battle pitted the Jacobite forces of Charles Edward

Stuart against an army commanded by William Augustus, Duke of Cumberland, loyal to the British government. The Jacobite cause of overthrowing the reigning House of Hanover and restoring the House of Stuart to the British throne was dealt a decisive defeat at Culloden; Charles Stuart never mounted any further attempts to challenge Hanoverian power in Britain. The conflict was the last pitched battle fought on British soil, occurring near Inverness in the Scottish Highlands.

Battle of Trenton - Took place on December 26, 1776, during the American Revolutionary War, after General George Washington's crossing of the Delaware River north of Trenton, New Jersey. The hazardous crossing in adverse weather made it possible for Washington to lead the main body of the Continental Army against Hessian soldiers garrisoned at Trenton. After a brief battle, nearly the entire Hessian force was captured, with negligible losses to the Americans.

BDM Girl - The League of German Girls or League of German Maidens (German: Bund Deutscher Mädel or BDM), was the girl's wing of the overall Nazi party youth movement, the Hitler Youth. It was the only female youth organization in Nazi Germany.

Black Shirt Militia - There were Fascist paramilitary groups in Italy during the period immediately following World War I and until the end of World War II. Black shirts were officially known as the Voluntary Militia for National Security (MVSN).

Blitzed - Attack or damage (a place or building) in a blitz: "Rotterdam had been blitzed."

Blitzkrieg - German, "lightning war" is an anglicized word describing all-mechanized force concentration of tanks, infantry, artillery and air power, concentrating overwhelming force at high speed to break through enemy lines, and once the latter is broken, proceeding without regard to its flank. Through constant motion, the blitzkrieg attempts to keep its enemy off-balance, making it difficult to respond effectively at any given point before the front has already moved on.

Bolshevik Party - The Communist Party of the Soviet Union was the only legal, ruling political party in the Soviet Union and one of the largest communist organizations in the world. It lost its dominance in the wake of the failed August 1991 coup d'état attempt led by authoritarian hardliners.

Brittany - Breton: is a cultural and administrative region in the north-west of France. Previously a kingdom and then a duchy, Brittany was united to the Kingdom of France in 1532 as a province. Brittany has also been referred to as Less, Lesser or Little Britain (as opposed to Great Britain). It is characterized as one of the six Celtic nations.

Bund – The German government's federal bond. The bund is issued to the public as a way for the German government to finance its spending.

Bureau of Securite Militaire – Bureau of the Secretary of the Military

Burgomeister - literally master of the town, borough or master of the fortress) or the chief magistrate or chairman of the executive council of a sub-national level of administration.

Cadre – Permanent staff

Calvinist - Calvinism (also called Reformed tradition, the Reformed faith, or Reformed theology) is a Protestant theological system and an approach to the Christian life.

Camp Ritchie – Special Agent training camp located at Ft. Meade, Maryland

Camp Robinson – Located in North Little Rock, Arkansas

Chinese Exclusion Act - This was a United States federal law signed by Chester A. Arthur on May 8, 1882, following revisions made in 1880 to the Burlingame Treaty of 1868. Those revisions allowed the U.S. to suspend immigration, and Congress subsequently acted quickly to implement the suspension of Chinese immigration, a ban that was intended to last 10 years. This law was repealed by the Magnuson Act on December 17, 1943.

Churchill, Winston - Sir Winston Leonard Spencer-Churchill, KG, OM, CH, TD, PC, DL, FRS, Hon. RA (30 November 1874 – 24 January 1965) was a British politician and statesman known for his leadership of the United Kingdom during the Second World War. He is widely regarded as one of the great wartime leaders and served as Prime Minister twice (1940–45 and 1951–55). A noted statesman and orator, Churchill was also an officer in the British Army, a historian, a writer, and an artist. To date, he is the only British prime minister to have received the Nobel Prize in Literature, and he was the first person to be made an honorary citizen of the United States.

CIB – Counter Intelligence Bureau

CIC – Counter Intelligence Corps

CIA - The Central Intelligence Agency (CIA) is a central intelligence agency of the United States government.

CID - United States Army Criminal Investigation Command (USACIDC), of which the operations division is commonly abbreviated to CID.

CIP – Counter Intelligence Police, 1st World War name of CIC.

Civil Affairs - While the concept of civil affairs has been around for centuries, it was not until WWII that the U.S. government institutionalized the program in the Army. The key missions of civil affairs during WWII consisted almost entirely of military governance. Civil affairs in WWII was successful in developing and instituting training programs, in deploying many small detachments specialized in installing the types of governance and infrastructure that were known to be in need of rebuilding, and in recognizing the end of military involvement in civil affairs when there was no longer interference from civilians or the need to support a military mission. (Source: Center for Strategic & International Studies.)

C.O. - Commanding Officer

Com Z. - Army Communications Zone ETO WWII

Commissaire Blandignieres – Police Commisioner

Communist Manifesto - Originally titled Manifesto of the Communist Party is a short 1848 book written by the German Marxist political theorists Karl Marx and Friedrich Engels. It has since been recognized as one of the world's most influential political manuscripts. Commissioned by the Communist League, it laid out the League's purposes and program.

CONQUER CIB – 9th Army Counter Intelligence Command

Corpus Delicti - (Latin: "body of crime") is a term from Western jurisprudence referring to the principle that a crime must have been proven to have occurred before a person can be convicted of committing that crime.

Daily Journal – The Mission, and Accomplishment descriptive of the planning and execution of Operation Overlord and a brief daily report of each day of the war from July 1944 – July 1945. This report also included the St. Germaine and the Braunschweig

Gestapo Reports. The reports were part of the official record of CIC CRT 4 – CONQUER.

Delilah - Standard Hebrew meaning "[One who] weakened or up-rooted or impoverished" from the root meaning "weak or poor") appears only in the Hebrew bible Book of Judges 16, where she is the "woman in the valley of Sorek" whom Samson loved, and who was his downfall. Her figure, one of several dangerous tempt-resses in the Hebrew bible, has become emblematic: "Samson loved Delilah, she betrayed him, and, what is worse, she did it for money", Madlyn Kahr begins her study of the Delilah motif in European painting.

Delta Eagle - Delta Eagle passenger train, custom built by Elec-tro-Motive Corporation with passenger or baggage space in the same body; built for the Missouri Pacific Railroad, with service which ran between Memphis, Tennessee and Tallulah, Louisiana.

Dope – Information

DF's – Direction Finders

DP's – Displaced Persons

Engels, Frederich - (28 November 1820 – 5 August 1895) was a German industrialist, social scientist, author, political theorist, philosopher, and father of Marxist theory, alongside Karl Marx. In 1845 he published The Condition of the Working Class in Eng-land, based on personal observations and research. In 1848 he produced with Marx The Communist Manifesto and later he sup-ported Marx financially to do research and write Das Kapital.

ETO – European Theatre of Operations

Fahndungs Department – Border Police Department

Fascis di Combaltimento - The rise of Mussolini and former pro-war agitators; the ex-Socialist journalist Benito Mussolini soon became even more prominent, founding his fasci di combattimento ("fighting leagues"), better known as Fascists, in Milan in March 1919. The group's first program was a mishmash of radical nationalist ideas

Firemen – CIC Agents

Fraternal Outlook - official organ of the International Workers Order. The International Workers Order (IWO) was a Communist Party-affiliated insurance, mutual benefit and fraternal organization founded in 1930 and disbanded in 1954 as the result of legal action undertaken by the state of New York in 1951. At its height in the years immediately following World War II, the IWO had almost 200,000 members and provided low-cost health and life insurance, medical and dental clinics, and supported foreign-language newspapers, cultural and educational activities. The organization also operated a summer camp and cemeteries for its members.

Fichte-Bund - The Deutscher Fichte-Bund also known as The Union for World Veracity was a German, nationalist, anti-Semitic organization, founded in Hamburg by Heinrich Kessemeier on January 29, 1914. In addition to standard propaganda the organization distributed translations of major speeches of Hitler, Goebbels, Rosenberg and other key National Socialist figures to interested parties around the world. (Source: Metipidia)

Fraternal Outlook - Official organ of the International Workers Order. The International Workers Order (IWO) was a Communist Party-affiliated insurance, mutual benefit and fraternal organization founded in 1930 and disbanded in 1954 as the result of legal action undertaken by the state of New York in 1951. At its height in the years immediately following World War II, the IWO had almost 200,000 members and provided low-cost health and life insurance, medical and dental clinics, and supported foreign-language newspapers, cultural and educational activities. The organization also operated a summer camp and cemeteries for its members.

Fragenbogen - A questionnaire (plural : questionnaire, even regionally. questionnaires, English questionnaire) is an instrument of data collection , especially in the psychology and the social sciences . Questionnaires are used here very broadly to social and political attitudes , opinions , interests and psychological properties to capture. A questionnaire is less expensive than a psychological interview , so that a large number of people easier for statistically reliable results can be examined. From simple lists of questions and the standardized test methodically constructed questionnaire can be distinguished.

Frederich Engels - (28 November 1820 – 5 August 1895) was a German industrialist, social scientist, author, political theorist, philosopher, and father of Marxist theory, alongside Karl Marx. In 1845 he published The Condition of the Working Class in England, based on personal observations and research. In 1848 he produced with Marx The Communist Manifesto and later he supported Marx financially to do research and write Das Kapital.

Frederick the Great - Frederick II (24 January 1712 – 17 August 1786) was a King in Prussia (1740–1772) and he became known as Frederick the Great (Friedrich der Große).

Ft. Leonard Wood – Located in Pulaski County, Missouri, United States. It is named in honor of Major General Leonard Wood, who was awarded the Medal of Honor.

Fuhrerschein - Driver's License

Gadgets – Air Force Pilots

Gestapo - was the official secret police of Nazi Germany.
Gestapo Polizei Obersekretar – Gestapo Police Senior Criminal Secretary

G-2 – Army Intelligence

G-2 TRAINING SCHOOL – Army Intelligence School located in Chicago, IL.

Genghis Kahn - Mongol: 1162? – August 1227, born Temujin and also known by the temple name Taizu, was the founder and Great Khan (emperor) of the Mongol Empire, which became the largest contiguous empire in history after his death. He started the Mongol invasions that would result in the conquest of most of Eurasia. These campaigns were often accompanied by wholesale massacres of the civilian populations – especially in Khwarezmia.

Gestapo Kriminal Kommissar – Gestapo Criminal Commissioner

G.I. - is a noun used to describe members of the United States armed forces or items of their equipment. The term is now used as an initialism of "Government Issue" (or often incorrectly "General Infantry"), but originally referred to galvanized iron.

Giliesmarode Hospital – Hospital in Braunschweig, Germany.

Gulpen territory – area in the Netherlands; taken over by the Germans.

Hague Tribunal - A popular name for the Permanent Court of Arbitration established in 1899.

Heinie – Slang for German individual.

Hindenburg - Paul Ludwig Hans Anton von Beneckendorff and von Hindenburg, known universally as Paul von Hindenburg; 2 October 1847 – 2 August 1934) was a German field marshal, statesman, and politician, and served as the second President of Germany from 1925 to 1934.

HJ Member - The Hitler Youth (German: Hitler-Jugend , abbreviated HJ) was a paramilitary organization of the Nazi Party. It existed from 1922 to 1945. The HJ was the second oldest paramilitary Nazi group, founded one year after its adult counterpart, the Sturmabteilung (the SA). It was made up of the Hitlerjugend proper, for male youth ages 14–18; the younger boys' section Deutsches Jungvolk for ages 10–14; and the girls' section Bund Deutscher Mädel (BDM, the League of German Girls).

Hoffman, Werner - (7 August 1920 – 7 February 1945) was a highly decorated Hauptmann in the Luftwaffe during World War II and a recipient of the Knight's Cross of the Iron Cross. The Knight's Cross of the Iron Cross was awarded to recognize extreme battlefield bravery or successful military leadership. During his career credited with flying 500+ missions.

Hoover, J. Edgar - John Edgar Hoover (January 1, 1895 – May 2, 1972) was the first director of the Federal Bureau of Investigation (FBI) of the United States. Appointed director of the Bureau of Investigation—predecessor to the FBI—in 1924, he was instrumental in founding the FBI in 1935, where he remained director until his death in 1972.

Hunnish Riders (horse riding warriors) - The Hunnic Empire (370-469) was an empire established by the Huns. The Huns were a confederation of Eurasian tribes from the steppes of Central Asia. Their mass migration into Europe, led by Attila, brought with it great ethnic and political upheaval.

Industrial Revolution - This was a period from the 18th to the 19th century where major changes in agriculture, manufacturing, mining, transportation, and technology had a profound effect on the socioeconomic and cultural conditions of the times. It began in the United Kingdom, then subsequently spread throughout Europe, North America, and eventually the world.

Internationale - (L'Internationale in French) is a famous socialist, communist, social-democratic and anarchist anthem. The Internationale became the anthem of international socialism, and gained particular fame under the Soviet Union from 1922 to 1944, when it was that communist state's de facto central anthem.

Islam – Islam is the monotheistic religion articulated by the Qur'an, a text considered by its adherents to be the verbatim word of God (Allāh), and by the teachings and normative example (called the Sunnah and composed of Hadith) of Muhammad, considered by them to be the last prophet of God. An adherent of Islam is called a Muslim.

I.W.W. - The Industrial Workers of the World (IWW or the Wobblies) is an international union. At its peak in 1923, the organization claimed some 100,000 members in good standing, and could marshal the support of perhaps 300,000 workers.

Jayhawk – VII Corps "nickname"

Jiu Jitsu - Martial art from Japan consisting of grappling and striking techniques.

Isle of Skye - Skye or the Isle of Skye (Scottish Gaelic: An t-Eilean Sgitheanach or Eilean a' Cheò) is the largest and most northerly island in the Inner Hebrides of Scotland. The island's peninsulas radiate out from a mountainous centre dominated by the Cuillin hills. Although it has been suggested that the first of these Gaelic names describes a "winged" shape there is no definitive agreement as to the name's origins.

IPW Personnel – Interogaters of Prisoners of War

Jacobin Club - was the most famous political club of the French Revolution, so-named because of the Dominican convent where they met, located in the Rue St. Jacques (Latin: Jacobus), Paris. The club originated as the Club Benthorn, formed at Versailles from a group of Breton deputies attending the Estates General of 1789. At the height of its influence, there were thousands of chapters throughout France, with a membership estimated at 420,000. JAG - Judge Advocate General's Corps, the judicial arm of a military force in some jurisdictions.

Judge Advocate - Judge Advocate General's Corps, also known as JAG or JAG Corps, refers to the legal branch or specialty of the Air Force, Army, Coast Guard, and Navy. Officers serving in the JAG Corps are typically called Judge Advocates. The Marine Corps and Coast Guard do not maintain separate JAG Corps per se and judge advocates in those services maintain their line officer-status. In the Army and Navy, JAG officers only serve in legal positions.

Marx, Karl - Karl Heinrich Marx (5 May 1818 – 14 March 1883) was a German philosopher, sociologist, economic historian, journalist, and revolutionary socialist who developed the socio-political theory of Marxism. His ideas have since played a significant role in the development of social science and the socialist political movement. He published various books during his lifetime, with the most notable being The Communist Manifesto (1848) and Capital (1867–1894), many of which were co-written with his friend, the fellow German revolutionary socialist Friedrich Engels.

Kennkarten - Kennkarte was the basic identity document in use during the Third Reich era, first introduced in July 1938. They were normally obtained through a police precinct and had the corresponding issuing office and official's stamps on them. Every German citizen was issued one and was expected to produce it when confronted by officials.

Kennkarten Oberregierungarat - was the identity document of a senior government official in use of the Third Reich.

K.P. - Kitchen Patrol

K-ration - An individual daily combat food ration which was introduced by the United States Army during World War II. Kreisleiterin of the NSF - NS-Frauenschaft, the women's wing of the former German Nazi party.

Kriminal Kommissar – Criminal Commissioner

Kriminal Sekretär – Criminal Secretary

KRIPO - Kriminal Polizei (criminal police, Germany)

KRIPO Angestellter – Security Police Staffer

KRIPO Beamter – Security Police Detective

Looeys – Lieutenants

Louis, Joe - Joseph Louis Barrow (May 13, 1914 – April 12, 1981), better known as Joe Louis, was the world heavyweight boxing champion from 1937 to 1949. He is considered to be one of the greatest heavyweights of all time.

Luncheon Menu – Ch. De'Gaulle repatriated to France – invited heads of his military and the counterparts of the Allied Forces were invited. Dave attended this gathering.

Malheureusement – Unlucky or unfortunate

Mein Kampf - (English: My Struggle or My Battle) is a book written by Nazi leader Adolf Hitler. It combines elements of autobiography with an exposition of Hitler's political ideology.

Mensheviks - A faction of the Russian revolutionary movement that emerged in 1904 after a dispute between Vladimir Lenin and Julius Martov, both members of the Russian Social-Democratic Labour Party. The dispute originated at the Second Congress of that party, ostensibly over minor issues of party organization. Martov's supporters, who were in the minority in a crucial vote on the question of party membership, came to be called "Mensheviks," whereas Lenin's adherents were known as "Bolsheviks," from bol'shinstvo ("majority").

Milan Populo di Italia - An Italian newspaper founded by Benito Mussolini on November 15, 1914, as a result of his split with the Italian Socialist Party. The paper, advocating militarism and irredentism, was subsidized by the French and industrialists on the pretext of influencing Italy to join the Entente Powers. This is also where Mussolini spread his ideas about how he wanted Italy to increase its birth rate. From 1936 to 1943 it was edited by Giorgio Pini.

Military Government "Fragebogen" - "The Questionaire"

Ministerialrat - An under secretary is an executive government official in many countries, frequently a career public servant, who typically acts as a senior administrator or second-in-command to a politically-appointed Cabinet Minister or other government official.

Modus Operandi - (plural modi operandi) is a Latin phrase, approximately translated as "mode of operating." The term is used to describe someone's habits or manner of working, their method of operating or functioning. In English, it is frequently shortened to M.O.

Mohamet - Muḥammad (Arabic) Muḥammad, pronounced [mħæmmæd], (or sometimes Muhammad) (ca. 26 April 570– 8

June 632), was the founder of the religion of Islam, and is considered by Muslims to be a messenger and prophet of God, the last law-bearer in a series of Islamic prophets, and, by most Muslims, the last prophet of God as taught by the Quran. Muslims thus consider him the restorer of an uncorrupted original monotheistic faith (islām) of Adam, Noah, Abraham, Moses, Jesus and other prophets. He was also active as a social reformer, diplomat, merchant, philosopher, orator, legislator, military leader, humanitarian, philanthropist, and, according to Muslim belief, an agent of divine action.

Mola, General Emilio y Vidal - Emilio Mola y Vidal, 1st Duke of Mola, Grandee of Spain (June 9, 1887 – June 3, 1937) was a Spanish Nationalist commander during the Spanish Civil War. He is best-known for having coined the term "fifth column".

Morgenthau, Hans Joachim - (February 17, 1904 – July 19, 1980) was one of the leading twentieth-century figures in the study of international politics.

M.P. - Military Police

Mussolini, **Benito Amilcare Andrea** - Mussolini (29 July 1883 – 28 April 1945) was an Italian politician who led the National Fascist Party and is credited with being one of the key figures in the creation of Fascism.

Napoleon Bonaparte (5 August 1769 – 5 May 1821) was a French military and political leader during the latter stages of the French Revolution. As Napoleon I, he was Emperor of the French from 1804 to 1815. His legal reform, the Napoleonic code, has been a major influence on many civil law jurisdictions worldwide, but he is best remembered for his role in the wars led against France by a series of coalitions, the so-called Napoleonic Wars, during which he established hegemony over most of continental Europe and sought to spread the ideals of the French Revolution, while consolidating an increasingly autocratic, hereditary empire. Due to his longtime success in these wars, often against numerically superior enemies, he is generally regarded as one of the greatest military commanders of all time.

National Origins Act - A law that severely restricted immigration by establishing a system of national quotas that blatantly discriminated against immigrants from southern and eastern Europe and virtually excluded Asians. The policy stayed in effect until the 1960s.

Nay, Marshall - Michel Ney, 1st Duc d'Elchingen, 1st Prince de la Moskowa (10 January 1769 – 7 December 1815) was a French soldier and military commander during the French Revolutionary Wars and the Napoleonic Wars. He was one of the original 18 Marshals of France created by Napoleon I. He was known as Le Rougeaud ("red faced" or "ruddy" by his men and nicknamed le Brave des Braves ("the bravest of the brave") by Napoleon.

Nazi - The National Socialist German Workers' Party (German: Nationalsozialistische Deutsche Arbeiterpartei (help·info), abbreviated NSDAP), commonly known in English as the Nazi Party, was a political party in Germany between 1919 and 1945. It was known as the German Workers' Party (DAP) prior to a change of name in 1920. The term Nazi is German and stems from Nationalsozialist.

N.B. - This is used at the start of several G-2 Training classes. The exact meaning is unknown to me however, it is easy to determine that it implies a humorous perspective of double-meanings applied to a single verbal exchange between two parties. The investigator must pick up on this anomaly in order to pursue all avenues for the answers to an investigation.

New Deal - The New Deal was a series of economic programs implemented in the United States between 1933 and 1936. They were passed by the U.S. Congress during the first term of President Franklin D. Roosevelt. The programs were responses to the Great Depression, and focused on what historians call the "3 Rs": Relief, Recovery, and Reform.

NKBD - Peoples Commissariat of Internal Affairs

Oberscharfuhrer - was a Nazi Party paramilitary rank that existed between the years of 1932 and 1945. Translated as "Senior Squad Leader", Oberscharführer was first used as a rank of the Sturmabteilung (SA) and was created due to an expansion of the enlisted positions required by growing SA membership in the late 1920s and early 1930s. The SA rank of Oberscharführer was senior to Scharführer and junior to the rank of Truppführer.

Obersturmbannfuhrer - Military rank of the Nazi SA and SS, corresponds with lieutenant colonel. Literally translates to "Senior Storm Unit Leader." Next in rank to Standartenführer, rank below is Sturmbannführer. Senior Assault (or Storm) Unit Leader" in the German Army.

OCS – Officers Candidate School

OD – Office Duty

OGPU – Basis of KGB (in KGB (agency, Union of Soviet Socialist Republics): Pre-KGB Soviet security services) In 1922 the Cheka was supplanted by the GPU (State Political Administration) in an effort by the Communist Party to reduce the scale of the Cheka's terror. A year later the GPU was renamed the OGPU (Unified State Political Administration) and given additional duties, including the administration of "corrective" labor camps and the surveillance of the population.

Omnibus Sedition Act – Sedition Act of July 14, 1798 made it a crime to utter or publish any false, scandalous and malicious writing or writings against the government of the United States, or either House of Congress of the United States with intent to defame.

Operation Over-Lord - was the code name for the Battle of Normandy, the operation that launched the invasion of German-occupied western Europe during World War II by Allied forces. The operation commenced on 6 June 1944 with the Normandy landings (Operation Neptune, commonly known as D-Day). A 12,000-plane airborne assault preceded an amphibious assault involving almost 7,000 vessels. Nearly 160,000 troops crossed the English Channel on 6 June; more than 3 million troops were in France by the end of August.

Ordinance Unit – The Military Materials Unit which handles such as weapons, ammunition, combat vehicles, and equipment.

Orpheus Choir - Sir Hugh S. Roberton founded the Glasgow Orpheus Choir and set new standards in choral technique and interpretation. The Glasgow Orpheus Choir had no equal in Britain and toured widely enjoying world acclaim. Their repertoire included many Scottish folk songs, Italian madrigals, English motets, and the music of the Russian Orthodox Church. The choir also performed the works of Bach, Handel, Mandelssohn, Cornelius, Brahms and others.

Ortsgruppenleiters - (Local Group Leader) was a Nazi Party political rank and title which existed between 1930 and 1945. The term first came into being during the German elections of 1930, and was held by the head Nazi of a town or city for the purposes of election district organization. After 1933, through the process of Gleichschaltung, the position of Ortsgruppenleiter evolved into the Nazi leader of a large town or city.

Ortsgruppenleiter of Ortsgruppe Ruehme - The chapter leaders (Ortsgruppenleiter). An Ortsgruppe (chapter) encompassed

1500 households--usually a city suburb or a few villages.

OVRA - (OVRA; Italian for "Organization for Vigilance and Repression of Anti-Fascism") was the secret police of the Kingdom of Italy, founded in 1927 under the regime of Fascist dictator Benito Mussolini and during the reign of King Victor Emmanuel III. The German Gestapo were the equivalent of the OVRA. Mussolini's secret police were assigned to stop any anti-Fascist activity or sentiment. Approximately 5,000 OVRA agents infiltrated most aspects of domestic life in Italy. The OVRA was headed by Arturo Bocchini.

Panzerfausts - (lit. "armor fist" or "tank fist", plural: Panzerfäuste) was an inexpensive, recoilless German anti-tank weapon of World War II. It consisted of a small, disposable preloaded launch tube firing a high explosive anti-tank warhead, operated by a single soldier.

Papist - A term, usually disparaging or an anti-Catholic slur, referring to the Catholic Church, its teaching, practices or adherents.

P.I.O. - Post Intelligence Office

Plato's Republic - The Republic is a Socratic dialogue written by Plato around 380 BC concerning the definition of justice and the order and character of the just city-state and the just man. It is Plato's best-known work and has proven to be one of the most intellectually and historically influential works of philosophy and political theory. In it, Socrates along with various Athenians and foreigners discuss the meaning of justice and examine whether or not the just man is happier than the unjust man by considering a series of different cities coming into existence "in speech", culminating in a city ruled by philosopher-kings; and by examining the nature of existing regimes. The participants also discuss the theory of forms, the immortality of the soul, and the roles of the philosopher and of poetry in society.

Pyle, Ernie - Ernest Taylor Pyle (August 3, 1900 – April 18, 1945) was an American journalist who wrote as a roving correspondent for the Scripps Howard newspaper chain from 1935 until his death in combat during World War II. He won the Pulitzer Prize in 1944. His articles, about the out-of-the-way places he visited and the people who lived there, were written in a folksy style, much like a personal letter to a friend. He enjoyed a following in some 300 newspapers.

Plizei Obersekretar – Police Administrator

Proletarian Dictatorship - n Marxist socio-political thought, the dictatorship of the proletariat refers to a socialist state in which the proletariat, or industrial working class, have control of political power.

PROMI – Propaganda ministry under Goebbels.

Provost Marshal General - is a United States Army staff position reporting to the Chief of Staff of the United States Army that handles investigations and incarcerations, bringing all aspects of law enforcement in the U.S. Army in a single office.

PWs – Prisoner(s) of War

PWE – Political Warfare Executive

PX – Post Exchange

Quisling - Quisling is a term used in reference to fascist and collaborationist political parties and military and paramilitary forces in occupied Allied countries which collaborated with Axis occupiers in World War II, as well as for their members and other collaborators.

RAF - The Royal Air Force is the aerial warfare service branch of the British Armed Forces. Formed on 1 April 1918, it is the oldest independent air force in the world. The RAF has taken a significant role in British military history, playing a large part in the Second World War.

Red Army - The Workers' and Peasants' Red Army started out as the Soviet Union's revolutionary communist combat groups during the Russian Civil War of 1918-1922. It grew into the national army of the Soviet Union.

Reich - A German word cognate with the English rich, but also used to designate an empire, realm, or nation. The qualitative connotation from the German is "(imperial) sovereign state." It is the word traditionally used for a variety of sovereign entities, including Germany in many periods of its history.

Reichssicherheitsamt - The Third Reich's Security Headquarters

Reichstag - Reichstag (legislative body) - the diets or parliaments of the Holy Roman Empire, of the Austrian-Hungarian monarchy, and of Germany from 1871 to 1945.

Ribbentrop - Ulrich Friedrich Wilhelm Joachim von Ribbentrop (30 April 1893 – 16 October 1946) was Foreign Minister of Germany from 1938 until 1945. He was later hanged for war crimes after the Nuremberg Trials.

Royal Mile - A succession of streets which form the main thoroughfare of the Old Town of the city of Edinburgh in Scotland.

Russo-German Pact - The Molotov–Ribbentrop Pact, named after the Soviet foreign minister Vyacheslav Molotov and the German foreign minister Joachim von Ribbentrop, was an agreement officially titled the Treaty of Non-Aggression between Germany and the Soviet Union and signed in Moscow in the late hours of

23 August 1939. It was a non-aggression pact under which the Soviet Union and Nazi Germany each pledged to remain neutral in the event that either nation were attacked by a third party. It remained in effect until 22 June 1941, when Germany invaded the Soviet Union.

SA ("The SA is always there - Are you?") - The Sturmabteilung (SA); English: Storm Detachment; or English: Stormtroopers) functioned as a paramilitary organization of the National Socialist German Workers' Party (or Nazi Party). It played a key role in Adolf Hitler's rise to power in the 1920s and 1930s. SA men were often called "brown shirts" for the color of their uniforms (similar to Benito Mussolini's blackshirts).

Schenck Case - Schenck v. United States, 249 U.S. 47 (1919), was a United States Supreme Court decision that upheld the Espionage Act of 1917 and concluded that a defendant did not have a First Amendment right to freedom of speech against the draft during World War I. Ultimately, the case established the "clear and present danger" test, which lasted until 1927 when its strength was diminished.

SD - The intelligence agency of the SS and the Nazi Party in Nazi Germany, fierce competition with German military intelligence.

SD Chief – German Police Squad Chief

SD Sturmhauptscharfuhrer - Sturmscharführer (Sergeant Major)

SD Untersturmfuhrer - Untersturmführer was a paramilitary rank of the German Schutzstaffel first created in July 1934. The rank can trace its origins to the older SA rank of Sturmführer which had existed since the founding of the SA in 1921. The rank of Untersturmführer was senior to Hauptscharführer (or Sturmscharführer in the Waffen-SS) and junior to the rank of Obersturmführer.

Service Command - Joint Services Command and Staff College (JSCSC) is a British military academic establishment providing training and education to experienced officers of the Royal Navy, Army, Royal Air Force, Ministry of Defence Civil Service, and serving officers of other states.

Seventh Service Command - The Seventh Army was the first American formation of Field Army size to see combat in World War II.

Sicherheitspolizei - The Sicherheitspolizei (English: Security Police), often abbreviated as SiPo, was a term used in Nazi Germany to describe the state political and criminal investigation security agencies. It was made up by the combined forces of the Gestapo (secret state police) and the Kripo (criminal police) between 1936 and 1939. As a formal agency, the SiPo was folded into the RSHA in 1939, but the term continued to be used informally until the end of the Third Reich.

Socialist Labor Party of America - Established in 1876 as the Workingman's Party, it is the oldest socialist political party in the United States and the second oldest socialist party in the world. Originally known as the Workingmen's Party of America, the party changed its name in 1877 and has operated continuously since that date, although its current existence is tenuous. The party advocates the ideology of "socialist industrial unionism" — belief in a fundamental transformation of society through the combined political and industrial action of the working class organized in industrial unions.

Socialist Party of America - The Socialist Party of America (SPA) was a multi-tendency democratic-socialist political party in the United States, formed in 1901 by a merger between the three-year-old Social Democratic Party of America and disaffected elements of the Socialist Labor Party which had split from the main organization in 1899.

Sonderfuhrer - Special guide is an entity appointed by the German Wehrmacht was created in 1937 in case of mobilization. With attraction as a special civilian leaders should special skills of soldiers who had no or only inadequate military training can be used. This group of people was taken in an officer or noncommissioned officer rank.

Special Service Officer - The Office of Strategic Services (OSS) was a United States intelligence officer.

SS Hauptscharfuhrer - A Nazi paramilitary rank which was used by the Schutzstaffel (SS) between the years of 1934 and 1945. The rank was the highest enlisted rank of the SS, with the exception of the special Waffen-SS rank of Sturmscharführer.
Translated as "Head/Chief Squad Leader", Hauptscharführer became an SS rank after a reorganization of the SS following the Night of the Long Knives. The first use of Hauptscharführer was in June 1934 when the rank replaced the older SA title of Obertruppführer.

SS Oberschaufuher – Forced Labor and Death Camp Comanders

SS Unterscharfuhrer - (English: Junior Squad Leader) was a paramilitary rank of the Nazi Party used by the Schutzstaffel (SS) between 1934 and 1945. The SS rank was created after the Night of the Long Knives. That event caused an SS reorganization and the creation of new ranks to separate the SS from the Sturmabteilung (SA).

SS Untersturmfuhrer - A paramilitary rank of the German Schutzstaffel first created in July 1934. The rank paramilitary trace its origins to the older SA rank of Sturmführer which had existed since the founding of the SA in 1921. The rank of Untersturmführer was senior to Hauptscharführer (or Sturmscharführer in the Waffen-SS) and junior to the rank of Obersturmführer.

Squib - A squib is a miniature explosive device used in a wide range of industries, from special effects to military applications. It resembles a tiny stick of dynamite, both in appearance and construction, although with considerably less explosive power.

Standartenfuhrur - was a Nazi Party rank that was used in both the SA and the SS. First founded as a title in 1925, in 1928 the rank became one of the first commissioned Nazi ranks and was bestowed upon those SA and SS officers who commanded units known as Standarten which were regiment-sized formations of between three hundred and five hundred men.

Stay-behind - Gestapo Wehrwolf Mission Operative

Stalin, Joseph Vissarionovich (18 December 1878– 5 March 1953) was the Premier of the Soviet Union from 6 May 1941 to 5 March 1953. He was among the Bolshevik revolutionaries who brought about the October Revolution and had held the position of first General Secretary of the Communist Party of the Soviet Union's Central Committee from 1922 until his death in 1953. Stalin's idea of socialism in one country became the primary line of the Soviet politics.

Stars and Stripes - The U.S. military's independent news source

Stuart Kings of Scotland - The House of Stewart (also known as the House of Stuart) is a European royal house. Founded by Robert II of Scotland, the Stewarts first became monarchs of the Kingdom of Scotland during the late 14th century, and subsequently held the position of the Kings of Great Britain and Ireland. Their direct ancestors (from Brittany) had held the title High Steward of Scotland since the 12th century, after arriving by way of Norman England. The dynasty inherited further territory by the 17th century which covered the entire British Isles, including the Kingdom of England and Kingdom of Ireland, also upholding a claim to the

Kingdom of France.

Supreme Headquarters G-5 - Army headquarters organization for civil affairs/military governments.

T-5 – T-Force Unit

TAC - Tactical Air Command

T-Force - was an elite British Army force that inspired Ian Flemming to write the James Bond novels and which operated during the final stages of World War II. Originally used to secure and exploit targets that could provide valuable intelligence of scientific and military value, they were later tasked with seizing Nazi German scientists and businessmen in the aftermath of VE Day.

Trotsky, Leon - (7 November 1879– 21 August 1940), born Lev Davidovich Bronshtein, was a Russian Marxist revolutionary and theorist, Soviet politician, and the founder and first leader of the Red Army.

TUSAG – the United States Army Group

Totenkaupfrebunde - SS-Totenkopfverbände (SS-TV), meaning "Death's-Head Units," was the SS organization responsible for administering the Nazi concentration camps for the Third Reich.

Unterscharfuhrer - Unterscharführer (English: Junior Squad Leader) was a paramilitary rank of the Nazi Party used by the Schutzstaffel (SS) between 1934 and 1945. The SS rank was created after the Night of the Long Knives. That event caused an SS reorganization and the creation of new ranks to separate the SS from the Sturmabteilung (SA). (Source: Wikapedia)

USO - Since 1941 the United Service Organizations Inc. (USO) is a private, non profit organization that provides morale and recreational services to members of the U.S. military, with programs in 140 centers worldwide.

Vanguard - Vanguard (military formation), the forward element of an advancing military formation.

V-bombs - The Fieseler Fi 103, better known as the V-1 (German: Vergeltungswaffe 1, "retaliation weapon 1") and Buzz Bomb, also colloquially known in Britain as the Doodlebug, was an early pulse-jet-powered predecessor of the cruise missile.

VE Day – Victory in Europe Day

Verdun – Verdun, France – Location of TUSAG and The Battle of Verdun was one of the major battles during the First World War on the Western Front. It was fought between the German and French armies, from 21 February-18 December 1916, on hilly terrain north of the city of Verdun-sur-Meuse in north-eastern France; it can also be considered a costly strategic stalemate.

Versailles Treaty - The Treaty of Versailles was one of the peace treaties at the end of World War I. It ended the state of war between Germany and the Allied Powers. It was signed on June 28, 1919, exactly five years after the assassination of Archduke Franz Ferdinand. The other Central Powers on the German side of World War I were dealt with in separate treaties. Although the armistice signed on November 11, 1918 ended the actual fighting, it took six months of negotiations at the Paris Peace Conference to conclude the peace treaty. The treaty was registered by the Secretariat of the League of Nations on October 21, 1919, and was printed in The League of Nations Treaty Series.

V-Mail -Short for Victory Mail, a hybrid mail process used during the Second World War in America as the primary and secure method to correspond with soldiers stationed abroad. To reduce the logistics of transferring an original letter across the military postal system, a V-mail letter would be censored, copied to film, and printed back to paper upon arrival at its destination. The V-mail process is based on the earlier British Airgraph process.

Volkasturm - "Storm of the people"; "People's Army" or "National Militia" was a German national militia of the last months of World War II. It was founded on Adolf Hitler's orders on October 18, 1944 and conscripted males between the ages of 16 to 60 years who were not already serving in some military unit as part of a German Home Guard.

Waffen (Photo Reference) - The shot gun I grew up with. The story was that a Frenchman was walking down the street with this shot gun and a scope. Dad asked what he was going to do with them and the Frenchman said, "I'm going to put this scope on the gun and shoot some Germans." Dad's reply, "if you don't care any more than that about them, give them both to me." My brother has the scope.

Wehrpasses – Military ID card, seervice record

Wehrwolf – The last Gestapo Mission of the Nazi Party in Germany.

Wehrwolfs - Members of the Gestapo Leave-Behind Mission, "Wehrwolf."

Weishaupt, Adam (1748–1830) German philosopher and founder of the Order of Illuminati.

Workers International Industrial Union - (WIIU) was a Revolutionary Industrial Union active in the United States, Canada, Britain and Australia. A revived version of the original WIIU was launched in the United States in 2009.